America's
TEST KITCHEN

America's Best LOST RECIPES

121 Kitchen-Tested Heirloom Recipes
Too Good to Forget

FROM THE EDITORS OF COOK'S COUNTRY MAGAZINE

COLOR PHOTOGRAPHY Keller + Keller
FOOD STYLING Mary Jane Sawyer
BLACK AND WHITE PHOTOGRAPHY Daniel J. van Ackere

AMERICA'S TEST KITCHEN • BROOKLINE, MASSACHUSETTS

Welcome to America's Test Kitchen

THIS BOOK HAS BEEN TESTED, WRITTEN, AND EDITED BY THE FOLKS AT America's Test Kitchen, a very real 2,500-square-foot kitchen located just outside of Boston. It is the home of *Cook's Illustrated* magazine and *Cook's Country* magazine and is the Monday-through-Friday destination for more than two dozen test cooks, editors, food scientists, tasters, and cookware specialists. Our mission is to test recipes over and over again until we understand how and why they work and until we arrive at the "best" version.

We start the process of testing a recipe with a complete lack of conviction, which means that we accept no claim, no theory, no technique, and no recipe at face value. We simply assemble as many variations as possible, test a half dozen of the most promising, and taste the results blind. We then construct our own hybrid recipe and continue to test it, varying ingredients, techniques, and cooking times until we reach a consensus. The result, we hope, is the best version of a particular recipe, but we realize that only you can be the final judge of our success (or failure). As we like to say in the test kitchen, "We make the mistakes, so you don't have to."

All of this would not be possible without a belief that good cooking, much like good music, is indeed based on a foundation of objective technique. Some people like spicy foods and others don't, but there is a right way to sauté, there is a best way to cook a pot roast, and there are measurable scientific principles involved in producing perfectly beaten, stable egg whites. This is our ultimate goal: to investigate the fundamental principles of cooking so that you become a better cook. It is as simple as that.

You can watch us work (in our actual test kitchen) by tuning in to *America's Test Kitchen* (www.americastestkitchen.com) on public television or by subscribing to *Cook's Illustrated* magazine (www.cooksillustrated.com) or *Cook's Country* magazine (www.cookscountry.com), which are each published every other month. We welcome you into our kitchen, where you can stand by our side as we test our way to the "best" recipes in America.

Introduction

SOME THINGS ARE JUST CRYING OUT TO BE LOST. BAD SUPERMARKET TOMATOES. SpongeBob SquarePants Cereal. Breakfast at McDonald's. Halftime at the Super Bowl. Any recipe that starts with a can of cream of mushroom soup. And don't forget children's books penned by celebrities and casseroles with overcooked broccoli.

Just because something is old doesn't mean it's any darn good. There are dozens of varieties of "heirloom" apples that have scabby rough skin and bitter fruit. The same can be said for many heirloom potatoes, carrots, lettuce, and anything else that is likely to grow in a kitchen garden. When it comes to recipes, your great-grandmother may have created a dish that is a family favorite, but that doesn't mean it is worthy of being considered a classic, a recipe that tells the story of a place, a generation, a style of cooking, and or even a family.

Here at *Cook's Country,* we are no strangers to the recipe contest. We do them in every issue. A few of the recipes are excellent, many are good, and others are simply variations on well-established themes. So when we approached the notion of seeking out "lost recipes" from around the country, we were looking for something special, recipes that tasted great but also recipes that told a story, that truly represented a special window into the American experience. But let's be clear, this was not to be simply a museum conservation project, in which recipes are bundled off to a dusty room in the basement of the Smithsonian. Each and every recipe had to be for food we would be eager to make that night for dinner. It had to be as appealing and exciting as on the day it was first made. That was a tall order.

So what happened? Well, we received over 2,800 entries in less than four months. The bigger surprise was that hundreds of these recipes were excellent and a large percentage of those needed very little, if any, fiddling by our test kitchen staff. Perhaps because this food had stood the test of time, the recipes were uniformly top notch and we had a difficult time sorting those special few that would make it into this book. We read and reread each and every recipe, prepared the 300 most promising dishes, and took it from there with additional testing, tastings, and discussions over a period of many months.

So how did we choose? That goes to the heart of what we consider a "lost recipe" to be. Just like a short story, a lost recipe has to have a narrative. Like a book title, the recipe name has to hold out a promise, an expectation of something unusual. Tennessee Stack Cake. Joe Froggers. Naked Ladies with Their Legs Crossed. Next, the recipe itself has to be the chronicle of an immigrant family adapting to the new world or perhaps the story of how cooks during wartime adapted recipes to a meager list of available ingredients. For example, Chocolate Sauerkraut Cake is an adaptation of German chocolate cake (but with an obvious surprise ingredient). Another favorite lost recipe is Wacky Cake, a WWII-era invention that calls for no eggs, milk, or butter, ingredients that were in short supply. Finally, a lost recipe is served and that first taste, like the last line of a good O. Henry story, is a reawakening, a connection to another cook, perhaps a long time ago, who lived a very different sort of life. In a way, a good lost recipe is about tasting the past and, many times, that experience is more immediate and fulfilling than simply reading history.

Of course there were many family recipes (Grandpa Cooley's Angry Deviled Eggs, Mama Honey's Strawberry Bread), classic European recipes adapted to the new world (Runsas, Hungarian Sweet Rolls, Hungarian Cabbage Noodles), recipes inspired by convenience foods (Mile High Bologna Pie, 7UP Cake), original regional American fare (Pioneer Bread, Chicken Corn Rivel Soup, Whoopie Pies), recipes with great names (Blueberry Boy Bait, Peach Puzzle, Mashed Potato Fudge), and then, of course, there were the cakes (Tipsy Squire, Cold Oven Pound Cake, Red Velvet Cake, Hummingbird Cake).

The world is full of copycats, hand-me-downs, and second-rate knockoffs, but once in a great while one comes across a true original. It might be a neighbor (like the Vermonter who used a divining rod—an apple branch—to help our family locate our well back in 1955; he referred to the rod as Mr. Stick and talked to it constantly), a place, an experience, or, in this case, a recipe. And this book, *America's Best Lost Recipes,* doesn't have just one good recipe or two. These really are the best of the lost recipes, the best of our immigrant experience, the best of home cooks being inventive with sometimes new ingredients and sometimes few ingredients.

Through America's Test Kitchen, we can also promise you that the recipes will work. Those that were out-of-date have been updated and those that needed a bit of tweaking got tweaked. You can approach these dishes just like any recipe from *Cook's Country* or *Cook's Illustrated*—you know that they are going to turn out. (Well, if you follow the directions!)

We had a great time with this book. We learned a lot about American cooking, found many recipes that were completely new to us, and loved cooking and eating the food. If you enjoy *Lost Recipes* only half as much as we have, then this book will become a cherished and important part of your cookbook collection.

Christopher Kimball
Founder and Editor, *Cook's Illustrated* and *Cook's Country*
Host, *America's Test Kitchen*

GRANDPA COOLEY'S ANGRY DEVILED EGGS

Starters, Salads, Sides, and Sauces

Brooklyn Cheese Puffs

JESSICA LYNN-LATO | WAXHAW, NORTH CAROLINA

At first glance, these light and airy cheese puffs look like fancy French gougères. But instead of relying on hard-to-make cream puff pastry and a fussy pastry bag, this clever recipe turns butter, ricotta cheese, shredded cheddar, egg, and flour into a thick dough that balloons magically in the oven. As with gougères, these cheese puffs require a really hot oven since they are leavened by steam pushing up from the interior.

After tasting them, we understood why Jessica felt they were one of her mother's defining recipes. "My fondest memories of my mother have always involved her cooking. The daughter of Italian immigrants, she was born and raised in Brooklyn, New York, and so food naturally defined family for her and consequently for us as well. My mother unexpectedly passed away when I was 13 years old. Years later, as a young woman just out of college, I sat down with my sister and began rifling through Mom's old, wooden, cluttered recipe box. In the midst of all those recipes was Mother's favorite: her Brooklyn Cheese Puffs."

MAKES 36 CHEESE PUFFS

- 4   tablespoons unsalted butter, cut into small pieces and softened
- 3/4 cup shredded sharp cheddar cheese
- 2/3 cup all-purpose flour
- 1 1/2 cups ricotta cheese
- 1   teaspoon salt, plus extra for sprinkling
- 1/4 teaspoon pepper
- 2   tablespoons chopped fresh parsley
- 1   large egg

1. Combine the butter and cheddar cheese in a large bowl. Add the flour, ricotta, salt, pepper, parsley, and egg, and stir until well combined. Drop rounded teaspoonfuls of the mixture onto a baking sheet, spacing the rounds about an inch apart. Transfer the baking sheet to the freezer and chill until the rounds are frozen solid, at least 30 minutes.

2. Adjust an oven rack to the middle position and heat the oven to 450 degrees. Transfer the baking sheet with the puffs directly to the oven and bake until lightly browned, about 10 minutes. Transfer the puffs to a serving platter and sprinkle lightly with salt. Serve immediately.

Notes from the Test Kitchen

We had a hard time keeping our hands off of these cheese puffs—they were that good. To make them a little less heavy, we reduced the amount of butter from 8 to 4 tablespoons. We also tried substituting other cheeses for the cheddar and found that 1/2 cup of crumbled goat cheese, feta, or blue cheese also made great cheese puffs. If you don't have space in your freezer for a baking sheet, freeze the rounds on two large dinner plates, then transfer them to a baking sheet when ready to bake.

Ma's Kichel

LAURA HOLLAND | HIGHLAND PARK, NEW JERSEY

Kichel, which means "cookies" in Yiddish, are crisp crackers that are either sweet or savory. Laura's family recipe, flavored with grated onion, is a traditional savory kichel (with a hint of sweetness from the sugar water brushed on the dough). Laura's great-grandmother used to make them for her daughter (Laura's grandmother), who described her memories of this recipe as follows: "When I came home from school, I would go to the sukkah and get an apple from a barrel and some kichel, too. Mama rolled the dough out thin, cut out circles with a floured glass, and then brushed the circles with sugar water before baking to give the kichel a nice shine. The crackers came out hard, so I used to bite off a piece and hold it in my mouth while it got soft. I used to love that!"

MAKES ABOUT 92 1½-INCH CRACKERS

- ¼ cup water
- ¼ cup sugar
- 2½ cups all-purpose flour
- 2 tablespoons poppy seeds
- 1 teaspoon salt, plus extra for sprinkling
- ⅛ teaspoon pepper
- ½ cup vegetable shortening
- 2 medium onions, grated and drained (see note)
- 1 large egg, lightly beaten

1. Adjust an oven rack to the middle position and heat the oven to 350 degrees. Line a baking sheet with parchment paper. Mix the water and sugar together in a small bowl and set aside.

2. Pulse the flour, poppy seeds, salt, and pepper in a food processor until blended. Add the shortening and pulse until the flour resembles coarse cornmeal. (To do this by hand, use a fork to cut the shortening into the flour mixture until the flour turns coarse.) Turn the mixture into a medium bowl. Add the drained onion and egg and mix until thoroughly combined.

3. Working with one-quarter of the dough at a time, roll it out on a lightly floured surface until it is ⅛ inch thick. Using a 2-inch cookie cutter, cut out the cracker rounds and space them close together on the prepared baking sheet. Brush the rounds with the reserved sugar water and sprinkle lightly with salt. Reroll the scraps and repeat.

4. Bake until the crackers are spotty brown and firm, 15 to 20 minutes. Cool on the baking sheet for 5 minutes, then transfer the parchment and crackers to a rack to cool completely, at least 20 minutes (the crackers will crisp as they cool). Repeat with the remaining dough. (The crackers will keep in an airtight container at room temperature for up to 5 days. If they become soft, re-crisp them by placing them in a 350-degree oven for 3 minutes. Allow to cool completely before serving.)

Notes from the Test Kitchen
We added a bit more fat to this recipe, making these addictive crackers a little easier on our teeth. Grate the onions on the large holes of a box grater and then place them in a fine sieve. Press out as much of the liquid as possible from the grated onions—excess liquid will prevent the crackers from becoming crisp. Laura's recipe called for using a 3-inch cookie cutter to make the cracker rounds, but we found that by using a 2-inch cookie cutter, the rounds were easier to handle, and we could make many more crackers—enough to serve a good crowd.

Cheese-Crusted Olive Balls

ROBIN PHILLIPS | SONORA, CALIFORNIA

Robin recalls this recipe for homemade cheese-crusted olive balls as being one of her parents' favorites. Her mother would make a quick dough out of cheddar cheese, butter, paprika, and flour and wrap it around a pimiento-stuffed olive. Says Robin: "They are very unusual and I've never seen anything like them. You can't eat just one."

MAKES 36 PIECES

- 1 cup finely shredded cheddar cheese
- 4 tablespoons unsalted butter, very soft
- 1/4 teaspoon paprika
- 3/4 cup all-purpose flour
- 2 (5.75-ounce) jars small Spanish olives, drained

1. Adjust an oven rack to the middle position and heat the oven to 375 degrees. Using a wooden spoon, stir the cheese, butter, and paprika in a medium bowl until well blended. Add the flour and mix in with your hands until incorporated. Cover the bowl with plastic wrap and let rest for 15 minutes.

2. Measure out a level teaspoon of dough and pat into a 1½-inch circle. Following the photos, place an olive in the center of the circle and bring the edges of the dough together to cover the olive. Roll the ball between your hands until smooth and transfer to a baking sheet. Repeat with the remaining dough and olives. Refrigerate until firm, about 10 minutes.

3. Bake until the exterior of the olive balls turns light golden brown, 20 to 25 minutes. Serve hot.

Notes from the Test Kitchen

When we pulled the baked olive balls from the oven they didn't look like much, but after one bite we were sold. The cheesy dough baked into a crisp cracker-like crust, and the hot Spanish olives were pungent with salty, briny flavor. Be sure to use small Spanish olives, sometimes called Manzanilla olives, for this recipe. Queen (large) Spanish olives are too large and will take too long to bake.

MAKING CHEESE-CRUSTED OLIVE BALLS

1. Pat a teaspoon of dough into a 1½-inch circle, place an olive in the center, and pinch the dough around it to seal.

2. Place the ball between the palms of your hands and roll until smooth.

Amish Pickled Beets and Eggs

LILLIAN JULOW | GAINESVILLE, FLORIDA

This traditional Pennsylvania Dutch recipe dates back to the 1800s and is still served at church lunches and in area restaurants. Commonly referred to as "red beet eggs," they are made by soaking hard-boiled eggs in a pickling brine made from beet juice, sugar, vinegar, and spices. This recipe has been a tradition for Lillian's family since the 1930s. She writes: "A large part of my childhood was spent in Lancaster County, Pennsylvania, and the Amish community were our neighbors. One of them, a little girl named Alma, was my best friend and we did everything together. Alma's mother and my mother became friends and she taught my mother how to make some of her Amish dishes, among them pickled beets and eggs. The brilliant color and sweet and sour taste brightened every meal it was served with."

SERVES 8 TO 10

- 8 large hard-cooked eggs, peeled
- 2 (16-ounce) cans sliced beets, drained (reserve 1 cup juice)
- 1 cup sugar
- 3/4 cup cider vinegar
- 1 tablespoon salt
- 1/8 teaspoon pepper
- 2 bay leaves
- 10 whole cloves

1. Place the eggs and drained beets in a large, nonstaining bowl (glass or stainless steel works well). Bring the 1 cup reserved beet juice, sugar, vinegar, salt, pepper, bay leaves, and cloves to a simmer in a medium saucepan over medium-high heat. Cook until the sugar is completely dissolved, about 3 minutes. Pour the beet juice mixture over the eggs and beets, cover with plastic wrap, and refrigerate for at least 24 hours or up to 3 days. (At 24 hours, the pink color will be halfway through the egg white, while after 48 or more hours the egg white will be fully pink.)

2. To serve, drain the eggs and beets (discard bay leaves and cloves). Slice the eggs in half lengthwise and arrange on a serving platter. Scatter the beets around the eggs. Serve.

Notes from the Test Kitchen

You could count on one hand the number of us in the test kitchen who had ever eaten a pickled egg. But that didn't stop us from taking a shine to these incredibly appetizing pickled beets and eggs. The most interesting part, though, is that the white of the egg becomes firm while in the pickle brine, making it much easier to eat off an appetizer tray. The longer the eggs spend in the pickle brine, the deeper the color. Refer to step 1 of Grandpa Cooley's Angry Deviled Eggs (page 7) for our preferred method of cooking hard-boiled eggs.

Grandpa Cooley's Angry Deviled Eggs

LAURA FISCHER | CHICAGO, ILLINOIS

Deviled eggs are an American tradition. This recipe caught our tasters' fancy because they are quite spicy. And Laura's story also won us over. "Grandpa Cooley didn't like kids—not even his grandkids. Or so it seemed. He was gruff at best, mean at worst, smoked two packs a day, and owned a cherished rack of hunting rifles that towered over my grandparents' basement. But Grandpa Cooley had a side I loved—he could cook. My favorite of his specialties was his deviled eggs. Like Grandpa, they were spicy (full of horseradish), and not to the taste of his other grandchildren. I gobbled them up like candy."

MAKES 2 DOZEN FILLED EGG HALVES

- 12 large eggs
- 1/4 cup mayonnaise
- 2–3 tablespoons prepared horseradish (see note)
- 2 teaspoons yellow mustard
- 2 teaspoons sugar
- 1 teaspoon white vinegar
- 1/2 teaspoon salt
- 1/4 teaspoon dry mustard
- 1/4 teaspoon pepper
-    Paprika for garnish

1. Place the eggs in a large saucepan, cover with an inch of water, and bring to a boil over high heat. Remove the pan from the heat, cover, and let stand 10 minutes. Meanwhile, fill a medium bowl with 1 quart water and a dozen ice cubes. Following the photos, pour off the water from the saucepan and gently shake the pan back and forth to crack the shells. Using a slotted spoon, transfer the eggs to the ice water and let cool 5 minutes.

2. Peel the eggs and slice them in half lengthwise. Transfer the yolks to a fine-mesh sieve and use a spatula to press them through the sieve and into a bowl. Add the remaining ingredients (except for the paprika) and mash the mixture against the sides of the bowl until smooth.

3. Arrange the whites on a serving platter and fill with the yolk mixture. Sprinkle with paprika and serve.

Notes from the Test Kitchen

To center the yolks before cooking, turn the carton of eggs on its side in the refrigerator the day before you plan to hard-cook them. Start with 2 tablespoons horseradish in the filling, then add more as desired.

EGG PEELING MADE EASIER

1. Once the eggs have finished cooking, pour out the boiling water and shake the pan back and forth to crack the shells.

2. Transfer the eggs to a bowl of ice water. Air and water will get in the cracks in the shells, making the eggs easier to peel.

Bloody Mary Terrine

SUSAN ASANOVIC | WILTON, CONNECTICUT

Recipes like this terrine (or aspic), where ingredients are suspended in gelatin, have a very long history dating back to the Middle Ages, when cooks first went through the labors of boiling animal bones to create a broth that thickened and set up when cooled. Fast forward to the 1890s, when Charles Knox introduced granulated gelatin and all manner of jelled concoctions came into vogue, most notably molded Jelly salads. This Bloody Mary terrine likely dates back to this era; in fact, we found an old *Fannie Farmer* recipe somewhat like it—Macèdoine of Aspic—in which tomatoes are simmered with seasonings and thickened with gelatin, and the aspic and its contents are artfully arranged in a mold that is chilled, then inverted, sliced, and served with a seasoned mayonnaise.

Susan's recipe (which comes from her aunt) takes the concept to new heights with the addition of vodka and seafood. "I had an aunt who liked a pre-dinner cocktail, and who found a way to serve it as an appetizer. For the children she left out the vodka (or so she said: I always wondered). I wish these jelled dishes hadn't gone out of style; one hardly ever sees these '50s-era showpieces today."

SERVES 8 TO 12

TERRINE
- 1/3 cup cold water
- 2 envelopes plain gelatin
- 4 pounds ripe tomatoes, cored and quartered
- 1/4 cup minced onion
- 1 garlic clove, minced
- 2 bay leaves
- 3 whole cloves
- Salt and pepper
- 1/4 cup vodka (see note on page 10)
- 2 tablespoons Worcestershire sauce
- 1 tablespoon lemon juice
- 1 tablespoon lime juice
- 1 teaspoon hot sauce, plus more if desired
- 1 small jalapeño chile, seeded and minced
- 3/4 cup sliced Spanish olives (jarred, not canned)
- 2 tablespoons capers, rinsed and dried
- 1/2 pound cooked, peeled, large shrimp (31 to 40 per pound)

FOR SERVING
Horseradish Mayonnaise (see page 10)

1. TO MAKE THE TERRINE: Place the water in a small bowl and sprinkle the gelatin over the water. Let stand 5 minutes to soften the gelatin.

2. Working in two batches, pulse the tomatoes in a food processor until finely chopped, then strain the tomatoes, reserving 4 cups of juice; discard any excess juice. Bring the chopped tomatoes, 4 cups tomato juice, onion, garlic, bay leaves, cloves, 1 teaspoon salt, and 1/4 teaspoon pepper to a simmer in a Dutch oven over medium heat. Reduce the heat to low and simmer until the flavors meld, about 10 minutes.

(Continued on page 10)

3. Strain the mixture into a bowl, discarding the solids. Stir the gelatin mixture into the hot tomato broth until completely dissolved. Add the vodka, Worcestershire sauce, lemon juice, lime juice, and hot sauce. Reserve 1 cup of the tomato mixture. Following the photos, stir the chile, olives, and capers into the remaining tomato mixture and refrigerate until just beginning to thicken (about the consistency of raw egg whites), about 1 hour. Pour the reserved tomato mixture into the bottom of a 9 by 5-inch loaf pan and refrigerate until slightly thickened but not set, about 30 minutes. Arrange the shrimp in the bottom of the loaf pan on top of the tomato mixture and refrigerate until ready to assemble.

4. Gently stir the slightly thickened gelatin mixture to redistribute the chile, olives, and capers, then spoon over the shrimp. Cover the terrine with plastic wrap and refrigerate until set, at least 8 hours, or preferably overnight. (The terrine can be refrigerated for up to 4 days.)

5. TO SERVE: Run a knife around the edges of the terrine, then dip the bottom of the terrine in hot water for 30 seconds. Unmold the terrine onto a platter and cut into ½-inch slices. Serve with Horseradish Mayonnaise.

HORSERADISH MAYONNAISE
MAKES ABOUT 1 CUP

- ³/₄ cup mayonnaise (see note)
- 3 tablespoons prepared horseradish, drained
- 2 tablespoons lemon juice
- 1½ teaspoons minced garlic

Combine all the ingredients and chill until the flavors meld, about 30 minutes. Serve.

Notes from the Test Kitchen
We took one look at this lengthy recipe and decided that it had better be worth the effort— and it sure was. Originally the recipe called for scallops, but we think it's easier for most cooks to find good shrimp, and their pink color looked pretty in the terrine. If you like a more potent punch, increase the amount of vodka to ¹/₃ cup. The horseradish mayonnaise can be prepared up to 3 days in advance. Do not use fat-free or low-fat mayonnaise. The terrine can be unmolded onto a lettuce-lined platter or simply garnished with parsley leaves.

ASSEMBLING THE TERRINE

1. Reserve 1 cup of the tomato mixture. Stir the chile, olives, and capers into the remaining tomato mixture and refrigerate until just beginning to thicken, about 1 hour.

2. Pour the reserved plain tomato mixture into the bottom of a loaf pan and refrigerate for 30 minutes or until thickened but not set.

3. Arrange the shrimp on top of the tomato mixture and refrigerate until ready to assemble.

4. Pour the tomato mixture with the chile, olives, and capers over the shrimp layer. Refrigerate until completely set, at least 8 hours or overnight.

Nine-Day Slaw

MERRIGAY SCHROER | PLAINFIELD, INDIANA

This unusual coleslaw was handed down via Merrigay's uncle's wife. "She grew up on a farm in Greenup, Illinois, and said that it was an easy way to use up the extra cabbage in the garden but also prepare a side dish that would feed field workers for several days, cutting down on food prep time. You can make a large batch and it will keep up to nine days in the fridge. And it only gets better and better after a few days in the fridge."

SERVES 8

- ³/₄ cup white vinegar
- ³/₄ cup sugar
- 1¹/₂ teaspoons salt
- ¹/₂ teaspoon celery seed
- ¹/₂ teaspoon mustard seed
- ¹/₂ teaspoon ground cumin
- ¹/₂ teaspoon pepper
- 1 large head green cabbage, cored and chopped medium
- 1 small onion, chopped fine
- 1 green bell pepper, stemmed, seeded, and chopped medium
- ¹/₄ cup diced pimientos

1. Bring the vinegar, sugar, salt, celery seed, mustard seed, cumin, and pepper to a boil in a medium saucepan over medium-high heat. Boil until the sugar dissolves, about 1 minute, then set aside to cool completely, at least 20 minutes.

2. Toss the cabbage, onion, bell pepper, and pimientos together in a large bowl. Add the dressing and stir to combine. Cover the surface with plastic wrap, pressing down on it so it touches the surface, then place a heavy plate on top of the plastic to keep the cabbage mixture submerged in the dressing. Refrigerate until most of the liquid is absorbed by the cabbage and the flavors meld, at least 24 hours. (The slaw can be refrigerated for up to 9 days.) Serve.

Notes from the Test Kitchen

This sweet and sour chopped slaw gets a kick from pimiento peppers, crisp green bell pepper, and abundant spices. Although most slaws improve with time, in this case it is essential; at least 24 hours are necessary to bring out the flavor of the celery and mustard seeds. Weighting down the cabbage so that it is submerged in the tangy dressing ensures that the cabbage is softened and flavored through and through.

PREPARING CABBAGE

1. Cut the cabbage into quarters, then trim and discard the hard core.

2. Separate the cabbage into small stacks of leaves that flatten when pressed.

3. Cut each stack of cabbage leaves into ¹/₄-inch strips.

4. Chop the strips into medium-sized pieces.

24-Hour Salad

HARRIET MATTES | HIGH POINT, NORTH CAROLINA

There is a tradition going back to the late 19th century of fruit salad married with a sweet custard and frozen. Then, in the 1930s, we began to see all sorts of creamy fruit salads with marshmallows and cream or whipped cream along with coconut—most notably a recipe called Ambrosia. This recipe differs from both, though it has the same spirit (and creamy appeal). The name, 24-Hour Salad, is sometimes attached to savory layered salads and sometimes to sweet salads like this one, which must sit for the flavors to meld.

SERVES 8 TO 10

- 2   large eggs
- 2   tablespoons sugar
- 1   cup heavy cream
- 2   tablespoons lemon juice
- 2   cups frozen sour cherries, drained (see note)
- 1   (20-ounce) can pineapple tidbits or crushed pineapple packed in juice, drained
- 2   (14.5-ounce) cans mandarin oranges packed in juice, drained
- 3   cups large marshmallows, quartered (see note)
- 1   cup sliced almonds, chopped coarse

1. Combine the eggs and sugar in a medium heatproof bowl. Set the bowl over a saucepan containing an inch of simmering water and whisk until the sugar begins to dissolve, about 1 minute. Whisk in ¼ cup of the heavy cream and the lemon juice and cook, whisking constantly, until the mixture begins to thicken slightly, about 5 minutes. Let cool completely, at least 30 minutes.

2. Meanwhile, with an electric mixer on high speed, beat the remaining ¾ cup heavy cream in a large bowl to soft peaks. Gently fold into the cooled egg mixture.

3. Toss the cherries, pineapple, oranges, marshmallows, and almonds together in a large bowl. Pour the egg and cream mixture over the fruit and toss gently until combined. Refrigerate until ready to serve, at least 24 hours and up to 2 days in advance. Serve.

Notes from the Test Kitchen

This take on a familiar holiday favorite was a pleasant surprise for the test kitchen. The tart cherries really cut the sweetness of the custard, and the almonds added some necessary texture to the salad. Fresh sour cherries will also work well in this recipe, but do not substitute canned cherries, which are too soft and will turn mushy. Originally the recipe called for 2 cups of fresh orange segments, a little too much work for a salad (in our opinion). Instead, we turned to mandarin orange slices, which are ready to go and taste great.

The recipe also called for whole chopped almonds, which we felt were too coarse for this elegant combination. Our version uses sliced almonds, which provide a more delicate crunch in the salad. We also tried substituting miniature marshmallows to avoid quartering large ones. Bad idea—the small marshmallows simply turned to mush. To make the prep work easier, we found that if we sprayed our chef's knife with cooking spray, the marshmallows did not cling to the blade (and were less likely to stick together).

Hungarian Cabbage Noodles (Kaposztas Taszta)

DANA FULMER | ACCORD, NEW YORK

This humble peasant dish, a staple in the Hungarian Jewish kitchen, traditionally marries sautéed cabbage with homemade noodles (*taszta* refers to the noodle dough while *kaposztas* means cabbage). According to Joan Nathan, a food writer with a focus on Jewish cooking, this is one of the famous dishes brought to the United States by the Satmar, the world's largest group of Hasidic Jews, who originated in Szatmárnémeti, Hungary, and settled in and around New York City.

The recipe came by way of Dana's grandmother, Margaret Czegledy, who was from a small village in Hungary but came to the United States at the age of 13. "She worked as a servant in a well-to-do household until the gentleman of the house became too familiar and then fibbed her way into a job at the Singer sewing factory. She could not sew at all, but luckily a coworker took her under her wing and my grandmother became a master seamstress who supported her family during the Depression with her work."

SERVES 4

- 2 tablespoons vegetable oil or rendered bacon fat
- ½ large head green cabbage, cored and sliced thin (see page 11)
  Salt
- 1 (16-ounce) bag wide egg noodles
- 1 tablespoon unsalted butter
  Pepper

1. Bring 4 quarts of water to a boil in a large pot for the noodles.

2. Meanwhile, heat 1 tablespoon of the oil in a large skillet over medium-high heat until shimmering. Add half of the cabbage, season with ¼ teaspoon salt, and cook, tossing frequently, until golden brown, 5 to 8 minutes. Transfer the cooked cabbage to a plate. Repeat with the remaining oil and cabbage.

3. Add 1 tablespoon salt and the noodles to the boiling water and cook until al dente. Drain the noodles and transfer back to the pot. Add the reserved cabbage and butter, toss to combine, and season to taste with salt and pepper. Serve.

Notes from the Test Kitchen
Although this recipe looks incredibly simple, the mingled flavors of the browned cabbage and the egg noodles are surprisingly complex. Be sure not to overcrowd the skillet when cooking the cabbage—the result will be steamed cabbage rather than browned. To make this dish just a bit richer, we took a note from other buttered egg noodle dishes, and added just 1 tablespoon of butter. These cabbage noodles are great served with pot roast.

Summary Squash Soufflé

CARY WING | RICHMOND, VIRGINIA

Although this dish is called a soufflé, it's really a baked casserole. Clearly a great way to use up a surplus of summer squash, this recipe was handed down to Cary by her late mother, Ada Stuart Holland, "a woman before her time, tackling the home chores and a job outside the house long before it was fashionable. Many of her recipes were quick and easy to prepare due to her busy lifestyle." Like many casseroles, this one uses saltines in the topping and as a binder in the filling. Saltines first became popular in Missouri in the late 19th century and were nationally available by the 1920s. Their distinctive perforations allow steam to escape as the crackers bake, ensuring an even rise.

SERVES 6

24	saltines, crushed fine
1/4	cup grated Parmesan cheese
4	tablespoons unsalted butter (with 1 tablespoon melted)
1	medium onion, chopped fine
3	pounds summer squash (about 6), ends trimmed and sliced thin
1	garlic clove, minced
1 1/2	cups milk
2	large eggs
2	tablespoons chopped fresh parsley
1	teaspoon salt
1/4	teaspoon pepper

1. Toss half the saltine crumbs with the Parmesan and melted butter in a medium bowl and set aside.

2. Adjust an oven rack to the middle position and heat the oven to 350 degrees. Grease a 2-quart baking dish. Melt 2 tablespoons butter in a large skillet over medium-high heat. Add the onion and cook until golden brown, about 5 minutes. Add half the squash and cook until completely softened and most of the liquid has evaporated, about 10 minutes. Transfer to a large bowl. Repeat with the remaining 2 tablespoons butter and squash. Stir in the garlic when the squash is completely softened and cook until fragrant, about 30 seconds.

3. Combine the remaining saltine crumbs, milk, eggs, parsley, salt, and pepper in a medium bowl, then add to the squash, stirring to combine. Transfer the mixture to the prepared baking dish. Top with the reserved saltine-Parmesan mixture and bake until the filling is hot and the topping is golden brown, about 30 minutes. Serve.

Notes from the Test Kitchen
Like many other squash dishes, this one suffered a bit from the large amount of liquid in the squash. Rather than boiling the squash (as originally called for), we sautéed it in butter until most of the liquid had evaporated, which also concentrated its flavor. This recipe can be made with an equal amount of zucchini as well.

Kentucky-Style Okra, Corn, and Tomato Stew

PHILLIP YATES | PORTLAND, OREGON

Okra arrived in the South in the 1700s from West Africa, and for generations it has played a starring role in many regional favorites, like Creole Gumbo and Brunswick Stew (see page 37). It's also often served as a side dish, breaded and fried or paired with tomatoes and other vegetables. This savory recipe was developed by Phillip's great aunt Trudy, "who ran a small reservation-only restaurant out of her home in Jeffersontown, Kentucky, in the early 1960s. Family lore has it that this was one of her most requested menu items. I still remember the smells and sounds of my grandmother preparing this recipe in her ancient cast-iron skillet when I was a child. When I finally learned the recipe from my mother, I was surprised that such fullness of flavor could come from such simple ingredients—no onions, no garlic, no spices—just okra, corn, tomatoes, and some salt and pepper."

SERVES 6 TO 8

- 4   large ears corn, husks and silk removed
- 2   cups okra, trimmed and cut into 1/2-inch rounds
- 2   tablespoons cornmeal, fine or medium grind
- 2   tablespoons unsalted butter
- 4   pounds ripe tomatoes, cored and chopped coarse
- 1   cup water
    Salt and pepper

1. Cut the kernels from the corn and transfer to a medium bowl. Scrape the cobs with the back of a knife (see page 18) to collect the milk in the same bowl and set aside.

2. Toss the okra with the cornmeal in a large bowl until evenly coated. Melt the butter in a large skillet over medium-high heat. Add the okra to the skillet (leaving the excess cornmeal behind) and fry until golden brown, about 2 minutes per side. Stir in the corn, tomatoes, water, and 1/2 teaspoon salt, bring to a simmer, then cook over medium-low heat until the tomatoes break down, most of the liquid has evaporated, and the sauce becomes very thick, 45 to 55 minutes. Season to taste with salt and pepper. Serve.

Notes from the Test Kitchen

More than a few of us have been put off by the somewhat slimy texture of okra, so we were suspicious of this dish at first. Boy were we surprised! The okra and tomatoes cooked down into a silky thick sauce, much like a ratatouille, and the bites of summer corn scattered within added a sweet, summery flavor. As there is very little fat in this stew—just 2 tablespoons—we thought that it was bright and fresh enough to serve alongside grilled meat and fish. Do not use stone- or coarse-ground cornmeal for dredging the okra as it will result in a gritty texture.

Cheesy Scalloped Carrots

ANNE EDGECOMB | WAYNESBORO, VIRGINIA

We've scalloped potatoes, corn, and even sweet potatoes—why not carrots? Recipes for scalloped carrots appeared in newspapers around the country in the 1930s; in most of them, first the carrots are boiled, a simple roux-based sauce is made, and then both are combined with shredded cheese and maybe a bread-crumb topping and baked. This particular recipe, which Anne's mother made every Thanksgiving, "came from someone at St. John's Episcopal Church in Waynesboro, Virginia, back in the 1960s. In our family we simply call it Carrot Casserole. It adds a punch of color next to the turkey, mashed potatoes, and dressing. When I was a girl I asked my mother why she didn't make Carrot Casserole in the summer. She said she did not want to heat up the kitchen. Would it taste as good in June?"

SERVES 6 TO 8

- 2 slices hearty white sandwich bread, torn into pieces
- 5 tablespoons unsalted butter (with 2 tablespoons melted)
- 2 teaspoons salt
- 2 pounds carrots, peeled and cut on the bias into $1/2$-inch slices
- 1 small onion, chopped fine
- 3 tablespoons all-purpose flour
- $1^1/2$ cups milk
- 1 teaspoon dry mustard
- $1/4$ teaspoon pepper
- $1/4$ teaspoon celery salt
- $2^1/2$ cups shredded sharp cheddar cheese

1. Process the bread in a food processor until finely ground. Transfer to a medium bowl and toss with the melted butter until evenly coated. Set aside.

2. Adjust an oven rack to the middle position and heat the oven to 350 degrees. Grease a 2-quart baking dish.

3. Bring 2 quarts of water to a boil in a large pot over medium-high heat. Add 1 teaspoon salt and the carrots and cook until barely tender, 6 to 8 minutes. Drain, then transfer the carrots to a paper-towel-lined plate.

4. Melt the remaining 3 tablespoons butter in a large skillet over medium-high heat. Add the onion and cook until softened but not browned, about 3 minutes. Stir in the flour and cook until it begins to brown, about 1 minute. Whisk in the milk, mustard, pepper, celery salt, and the remaining 1 teaspoon salt, bring to a simmer, and cook until the mixture begins to thicken, about 2 minutes. Off the heat, stir in the cheese until melted, then stir in the carrots.

5. Transfer the mixture to the prepared baking dish, top with the reserved crumb mixture, and bake until the filling is hot and the topping is golden brown, about 30 minutes. Serve.

Notes from the Test Kitchen

To enhance the flavor of the carrots, we reduced the original amount of the white sauce but increased the amount of black pepper and mustard called for in the recipe. And we found that boiling the carrots for just 6 minutes, then baking the casserole for 30 minutes, yielded carrots with just the right amount of bite. Comfort food at its best, this casserole could convince even the finicky to eat their vegetables. Serve with any type of roast meat.

Corn Oysters

LOIS BLUMENTHAL | YORK, PENNSYLVANIA

Corn oysters date back to the late 1800s. Some of the early recipes were made with "Indian" green corn and the taste was thought to resemble that of oysters. When these fritters hit the hot oil, the batter sputters and invariably a stream of it trails behind, making them look even more like fried oysters. According to Lois, whose family settled in Maryland in the 1600s, "this recipe is the original and makes truly tender, full of corn flavor, delicate corn oysters."

SERVES 6

- 4 medium ears corn, husks and silk removed
- 1/2 cup all-purpose flour
- 1/4 cup cornstarch
- 4 large eggs
- 1/2 teaspoon salt, plus extra for sprinkling
- 1/4 teaspoon baking powder
- 2 quarts vegetable oil

1. Following the photos, grate the kernels from the corn into a medium bowl using the large holes of a box grater. Using the back of a knife, scrape any pulp remaining on the cobs into the bowl with the grated corn. Stir in the flour, cornstarch, eggs, salt, and baking powder until well blended.

2. Heat the oil in a Dutch oven over medium heat until it registers 350 degrees. Carefully drop 13 to 15 heaping tablespoons of batter into the hot oil and fry, turning once, until the corn oysters puff and are golden brown on both sides, about 2 minutes. Transfer to a paper-towel-lined plate. Add more oil to the pot if necessary and heat to 350 degrees. Repeat with the remaining batter. Sprinkle the corn oysters with salt. Serve immediately.

Notes from the Test Kitchen

Use only fresh corn for this recipe—frozen corn is too dry to produce a creamy batter. The key to this recipe is getting the oil temperature just right. Above 360 degrees and the exterior of the "oysters" will darken quickly before the interior is cooked through. Too low a temperature (starting under 340 degrees) and they will be sodden with oil. Avoid guesswork by using a deep-fat thermometer. These corn oysters are great with fried fish or any barbecue—serve with tartar sauce, hot sauce, or maple syrup.

PREPARING THE CORN

1. Using the large holes on a box grater, grate the kernels into a medium bowl.

2. To extract maximum flavor, use the back of a knife to scrape the pulp remaining into the bowl.

G-Mom's Spanish Dressing

JULIE LONGABACH | BRADENTON, FLORIDA

The unmistakable taste of saffron adds an unexpected and refreshing flavor to this otherwise traditional sausage dressing. Julie's grandmother (G-Mom) concocted this savory recipe for her husband, a Spaniard whom she met when they were both visiting Cuba in the 1940s.

SERVES 8 TO 10

6–7 slices hearty white sandwich bread, cut into
¹/₂-inch cubes (about 7 cups)
1 (16-ounce) package ground breakfast sausage
2 tablespoons olive oil
1 large onion, chopped medium
¹/₂ small green bell pepper, stemmed, seeded, and chopped fine
1 large tomato, cored and chopped medium
2 garlic cloves, minced
1¹/₂ cups low-sodium chicken broth
¹/₄ cup chopped fresh parsley
¹/₈ teaspoon saffron threads, crumbled, or ¹/₁₆ teaspoon powdered saffron
1 bay leaf
¹/₂ teaspoon salt
¹/₄ teaspoon pepper
1 egg white, lightly beaten

1. Adjust an oven rack to the middle position and heat the oven to 350 degrees. Spread the bread cubes onto a baking sheet and bake, tossing occasionally, until golden brown, 20 to 25 minutes. Cool completely before using, at least 20 minutes. Transfer to a large bowl.

2. Brown the sausage in a large skillet over medium heat, breaking it into small pieces with a spoon. Using a slotted spoon, transfer the sausage to a paper-towel-lined plate and pour off the fat from the skillet. Heat the olive oil in the now-empty skillet over medium-high heat until shimmering. Cook the onion and bell pepper until softened, about 5 minutes. Add the tomato and garlic and cook until the tomato softens, about 5 minutes. Stir in 1 cup of the broth along with the parsley, saffron, bay leaf, salt, and pepper and bring to a simmer. Reduce the heat to medium-low and simmer until the flavors meld, about 10 minutes. Discard the bay leaf.

3. Beat the remaining ¹/₂ cup of broth with the egg white, then toss with the vegetable mixture, sausage, and bread cubes until well combined. (The mixture should be moist but not wet.) Transfer the mixture to a 13 by 9-inch baking dish and bake until the dressing is hot and the top is golden brown, about 30 minutes. Serve.

Notes from the Test Kitchen

Simmering the saffron and bay leaf in the chicken broth allows their heady flavors to penetrate the dressing. When shopping for saffron, look for dark threads, which have much more flavor than the lighter threads, or buy powdered saffron, which has plenty of flavor (and is more economical). Julie's original recipe called for a mixture of white sandwich bread and bakery Cuban bread, but we found that good-quality, sturdy sandwich bread, such as Pepperidge Farm, was just fine on its own in this flavorful dressing.

Celery Seed Dressing

PHYLLIS KIRIGIN | CROTON-ON-HUDSON, NEW YORK

Department store eateries, whether the humble lunch counters at Woolworths or the elegant dining rooms of upscale stores like Lord and Taylor or Saks Fifth Avenue, had a definite place in our culture in the 1950s and 1960s; many of the fancier ones became destinations apart from the shopping experience because the food was often that good. We loved this detailed description of a Midwestern department store restaurant:

"In the 1950s, my mother worked as a waitress in a restaurant called the Coin Room in Rike's Department Store in Dayton, Ohio. The restaurant featured light, well-prepared meals for 99 cents plus the 3-cent sales tax, bringing the total for a wonderful cooked-from-scratch luncheon to $1.02. It was great for shoppers who wanted a quick, inexpensive, and tasty meal. My mother brought home the Coin Room recipe for Celery Seed Dressing, which was a big hit there and in our home. It was a dressing for a fruit salad. It tasted great on grapefruit, pears, apples—just about any fruit, as well as greens, nuts, and other fruit salad accompaniments. However, somewhere along the line it got lost. Rike's was sold to a conglomerate, the Coin Room disappeared, and, in 1986, my mother died. Then, just this year, tucked in an old cookbook left to me by my mother, there it was."

MAKES ABOUT 1 CUP

- $1/4$ cup sugar
- $1/2$ teaspoon dry mustard
- $1/2$ teaspoon salt
- $1/2$ teaspoon celery seed
- 2 tablespoons grated yellow onion
- $2^1/2$ tablespoons white vinegar
- $1/2$ cup peanut or canola oil

Stir the sugar, mustard, salt, and celery seed together in a medium bowl. Add the onion and the vinegar and stir until the sugar is dissolved. Slowly whisk in the oil until well blended. Cover and refrigerate until the flavors meld, about 1 hour. (The dressing can be covered and refrigerated for up to 3 days. Whisk before serving.)

Notes from the Test Kitchen
The test kitchen loved the sweet and sour flavors of this dressing and tasted it on everything from apples to greens (we especially loved it on Bibb lettuce) to a cucumber and radish salad. The taste gets better as it sits, so be sure to allow it the full hour (or days) to develop all of its potential flavor. Also, be sure to use celery seed, not celery salt, for this recipe.

Josephine Draper's Chili Sauce

SHEILA DRAPER OREFICE | BRISTOL, CONNECTICUT

The simple, time-honored practice of putting up jams, jellies, relishes, and fruits and vegetables goes back to John Mason's invention of his "fruit jar" in 1858. Sheila's recipe goes back to the early part of the 20th century: "In September, during the '30s and '40s, my parents did the tedious job of canning. At the end of the summer, when there was an excess of fresh fruits and vegetables, they spent many hours canning tomatoes, peaches, and pears. The jars were cleaned, the produce peeled and sliced. Then the jars were filled and covers and seals were put on. Next, they were put into a rack that fit into the canner, and boiled. The jars were put on special shelves in the cellar, looking very colorful. All winter long, they were a welcome addition to our meals.

"One recipe they made was Chili Sauce—a vegetable relish. The vegetables were put, one at a time, into our old-fashioned 'food chopper.' My job was to turn the handle. Every Sunday during the winter, Dad made pot roast, which he browned in an iron Dutch oven. The scrapings in that pot made wonderful dark gravy for the mashed potatoes and turnips. This Chili Sauce was served as a garnish."

MAKES ABOUT 3 QUARTS

- 8 pounds ripe beefsteak tomatoes, cored, peeled, and chopped coarse
- 8 celery ribs, chopped coarse
- 4 large onions, chopped coarse
- 2 green bell peppers, stemmed, seeded, and chopped coarse
- 1 jalapeño chile, seeded and minced
- 1 cup sugar
- 2 cups white vinegar
- 2 tablespoons salt
- 1 teaspoon ground cinnamon
- 1 teaspoon mustard seed
- 1/2 teaspoon ground cloves

1. Working in batches, pulse the tomatoes, celery, onions, and bell peppers separately in a food processor until finely chopped. Transfer each batch to a large Dutch oven.

2. Stir in the remaining ingredients and cook over low heat, stirring often, until the sauce is very thick and the vegetables are completely soft, about 2 hours.

3. Cool the sauce completely, at least 1 hour. Then transfer to airtight containers. The relish will keep refrigerated for up to 2 weeks or can be frozen for up to 3 months. If freezing, press plastic wrap directly on the surface of the sauce before sealing.

Notes from the Test Kitchen

We were intimidated by the work it would take to make this sauce. But after making it, we thought the recipe was worthy of saving, and set out to simplify it wherever we could. So out came the food processor to chop the vegetables in record time. This recipe was of course originally designed to go through the canning process for long storage, so if you prefer you can follow standard canning/processing procedures rather than freezing the excess.

MILE HIGH BOLOGNA PIE

Soups, Stews, and Main Courses

Chicken Corn Rivel Soup

ANNE STEVENS | BOALSBURG, PENNSYLVANIA

This savory chicken soup with small dumplings called rivels is classic Pennsylvania Dutch fare. Anne wrote us about her grandmother's version of this soup: "At my grandmother Weiss's house, when dinner was a roasted chicken, within the next few days we could expect chicken rivel soup. In summer during corn season, the leftover corn on the cob was added and the result was chicken corn rivel soup. I assume that because of my grandmother's French grandmother, the butter for the rivels was browned."

SERVES 6

- 3 pounds bone-in, skin-on chicken thighs
  Salt and pepper
- 1 tablespoon vegetable oil
- 1 onion, chopped
- 2 celery ribs, chopped
- 2 quarts water
- 2 bay leaves
  Pinch saffron threads
- 1 pound boneless, skinless chicken breasts
- 6 tablespoons unsalted butter
- 1½ cups all-purpose flour
- 1 large egg yolk, beaten with 1 tablespoon water
- 2 ears fresh corn, kernels removed from cobs, or 1 cup frozen corn

1. Pat the thighs dry with paper towels and season with salt and pepper. Heat the oil in a large Dutch oven over medium-high heat until just smoking. Working in two batches, brown the thighs, about 8 minutes. Transfer to a paper-towel-lined plate. Pour off all but 1 tablespoon fat from the pot. Cook the onion and celery over medium heat until softened, about 5 minutes. Meanwhile, remove and discard the skin from the thighs. Add the thighs, water, bay leaves, saffron, and 1 tablespoon salt to the pot. Cover and simmer until the broth is flavorful, about 30 minutes. Add the chicken breasts and simmer until cooked through, about 15 minutes.

2. Strain the broth into a large container, let stand at least 10 minutes, then skim the fat from the surface. Reserve the thigh meat for another use. Shred the breast meat and reserve for the soup.

3. Melt the butter in a small saucepan over medium heat until nutty brown, about 3 minutes. Let cool. Add the broth and ¼ teaspoon salt to the now-empty Dutch oven and set over medium-high heat. Meanwhile, place the flour in a bowl and make a well in the center. Add the yolk mixture and 2 tablespoons of the browned butter to the well and, using your hands, mix until incorporated. Following the photos, pinch the dough between your fingers to form ½-inch pieces (the rivels). Place on a baking sheet and repeat with the remaining dough. Add the rivels, one at a time, to the simmering soup. Gently stir in the corn and reserved shredded chicken and simmer until the rivels are tender, 15 to 20 minutes. Serve, drizzling each portion with the remaining browned butter.

HOW TO MAKE RIVELS

1. Pinch small pieces of the dough between your fingers to form ½-inch rivels.

2. Drop the rivels into the simmering soup, stirring them gently so they don't stick together.

German Potato Soup

THEDA SULLICK | OCEAN VIEW, NEW JERSEY

The only thing that seems consistent among German Potato Soup recipes is that they are heartier than most other potato soups and rely on a flavor base of bacon or sausage, onions, and beef broth. Sometimes the potatoes are cooked in the broth, removed, and then mashed, thickening the soup. Other times, homemade dumplings or egg noodles are added. Here, egg yolks combined with sour cream and tempered with some hot broth both thicken and enrich the soup. This recipe was passed down in Theda's family from her German grandmother. "It is the soup that is most asked for around my home. I like to serve rye and pumpernickel bread with it."

SERVES 8

- 8 slices bacon, chopped
- 3 large onions, chopped medium
- 2 garlic cloves, minced
- 3 tablespoons all-purpose flour
- 5 cups low-sodium beef broth
- 3 cups water
- 3½ pounds russet potatoes, peeled, halved lengthwise, and sliced thin
- 3 large egg yolks
- 2 cups sour cream
- 2 tablespoons chopped fresh parsley
- 2 tablespoons chopped fresh basil

1. Cook the bacon in a large Dutch oven over medium heat until crisp, about 8 minutes. Using a slotted spoon, transfer the bacon to a paper-towel-lined plate. Cook the onions in the bacon fat until golden, about 5 minutes. Add the garlic and cook until fragrant, about 30 seconds. Stir in the flour and cook until it begins to brown, about 1 minute. Stir in the broth, water, and potatoes and simmer until the potatoes break down and the soup is slightly thickened, about 45 minutes.

2. Beat the egg yolks and sour cream together in a medium bowl. Whisk 1 cup of the hot soup into the egg mixture, then stir the egg mixture back into the soup pot. Add the herbs and stir constantly (see note) over medium-low heat until thick and creamy, about 5 minutes. Stir in the bacon. Serve.

Notes from the Test Kitchen
With all the flavors of a good German potato salad, this soup was hard to beat. But some in the test kitchen thought that the texture was too thick and the flavor too beefy. The solution was simple. After cutting some of the beef broth with water and adding more water to thin down the soup, tasters lined up to eat it by the bowlful. After the eggs and sour cream are added in step 2, do not allow the soup to come back to a simmer. If it does, the eggs and sour cream will curdle.

Grandma June's Sauerkraut Soup

HEATHER CLARK | COLUMBUS, OHIO

Sauerkraut soup is German in origin, though this family recipe came from Czechoslovakia via Heather's great-great-great-grandmother, who immigrated to the United States in the late 1880s. Many sauerkraut soups include potatoes, but this one has simple, small potato dumplings instead.

SERVES 6

- 4 smoked ham hocks (see note)
- 4 quarts water
- 1 (10-ounce) jar sauerkraut, drained and rinsed
- 1 tablespoon caraway seeds
- 1 large egg, lightly beaten
- 1 russet potato, peeled and grated on the large holes of a box grater
- 3 tablespoons finely grated onion
- 1/4 teaspoon pepper
- 1/2 cup all-purpose flour
  Sour cream, for serving

1. Bring the ham hocks and water to a boil in a large Dutch oven over medium-high heat. Reduce the heat to medium-low and simmer, partially covered, until the broth is richly flavored, 1½ to 2 hours. (You should have about 3 quarts of broth.) Cool to room temperature (leaving the hocks in the broth), then refrigerate for at least 8 hours or up to 2 days.

2. Skim the congealed fat from the broth and bring the broth to a simmer over medium heat. Using a slotted spoon, transfer the hocks to a cutting board and carefully remove any meat; discard the bones and skin. Add the meat from the hocks, sauerkraut, and caraway seeds to the pot and simmer, covered, until the flavors meld, about 30 minutes.

3. While the soup simmers, combine the egg, potato, onion, and pepper in a large bowl. Add the flour and stir to combine. Following the photos, shape the dumpling mixture into heaping teaspoonfuls and drop into the simmering soup, cooking until tender, about 20 minutes. Serve, passing the sour cream at the table.

Notes from the Test Kitchen
The method here is simple, but it takes some advance planning as the broth must both simmer for a couple of hours and then sit for a minimum of eight hours (best done overnight) to deepen in flavor. Be sure to buy the smoked ham hocks for this recipe as they add such a rich, deep flavor to the broth.

HOW TO MAKE DUMPLINGS

1. After making the dumpling batter, scoop it out in heaping teaspoon-sized portions.

2. Using a second spoon, slide the dumplings into the simmering soup.

Bobbi's Beefy Bean and Barley Soup

DIANE HALFERTY | CORPUS CHRISTI, TEXAS

Although barley has a long history in the United States (and turns up in many late-18th-century recipe books), Diane's recipe has its roots back in Russia. Barley was a food staple in Russia and the Baltics and was used in soups as a matter of economy, as it could transform a soup made with nothing more than meat bones into a nutritious and filling meal. This humble though satisfying soup follows in that tradition. "My paternal grandparents came to the U.S. from Russia, to escape persecution and conscription, and passed through Ellis Island at the turn of the century. Their marriage lasted almost 50 years, until my grandmother's death in 1957. My grandfather lived to be 94, and was very successful in business. This was one of my grandmother's favorite recipes, and she continued to cook it even after they enjoyed their new-found material wealth."

SERVES 8

1½ pounds beef stew meat (preferably chuck), trimmed and cut into ½-inch pieces
    Salt and pepper
2   tablespoons vegetable oil
1½ pounds beef marrowbones (see note)
2   onions, chopped fine
2   celery ribs, chopped fine
4   carrots, peeled and cut into ¼-inch slices
6   garlic cloves, minced
2   tablespoons all-purpose flour
8   cups low-sodium beef broth
4   cups water
1   cup dried white beans, rinsed and picked over
1   cup pearl barley

1. Pat the beef dry with paper towels and season with salt and pepper. Heat the oil in a large Dutch oven over medium-high heat until just smoking. Working in two batches, cook the beef and bones until well browned, about 8 minutes. Transfer to a paper-towel-lined plate.

2. Add the onions, celery, carrots, and garlic to the now-empty pot and cook until softened, about 8 minutes. Add the flour and cook until it begins to brown, about 1 minute. Stir in the broth, water, beans, and beef and bring to a simmer. Reduce the heat to medium-low, cover, and simmer until the beans begin to soften, about 1 hour.

3. Add the barley and continue to cook, covered, until the barley, beans, and beef are fully tender, about 1 hour. Season to taste with salt and pepper. Serve. (The soup can be refrigerated for up to 3 days or frozen for up to 2 months. Thin with water as necessary before reheating.)

Notes from the Test Kitchen
We couldn't believe that just a little meat could flavor a soup so much, but thanks to a few marrowbones, this soup is rich with beef flavor. It was, however, so thick that we could stand a spoon up straight in it, so we added a bit more water and the problem was solved. Either beef marrowbones or shinbones will work in this recipe. Dried Great Northern beans, navy beans, or cannellini beans can be used here.

Kolotny Borscht

JEAN SOHRAKOFF | AURORA, OREGON

This savory chilled soup is based on the Polish *chlodnik*, a cold cucumber soup with sour cream as its base and beet greens and stems for color. This recipe is somewhat unusual because it replaces the beets with radishes. "My husband's grandmother, who immigrated to the United States just before the Russian Revolution, developed the recipe for this delicious, cold soup. My husband fondly recalls grating the vegetables next to the wood cookstove in his grandmother's kitchen when he was a boy while she talked to him in Russian."

SERVES 4

- 3 cucumbers, peeled, seeded, and grated (see note)
- 3 celery ribs, chopped
- 8 radishes, trimmed and grated (see note)
- 6 scallions, chopped
- 2 cups ice cubes
- 2 cups half-and-half
- 1/2 cup white vinegar
- 1/2 cup water
- 3 hard-cooked eggs, peeled and chopped (see page 7)
  Salt and pepper

1. Place the cucumbers, celery, radishes, and scallions in a medium bowl. Cover with the ice cubes and refrigerate until the vegetables are crisp, 1 to 2 hours.

2. Remove any unmelted ice cubes. Stir in the half-and-half, vinegar, water, and eggs, and season to taste with salt and pepper. Serve immediately.

Notes from the Test Kitchen

We've had our share of stodgy beet borscht, so we were thrilled with this light (beet-free) rendition. With crisp cucumbers and peppery radishes, this soup is more like a gazpacho than what we think of as borscht. The eggs give it plenty of flavor without making it noticeably eggy. Grate the cucumbers and radishes on the large holes of a box grater, or use a food processor fitted with the grating disk.

SEEDING AND GRATING CUCUMBERS

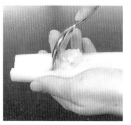

1. Peel and halve each cucumber lengthwise. With a spoon, use just enough pressure to scoop away the seeds and the surrounding liquid.

2. Grate each cucumber on the large holes of a box grater (or use a food processor fitted with a grating disk).

32 AMERICA'S BEST LOST RECIPES

Grandma's Pepper Pot Soup

ELIZABETH A. GIBSON | NORTH BRENTWOOD, MARYLAND

Legend has it that pepper pot soup was created by George Washington's cook during the harsh winter of 1778 at Valley Forge, when available rations included only tripe and peppercorns. This variation on a pepper pot theme was handed down by Elizabeth's great-grandmother, who would go out in the yard and wring a chicken's neck to make it when "someone was not feeling up to par." Rather than peppercorns, this soup relies on red pepper flakes, which make it especially spicy.

SERVES 6

CHICKEN BROTH
- 3 pounds bone-in, skin-on chicken thighs
- Salt and pepper
- 1 tablespoon vegetable oil
- 1 onion, chopped
- 2 quarts water
- 3 bay leaves
- 3 garlic cloves, peeled
- 2 teaspoons red pepper flakes
- 1 pound boneless, skinless chicken breasts

SOUP
- 1 tablespoon vegetable oil
- 1 onion, chopped
- 1 celery rib, chopped
- 2 carrots, peeled and chopped
- 4 garlic cloves, minced
- 2 cups egg noodles
- 1/2 cup chopped fresh parsley
- 1–2 teaspoons red pepper flakes (see note)

1. FOR THE BROTH: Pat the thighs dry with paper towels and season with salt and pepper. Heat the oil in a large Dutch oven over medium-high heat until just smoking. Working in two batches, brown the thighs, about 8 minutes. Transfer to a paper-towel-lined plate. Pour off all but 1 tablespoon fat from the pot. Cook the onion over medium heat until softened, about 5 minutes. Meanwhile, remove and discard the skin from the thighs. Add the thighs, water, bay leaves, garlic, pepper flakes, and 1 tablespoon salt to the pot. Cover and simmer until the broth is flavorful, about 30 minutes. Add the chicken breasts and simmer until cooked through, about 15 minutes.

2. Strain the broth into a large container, let stand at least 10 minutes, then skim the fat from the surface. Meanwhile, transfer the chicken to a cutting board to cool. Reserve the thigh meat for another use. Shred the breast meat and reserve for the soup.

3. FOR THE SOUP: Wipe out the Dutch oven and heat the oil over medium heat until shimmering. Cook the onion, celery, and carrots until lightly browned, about 5 minutes. Add the garlic and cook until fragrant, about 30 seconds. Add the reserved broth and simmer until the vegetables are nearly tender, about 10 minutes. Stir in the noodles and cook until tender, 8 to 10 minutes. Add the reserved shredded chicken, parsley, and pepper flakes and simmer until heated through, about 2 minutes. Serve.

Notes from the Test Kitchen
Although Elizabeth made this soup with a whole chicken as her starting point, we streamlined it a bit by using chicken thighs to build a flavor base and boneless chicken breasts for their tender meat for the finished soup. If you prefer, use the thigh meat in the soup and omit the chicken breasts. You can adjust the amount of red pepper flakes to your liking.

The Phantom Stew

BARBARA KAY SCHICK | MESA, ARIZONA

When we made this simple stew, we were drawn in by the story behind it as well as its rich tomato flavor. So where did the name come from? In short, when Barbara was a toddler, her father returned from dangerous duty in the Korean War and the local Chicago media made him an instant celebrity. Coming to Barbara's home to stage a homecoming photo, they stationed his young wife and children near the stove to show them making his favorite stew. Upon looking into the pot, Barbara's unhappy face, as captured in the photo, told the *real* story: the Dutch oven was empty—hence the "phantom" stew.

SERVES 6 TO 8

- 3 pounds beef stew meat (preferably chuck), trimmed and cut into 1- to 1$\frac{1}{2}$-inch pieces
  Salt and pepper
- 2 tablespoons olive oil
- 1 onion, chopped medium
- 2 garlic cloves, minced
- 1$\frac{1}{4}$ cups water
- 1$\frac{1}{4}$ cups dry red wine
- 2 (15-ounce) cans tomato sauce
- 1 teaspoon dried thyme
- $\frac{1}{4}$ cup ketchup
- 6 celery ribs, cut into 2-inch pieces
- 6 carrots, peeled and cut into 2-inch pieces
- 2 pounds large red potatoes, scrubbed and quartered
- 2 tablespoons unsalted butter

1. Pat the beef dry with paper towels and season with salt and pepper. Heat 1 tablespoon of the oil in a large Dutch oven over medium-high heat until just smoking. Cook half of the beef until well browned, about 8 minutes. Transfer to a plate. Repeat with the remaining oil and beef.

2. Add the onion to the now-empty pot and cook until softened, about 3 minutes. Add the garlic and cook until fragrant, about 30 seconds. Stir in the water, wine, tomato sauce, thyme, beef, and any accumulated juices and bring to a simmer. Reduce the heat to medium-low, cover the pot, and simmer for 1½ hours.

3. Stir in the ketchup. Add the celery, carrots, and potatoes and stir to combine. Cook until the vegetables and meat are tender, about 1 hour. Stir in the butter. Serve. (The stew can be refrigerated for up to 3 days or frozen for up to 2 months. Thin with water as necessary before reheating.)

Notes from the Test Kitchen
Barbara's original recipe called for 2 cans of condensed tomato soup. While we liked the tomato flavor, we had a hard time getting around the inherent sweetness of the soup. To counter that, we decided to use 2 cans of tomato sauce instead (not jarred spaghetti sauce). The result was a fork-tender beef stew with plenty of rich tomato flavor.

Brunswick Stew

ELIZABETH DORN | RICHMOND, VIRGINIA

There is one thing about Brunswick Stew about which there is no argument: It's Southern in origin. The consensus ends there, however. Everything else—what kind of meat is included (rabbit, squirrel, chicken, pork, or some combination thereof), the vegetables (okra or no okra, the type of beans, and corn), and the specific origin (does the honor go to Brunswick, Georgia, or Brunswick County, Virginia?)—is up for grabs.

Elizabeth recalls her mother's stew, which originated with a branch of her family that settled in Brunswick County, Virginia: "It contained anything she had on hand, which sometimes included squirrel and/or rabbit meat my father brought home from a hunting trip. She added corn and lima beans and tomatoes that she had canned and white potatoes, onions, and spices."

SERVES 10

- 3 pounds bone-in, skin-on chicken thighs
- 1 pound boneless pork loin, cut into 1-inch pieces
  Salt and pepper
- 2 tablespoons vegetable oil
- 2 large onions, chopped fine
- 1 red bell pepper, stemmed, seeded, and chopped medium
- 2 tablespoons all-purpose flour
- 8 cups low-sodium chicken broth
- 2 cups water
- 1 bay leaf
- 1/2 teaspoon dried oregano
- 1/2 teaspoon dried thyme
- 1 pound boneless, skinless chicken breasts
- 1 (28-ounce) can crushed tomatoes
- 2 large red potatoes, scrubbed and cut into small cubes
- 2 cups frozen baby lima beans
- 2 cups frozen white corn
  Hot sauce

1. Pat the chicken thighs and pork dry with paper towels and season with salt and pepper. Heat the oil in a large Dutch oven over medium-high heat until just smoking. Working in two batches, brown the thighs, about 8 minutes.

Transfer to a paper-towel-lined plate and when cool enough to handle remove the skin. Add the pork to the pot and cook until browned on all sides, about 5 minutes. Transfer to a plate. Pour off all but 1 tablespoon fat from the pot.

2. Cook the onions and bell pepper until softened, about 5 minutes. Add the flour and cook until it begins to brown, about 1 minute. Stir in the broth, water, chicken thighs, pork, any accumulated juices, bay leaf, oregano, and thyme and simmer until the thighs are tender, about 40 minutes. Add the chicken breasts and simmer until cooked through, about 15 minutes.

3. Transfer the thighs and breasts to a cutting board to cool. Stir in the tomatoes, potatoes, lima beans, and corn and simmer until the potatoes and beans are tender, about 15 minutes.

4. Meanwhile, shred the chicken thighs and cut the chicken breasts into bite-sized pieces. Stir the chicken back into the stew and season with hot sauce. Serve.

Notes from the Test Kitchen
You can certainly substitute ham for the pork loin. We recommend using Virginia ham from the deli—just ask for a pound of thick-cut ham and cut it into 1-inch pieces.

Székely Goulash (Pork Stew with Sauerkraut)

KEITH SAKOWSKY | AUSTIN, TEXAS

Also known as *székelykáposzta* or Székely cabbage, this hearty, peasant-style stew has deep roots in Hungarian culture. A simple marriage of pork (or beef), onions, paprika, and sauerkraut, it gets its name from the Székely Hungarians, an ethnic minority group in Romania whose name, *Szekler,* means frontier guard. They guarded the eastern flank of Hungary, which was prone to invasion because of its geographic position in Europe as a crossroads. This is one of Keith's family recipes, made by his grandparents when he was growing up.

SERVES 6

- 2 pounds boneless pork loin, cut into 1-inch pieces
  Salt and pepper
- 2 tablespoons unsalted butter
- 1 tablespoon vegetable oil
- 2 large onions, chopped fine
- 2 garlic cloves, minced
- 2 tablespoons sweet paprika
- 1½ cups low-sodium chicken broth
- 1 tablespoon chopped fresh dill, plus extra for garnish
- 2 pounds sauerkraut, drained and rinsed (see note)
- 2 teaspoons sugar
- 2 cups sour cream

1. Adjust an oven rack to the middle position and heat the oven to 300 degrees. Pat the pork dry with paper towels and season with salt and pepper. Heat the butter and oil in a large Dutch oven over medium-high heat until the foaming subsides. Working in two batches, cook the pork until browned on all sides, about 5 minutes. Transfer to a plate.

2. Pour off all but 1 tablespoon fat from the pot. Cook the onions until softened, about 3 minutes. Add the garlic and paprika and cook until fragrant, about 30 seconds. Stir in the pork, broth, dill, 1 teaspoon salt, and ½ teaspoon pepper and bring to a simmer. Cover, transfer the pot to the oven, and cook until the meat is just tender, about 1½ hours.

3. Stir in the sauerkraut and sugar, cover, and return the pot to the oven. Cook until the pork is fork-tender, about 45 minutes. Off the heat, stir in the sour cream. Serve, sprinkling individual bowls with extra chopped dill.

Notes from the Test Kitchen

We've had our share of goulash—with lots of beef and a tangy sour cream and paprika sauce. But this bright version made with lean pork loin and tangy sauerkraut (not to mention lots of sour cream) really surprised us. We loved it—especially when we added a little more dill for freshness. Be sure to use sweet, not hot, paprika and don't let the stew simmer once the sour cream has been added. Serve this dish with spätzle, boiled potatoes, or hot buttered noodles. Try to buy fresh sauerkraut sold at the delicatessen or in vacuum-sealed packages rather than canned or jarred cooked sauerkraut.

Poor Boy Stroganoff

CAROLE WEINBERGER | ORLANDO, FLORIDA

Classic Beef Stroganoff, which dates back to the 1890s and a Russian count of the same name (only spelled Stroganov), is essentially a fancy stew made with filet mignon, mushrooms, onions, and sour cream. This version, which is made with ground beef, won't break the bank and is good for everyday meals. Rather than serving the stew over egg noodles, the noodles, beef, and sauce are layered into a baking dish, topped with a little cheese, and baked as a hearty casserole.

SERVES 6

Salt
8 ounces egg noodles
2 tablespoons unsalted butter
1 pound 85% lean ground beef
1 small onion, chopped fine
8 ounces white mushrooms, sliced
1/4 teaspoon pepper
2 tablespoons all-purpose flour
1 garlic clove, minced
1 (8-ounce) can tomato sauce
1/4 cup dry red wine
1 1/4 cups low-sodium beef broth
1 cup sour cream
1/2 cup grated Parmesan cheese

1. Adjust an oven rack to the middle position and heat the oven to 375 degrees. Bring 2 quarts water to a boil in a large pot over medium-high heat. Add 1 tablespoon salt and the noodles and cook until nearly tender, 5 to 7 minutes. Drain and set aside in a colander.

2. Meanwhile, melt the butter in a large skillet over medium-high heat. Cook the beef, breaking up any large clumps with a wooden spoon, until lightly browned, about 8 minutes. Using a slotted spoon, transfer the beef to a paper-towel-lined plate.

3. Pour off all but 2 tablespoons fat from the pan, add the onion, and cook until golden, about 5 minutes. Add the mushrooms, 1/2 teaspoon salt, and pepper, and cook until the mushrooms begin to brown, about 7 minutes.

4. Add the flour and cook until it begins to brown, about 1 minute. Add the garlic and cook until fragrant, about 30 seconds. Stir in the tomato sauce, wine, broth, and beef and bring to a simmer; cook until slightly thickened, about 5 minutes. Off the heat, stir in the sour cream.

5. Spread one-third of the sauce over the bottom of an 8-inch baking dish and top with half the noodles. Repeat with half of the remaining sauce and the remaining noodles. Finish with the remaining sauce. Sprinkle the Parmesan evenly over the top and bake until the filling is hot and the top is browned, about 20 minutes. Let cool 5 minutes. Serve.

Notes from the Test Kitchen
Although we found it clever to use ground beef to make a family-friendly Stroganoff, we did find that it had one major problem—too much fat from the rendered beef. So instead of keeping the beef in the pan, we chose to brown it, then remove it to paper towels to drain. This step worked—and although there was still enough fat in the dish to make it rich, it was no longer greasy.

Texas Chili Dogs

MELANIE PRESCHUTTI | BOALSBURG, PENNSYLVANIA

Texas Chili Dogs are slathered with yellow mustard and topped with a chunky and aromatic meat chili. You'd think they were from Texas, but they actually were the invention of an un-named Greek gentleman who owned a small restaurant in Paterson, New Jersey. Around 1924, he devised a chili sauce that drew upon his own heritage. Much like Cincinnati chili, a dish also created by Greek immigrants, this chili included cloves as well as garlic and other spices. According to legend, because the chili was made with steak, not ground meat, it earned the "Texas" part of its name. These hot dogs caught on and spread from Paterson to western Connecticut and Pennsylvania, where Melanie first tasted them. "In the 1950s, '60s, and '70s, my hometown of Tamaqua, Pennsylvania, had two 'hot spots' to eat hot dogs: The Coney Island and The Texas Lunch. Both places served daily lunch to at least 100 people, but only had seats for 10 and six, respectively. Hot dogs were literally passed out the doors to customers standing on the sidewalk, like buckets of water to a fire, while orders and money were shouted and passed up the line! Both luncheonettes had sweltering, year-round internal temperatures and 'sweaty' windows, caused by steam billowing off the grills. The similarities ended there. Those who ate at The Coney Island NEVER ate at The Texas Lunch, and vice versa. My family ate at The Texas Lunch."

MAKES 4 CUPS SAUCE, ENOUGH FOR 16 HOT DOGS

- 1 **pound bottom round steak, trimmed and cut into 1-inch pieces**
- 2 **tablespoons vegetable oil**
- 1 **medium onion, chopped fine**
- 2 **celery ribs, chopped fine**
- 2 **garlic cloves, minced**
- 1 **tablespoon chili powder**
- 1/4 **teaspoon ground cloves**
- 1/2 **cup ketchup**
- 1/2 **cup chili sauce**
- 2 **tablespoons yellow mustard**
- 2 **tablespoons hot sauce**
- 1 **tablespoon Worcestershire sauce**

Process the steak in a food processor until finely ground. Heat the oil in a large Dutch oven over medium heat until shimmering. Add the ground steak, onion, celery, garlic, chili powder, and cloves and cook until the meat is no longer pink, about 5 minutes, breaking up any large pieces with a wooden spoon. Stir in the ketchup, chili sauce, mustard, hot sauce, and Worcestershire and bring to a simmer. Reduce the heat to medium-low and cook until thickened, about 30 minutes. Serve over hot dogs. (The sauce can be refrigerated for up to 5 days or frozen for up to 2 months.)

Notes from the Test Kitchen
Processing the steak gave it almost a shredded texture, making it much better than just using ground beef. Bottom round steaks are sometimes sold under the name London broil. Use yellow mustard (not Dijon) for this recipe.

German-American Hamburgers

JOHN SCHAG | BUFFALO, NEW YORK

A variation on Salisbury Steak, these hearty burgers are made with mashed potato and a little sour cream and topped with a simple gravy. What makes them German? Here's what John told us: "My grandparents were Schwabians and came to New York City around 1900. Although my father grew up in New York, he worked for the post office on the New York Central mail train that ran from New York City to Buffalo. While on a layover in Buffalo, he met my mother and settled here, so I didn't get to see my grandparents very often. But what I still remember about my visits there is the smell of good cooking that would greet me in the hallway. This was my father's favorite dish. He continued to work the mail train while my sister and I were young. He would be gone every other week. My mother would make this for him when he returned, so I have happy memories of this dish. True comfort food."

SERVES 4

- 1 large russet potato, peeled and cut into 1-inch chunks
- 2 tablespoons unsalted butter
- 1 small onion, chopped fine
- 1 pound 90% lean ground beef
- 1 tablespoon sour cream
- 1/2 teaspoon salt
- 1/4 teaspoon pepper
- 1 tablespoon all-purpose flour
- 1/2 cup low-sodium beef broth

1. Cover the potato with an inch of cold water in a small saucepan. Bring to a simmer over medium-high heat. Reduce the heat and simmer until the potato is tender, about 15 minutes. Drain the potato, then mash until smooth. Let cool completely, at least 30 minutes.

2. Adjust an oven rack to the middle position and heat the oven to 300 degrees. Melt 1 tablespoon of the butter in a large skillet over medium-high heat. Add half the onion and cook until golden, about 5 minutes. Transfer to a bowl and stir in the potato, beef, sour cream, salt, and pepper. Divide the mixture into four equal portions and lightly pack into 1-inch-thick patties.

3. Melt the remaining tablespoon butter in the now-empty skillet over medium-high heat. Cook the patties until browned on both sides and just cooked through, 3 to 4 minutes per side. Transfer the patties to a large plate and wrap tightly with foil (do not wash the skillet).

4. Add the remaining chopped onion to the fat in the skillet and cook until golden, about 5 minutes. Stir in the flour and cook until it begins to brown, about 1 minute. Stir in the broth and any accumulated burger juices and bring to a simmer, scraping the pan bottom with a wooden spoon, until the sauce thickens, 3 to 5 minutes. Pour over the burgers. Serve.

Notes from the Test Kitchen

To deepen the overall flavor, we browned the onions (and added some of those browned onions to the sauce). We also cooked the flour for the sauce. We'd serve these burgers with buttered egg noodles.

Just Chicken Pie

DEENA STOVALL | GURNEE, ILLINOIS

This is no ordinary chicken pot pie. It's a hearty double-crust pie packed with chicken (and cheese)—and with nary a pea or carrot in sight. Deena first sampled a pie like this in 1979 in Keokuk, Iowa. New to the area, she attended a spring bazaar where the line to get in wound around the building. Recalling the moment, Deena said, "After waiting for 10 minutes or so, I asked the woman in front of me, 'Is the line to get in always this long?' She replied, 'This isn't the line to get in. This is the line for the best chicken pie you will ever eat.' And yes, it WAS worth the wait in line. I had never eaten a 'chicken only' pie, and spent about two years looking for a recipe. I raised seven daughters on this pie and also ran a catering business. I've sold hundreds, maybe thousands, of my version of the Keokuk Bazaar Chicken Pie."

SERVES 6 TO 8

2½ pounds bone-in, skin-on split chicken breasts
    Salt and pepper
8   tablespoons (1 stick) unsalted butter
1   celery rib, chopped fine
2   garlic cloves, minced
⅓   cup all-purpose flour
1   (12-ounce) can evaporated milk
2   cups low-sodium chicken broth
1   teaspoon grated lemon zest
3   scallions, chopped
1   recipe Double-Crust Pie Dough,
    bottom crust fit into a 9-inch pie plate, top crust
    rolled to a 12-inch circle and refrigerated
    (see page 175)
¾   cup shredded sharp cheddar cheese
1   large egg, beaten, for brushing the top of the pie

1. Adjust an oven rack to the middle position and heat the oven to 400 degrees. Cover a rimmed baking sheet with foil.

2. Pat the chicken dry with paper towels and season with salt and pepper. Place on the prepared pan, skin-side up, and roast until the temperature registers 160 degrees, 35 to 40 minutes. Let cool to room temperature, remove and discard the skin, and cut the meat from the bone and shred the chicken into 2-inch pieces. Reduce the oven temperature to 350 degrees.

3. Melt the butter in a large saucepan over medium heat. Cook the celery until softened, about 5 minutes. Add the garlic and cook until fragrant, about 30 seconds. Stir in the flour and cook until it begins to brown, about 1 minute. Stir in the milk, broth, and zest and bring to a boil. Reduce the heat to low and simmer until thickened, about 5 minutes. Strain the sauce into a large bowl (discard the vegetables), stir in the chicken and scallions, and season to taste with salt and pepper. Let the filling cool until just warm, about 30 minutes.

4. Spoon the chicken mixture into the pie shell and sprinkle with the cheese. Top with the remaining chilled circle of dough. Trim all but ½ inch of the dough overhanging the edge of the pie plate. Press the top and bottom crusts together, then tuck the edges underneath. Crimp the dough evenly around the edge of the pie, using your fingers.

5. Cut four 2-inch slits in the top of the dough, brush with the beaten egg, and bake until the crust is deep golden brown, 45 to 55 minutes. Let cool 10 minutes. Serve.

Ham Pie

KATE WORLEY | BLOOMINGTON, INDIANA

Recipes for ham pie abound and while they are all different, they have one thing in common: They're a great way to stretch your food budget (or make quick work of leftover ham). Many are quiche-like affairs (with lots of eggs), while others are more akin to a pot pie and rely on cream-of-something soup. We zeroed in on this rendition because it was fresh tasting and has an inventive and cheesy dough for the topping. Says Kate of this recipe: "Growing up, we ate a lot of casseroles, some of which have thankfully been laid to rest. This one, though, with a quick, fresh sauce, rather than one from a can, and an equally quick homemade cheese crust, is still a favorite."

SERVES 6 TO 8

FILLING

- 3 tablespoons unsalted butter
- 1 medium onion, chopped fine
- 1 pound white mushrooms, sliced
- 1/2 teaspoon salt
- 1/4 teaspoon pepper
- 1/4 cup all-purpose flour
- 1/2 teaspoon dry mustard
- 2 cups milk
- 1 pound thick-sliced deli ham, chopped
- 1 cup frozen peas

DOUGH

- 1 cup all-purpose flour
- 1/4 teaspoon cayenne pepper
- 6 tablespoons unsalted butter, softened
- 1 cup shredded sharp cheddar cheese

1. FOR THE FILLING: Adjust an oven rack to the middle position and heat the oven to 375 degrees. Melt the butter in a large skillet over medium-high heat. Cook the onion until softened, about 3 minutes. Add the mushrooms, salt, and pepper, and cook until the mushrooms are soft and most of the liquid is absorbed, about 7 minutes. Stir in the flour and mustard and cook until it begins to brown, about 1 minute. Stir in the milk, bring to a simmer, and cook until slightly thickened, about 5 minutes. Add the ham and peas, then transfer the mixture to a 13 by 9-inch baking dish. Set aside.

2. FOR THE DOUGH: Pulse the flour and cayenne in a food processor. Add the butter and pulse until the flour is pale yellow and resembles coarse cornmeal. Transfer the dough to a floured work surface, sprinkle with the cheese, and knead until the cheese is well incorporated. Pinch off 1-inch pieces of the dough, roll each into a ball, and pat into 1/8-inch-thick rounds. Place on top of the ham mixture, covering the top completely. Bake until the filling is hot and the top is deep golden brown, about 35 minutes. Let cool for 5 minutes. Serve.

Notes from the Test Kitchen

This is one of those dishes that you don't expect to like as much as you do. The cheese crust on this casserole is reminiscent of spicy cheese crackers. Plus, we loved the easy, hodge-podge manner in which the crust was formed: Pinch off pieces of the dough, roll them into balls, pat them into circles, and place them on the filling, like patchwork. You can vary the amount of cayenne in the crust to your liking. The amount here will provide a little bite without setting your mouth on fire. If you don't have a food processor, grate frozen butter on the large holes of a box grater into a bowl containing the flour and cayenne.

Napoli Country Cheese Pie

PHYLLIS COSTELLO | CHAPEL HILL, TENNESSEE

This rustic Italian dish, a double-crust quiche-like pie, is also known as Easter Pie and Pizza Rustica, and there are countless versions—all of them rich and filling. Most feature an eggy custard enriched with ricotta, a generous complement of mozzarella and Parmesan, and one or more cured meats. It's no wonder these pies were sliced up and served as an antidote to the scaled-back, observant meals of Lent. This recipe came to America with Phyllis's grandparents, who emigrated from Italy to the South Side of Chicago.

SERVES 8 TO 10

- 1 pound ricotta cheese
- 2 cups shredded mozzarella cheese
- 3/4 cup grated Parmesan cheese
- 1/4 pound thinly sliced prosciutto, chopped fine
- 1/2 teaspoon pepper
- 1/4 teaspoon salt
- 2 tablespoons chopped fresh parsley
- 4 large eggs
- 1 recipe Double-Crust Pie Dough, bottom crust fit into a 9-inch pie plate, top crust rolled to a 12-inch circle and refrigerated (see page 175)

1. Adjust an oven rack to the lowest position and heat the oven to 375 degrees. Process the ricotta in a food processor until smooth. Transfer to a large bowl and mix in the mozzarella, Parmesan, prosciutto, pepper, salt, and parsley until incorporated. Beat 3 eggs in a medium bowl until well combined and add to the ricotta mixture. Cover and refrigerate until ready to use. (The mixture can be refrigerated for up to 24 hours.)

2. Spoon the filling into the pie crust. Top with the remaining chilled circle of dough. Trim all but 1/2 inch of the dough overhanging the edge of the pie plate. Press the top and bottom crusts together, then tuck the edges underneath. Crimp the dough evenly around the edge of the pie, using your fingers.

3. Beat the remaining egg in a small bowl. Cut four 2-inch slits in the top of the dough, brush with the beaten egg, and bake until the crust is deep golden brown, 45 to 55 minutes. Cool to room temperature, at least 1 1/2 hours. Serve. (The pie may be refrigerated for up to 2 days. Bring the pie back to room temperature before serving.)

Notes from the Test Kitchen
This cheesy pie had one downfall: The texture was grainy, no doubt because we were using super-market rather than fresh, locally made ricotta cheese. A simple spin of the ricotta cheese in the food processor eliminated this problem.

Vidalia Onion Pie

CYNTHIA DRUMMOND | BRUNSWICK, GEORGIA

There's no doubt that Georgia's Vidalia onions are the world's sweetest. And they definitely make a great pie. Often, these pies have a simple pressed crumb crust made with Ritz crackers and a rich filling of sautéed sliced Vidalias, egg, milk, and plenty of cheese. This recipe is a little different—more quiche-like, with bacon, sour cream instead of milk, and a traditional blind-baked pie crust. It came from Cynthia's grandmother, who had a farm in rural Toombs County, Georgia, where the small town of Vidalia is located. "My grandmother, better known as Mama Sapp, never knew that she was teaching me to cook, as well as many other things, but she did! I thank her and miss her. This fine Southern woman of little means, who split thumbnails from shelling peas and butterbeans and acquired a stooped back from hard labors, could cook anything from nothing!"

SERVES 6 TO 8

- 1 recipe Single-Crust Pie Dough, fully baked and cooled (see page 174)
- 6 slices bacon, chopped
- 2 medium Vidalia onions, sliced thin (about 3 cups)
- 3 large eggs, lightly beaten
- ½ cup sour cream
- ½ cup heavy cream
- ¾ teaspoon salt
- ½ teaspoon pepper
- 2 teaspoons chopped fresh chives

1. Adjust an oven rack to the lowest position and heat the oven to 350 degrees. Cook the bacon in a large skillet over medium heat until crisp, about 8 minutes. Using a slotted spoon, transfer the bacon to a paper-towel-lined plate and set aside. Cook the onions in the bacon fat until browned, about 12 minutes. Transfer to a medium bowl. Whisk the eggs, sour cream, heavy cream, salt, pepper, and 1 teaspoon chives in a large bowl, then add the reserved bacon and onions.

2. Pour into the prepared pie shell and bake until the filling is puffed and cracked around the edges and the center barely jiggles when the pie is shaken, 25 to 30 minutes. Let cool for 10 minutes and sprinkle with the remaining teaspoon chives. Serve. (The pie can be refrigerated for up to 3 days.)

Notes from the Test Kitchen

A pie packed with onions might not sound that special, but when those onions are sweet Vidalias, you know the pie will be good. When testers got a look at this pie recipe we suspected it was basically a quiche, and wondered where the cheese was. But the sour cream added all the tang that we could have asked for and was a pleasant foil for the sweet onions.

Mile High Bologna Pie

BARBARA ESTABROOK | RHINELANDER, WISCONSIN

If you like bologna, then this is the pie for you. We could find no precedent for this particular recipe and had to rely on Barbara to give us a few clues as to its origin: "As a young homemaker on a tight budget, I became very inventive when it came to stretching a pound of meat to feed my family. This recipe was a spin-off of the Michigan Pasty, a ground beef, potato, and onion combination wrapped in pie crust. My first version did not include a crust; I cooked the ingredients in an electric fry pan, then served it from the pan. Sometime later, I decided to change its presentation and piled the browned and partially cooked ingredients into a pie plate, added a top crust, and baked it. My creation became Mile High Bologna Pie. When my daughter-in-law asked me how to make this dish, I knew my son, who is fussy about his food, really did like it."

SERVES 6 TO 8

- 2 tablespoons vegetable oil
- 1 (1-pound) piece deli bologna, peeled and cut into ¹/₂-inch-thick rounds
- 1 small onion, halved and sliced thin
- 2 large russet potatoes, peeled, halved lengthwise, and sliced thin
- 2 carrots, peeled and sliced thin
- 2 garlic cloves, minced
- ¹/₄ cup water
- 1 cup frozen peas
  Salt and pepper
- 1 recipe Double-Crust Pie Dough, bottom crust fit into a 9-inch pie plate, top crust rolled into a 12-inch circle and refrigerated (see page 175)
- 1 large egg, beaten, for brushing the top of the pie
  Ketchup, for serving

1. Adjust an oven rack to the middle position and heat the oven to 425 degrees. Heat 1 tablespoon oil in a large nonstick skillet until shimmering. Working in two batches, cook the bologna in a large skillet over medium heat until lightly browned on both sides, about 6 minutes. Transfer to a large plate. Heat the remaining tablespoon oil in the now-empty skillet until shimmering. Cook the onion until softened, about 3 minutes. Add the potatoes and carrots and cook, tossing occasionally, until just beginning to brown, about 8 minutes. Add the garlic and cook until fragrant, about 30 seconds. Stir in the water, cover, and cook until the potatoes and carrots are just tender, about 15 minutes. Stir in the peas and season to taste with salt and pepper. Let the vegetables cool until just warm, about 30 minutes.

2. Spoon the vegetables into the pie shell. Arrange the bologna over the top of the vegetables. Top with the remaining chilled circle of dough and crimp the edges as desired. Cut four 2-inch slits in the top of the dough, brush with the beaten egg, and bake until the crust is golden brown, about 30 minutes. Let cool for 5 minutes. Serve, drizzling ketchup over the top.

Notes from the Test Kitchen
Whether it was a guilty pleasure or a culinary rebellion, the test kitchen staff devoured this pie in record time. The trick is searing the bologna first, which gives it a heartier flavor—much like kielbasa sausage. While Barbara's recipe had only a top crust, we liked this recipe better with a double crust.

Pagache (Polish Pizza)

NADINE JOHNSON | SAN CARLOS, CALIFORNIA

Pagache, known variously as pagash, Polish pizza, and pierogi pizza, is a giant stuffed pizza that is a local specialty in Pennsylvania. Nadine's recipe was handed down from her mother: "My mother comes from the coal-mining country of rural Pennsylvania, where family and traditions are the threads that hold the community together. When she migrated to the West Coast, she brought these values and some wonderful recipes with her. My favorite is pagache—a not-so-healthful, yet satisfyingly yummy dish made from the things I love—potatoes, cheese, and bread. Preparation began first thing in the morning with homemade pizza dough. As the dough sat by the wood stove to rise, we peeled potatoes, grated cheese, and made the filling, always allowing extra for 'tasting.' It took at least two people to get the pagache ready, with one person stretching the dough into a rectangle and the other spreading the filling. As it came out of the oven, Mom would rub a stick of butter over the top and add some salt. We could hardy wait to eat it—and always burned our tongues in our haste."

SERVES 8 TO 10

2	cups warm water (110 degrees)
2	tablespoons olive oil
1	teaspoon sugar
6–6½	cups all-purpose flour
2	packages rapid-rise or instant yeast
	Salt
2	pounds russet potatoes, peeled and cut into 1-inch chunks
4	cups shredded sharp cheddar cheese
6	tablespoons unsalted butter
	Pepper

1. Lightly grease a large bowl with cooking spray. Mix the water, oil, and sugar together in a large measuring cup. Mix 6 cups of the flour, the yeast, and 1 teaspoon salt in the bowl of a standing mixer fitted with the dough hook.

With the mixer on low, add the water mixture. After the dough comes together, increase the speed to medium and mix until shiny and smooth, 5 to 7 minutes. (If the dough is too sticky after 3 minutes, add the remaining ½ cup flour, 2 tablespoons at a time.) Turn the dough out onto a heavily floured work surface, shape into a ball, and place in the greased bowl. (To make the dough by hand, see page 74.) Cover the bowl with plastic wrap and let rest in a warm place until doubled in size, about 1 hour.

2. Cover the potatoes with 1 inch of water in a large saucepan. Bring to a simmer over medium-high heat. Reduce the heat to medium and simmer until the potatoes are tender, about 15 minutes. Drain, then mash until smooth. Stir in the cheese and 4 tablespoons of the butter and season with salt and pepper.

(Continued on page 50)

3. Adjust an oven rack to the middle position and heat the oven to 400 degrees. Following the photos and working on a lightly floured work surface, roll the dough into a large rectangle about 20 by 14 inches, with the short side facing you. Spread the potato filling on the bottom half of the dough (the half facing you) and fold the other half of the dough over the filling. Pinch the edges to seal and transfer to a 13 by 9-inch baking dish. Gently press down on the top of the dough until it touches the sides of the dish. Prick the top of the dough several times with a fork and bake until golden brown, about 40 minutes.

4. Turn the pagache out onto a cooling rack. Melt the remaining 2 tablespoons butter in a small saucepan. Brush the pagache with the melted butter and sprinkle with 1 teaspoon salt. Let cool 10 minutes. Cut in half lengthwise, then slice into 2-inch-wide strips. Serve.

Notes from the Test Kitchen

Somewhere between a big potato calzone and a huge pierogi, pagache features cheesy mashed potatoes encased in a light, yeasted crust. We loved the flavor of a sharp cheddar in the filling, but we found that gouda worked equally well. When the top is golden brown, you can be sure the pagache is done. Also, it should feel firm to the touch—if you press lightly on the top and the dough yields, then it needs more time.

MAKING PAGACHE

1. Roll the dough into a large rectangle, about 20 by 14 inches, with the short side facing you. Spread the potato filling over the bottom half of the dough.

2. Fold the dough over the potato filling.

3. Pinch the edges of the dough together.

4. Transfer the filled dough to a 13 by 9-inch baking dish, then press on the dough to make sure it touches all the sides of the dish.

Runsas (Beef and Cabbage Buns with Cheese)

PAM PATTERSON | LEON, KANSAS

Calling *runsas* "beef and cabbage buns" doesn't really do them justice. For this old-fashioned Midwestern recipe, a simple filling made with ground beef, browned cabbage, and chopped onion is encased in a rectangle of soft, slightly sweet yeast dough. The combination is both unexpected and addictive.

Runsas were brought to Nebraska by Volga Germans, ethnic German farmers who settled in Russia and then immigrated to the Midwest. Runsas were popularized by the Runza Drive-Inn, a fast-food restaurant that opened in Lincoln, Nebraska, in 1945; there are now dozens of Runza franchises, mostly in Nebraska, but also in Kansas, Iowa, and Colorado.

So how did runsas become a favorite recipe in Pam's household? She credits her sister for developing the family's first recipe back in the late 1960s. "I'm not sure how Jeanne thought of adding sweetened condensed milk to the dough, but it's a brilliant idea." Pam now lives in Kansas, where she says these buns are round, not rectangular, and go by the name "bierocks." Over the years, Pam has adopted the round shape (they are easier to make) and added a slice of American cheese to the filling.

SERVES 8

DOUGH
- ³/₄ cup warm water (110 degrees)
- ¹/₂ cup sweetened condensed milk
- ¹/₄ cup vegetable oil
- 2 tablespoons sugar
- 1 large egg
- 3¹/₂ cups all-purpose flour
- 2 packages rapid-rise or instant yeast
- 1 teaspoon salt

FILLING
- 3 tablespoons unsalted butter (with 2 tablespoons melted)
- 1¹/₂ pounds 90% lean ground beef
- 1 large onion, chopped fine
- ¹/₂ small head cabbage, cored and chopped (about 3 cups) (see page 11)
- Salt and pepper
- 8 slices deli American cheese

1. FOR THE DOUGH: Lightly grease a large bowl with cooking spray. Mix the water, condensed milk, oil, sugar, and egg in a large measuring cup. Mix the flour, yeast, and salt in the bowl of a standing mixer fitted with the dough hook. With the mixer on low, add the water mixture. After the dough comes together, increase the speed to medium and mix until shiny and smooth, 4 to 6 minutes. Turn the dough out onto a heavily floured work surface, shape into a ball, and place in the greased bowl. (To make the dough by hand, see page 74.) Cover the bowl with plastic wrap and let rest in a warm place until doubled in size, about 1 hour.

2. FOR THE FILLING: Melt 1 tablespoon of the butter in a large skillet over medium-high heat. Add the beef and cook until just beginning to brown, about 6 minutes, breaking up any large clumps. Using a slotted spoon, transfer the beef to a paper-towel-lined plate.

(Continued on page 54)

3. Pour off all but 2 tablespoons fat from the pan. Add the onion and cook until softened, about 3 minutes. Add the cabbage and toss until just beginning to wilt, 2 to 4 minutes. Return the beef to the pan and season with salt and pepper.

4. TO ASSEMBLE AND BAKE: Adjust two oven racks to the upper-middle and lower-middle positions and heat the oven to 350 degrees. Coat two baking sheets with cooking spray. Following the photos, divide the dough into eight equal pieces. Working on a lightly floured work surface, roll each piece of dough into a 7-inch circle. Place one dough round in a deep cereal bowl and top with one slice of cheese. Spoon ¾ cup filling over the cheese and pinch the edges of the dough together to form a bun. Transfer the bun, seam-side down, to a prepared baking sheet. Repeat with the remaining dough, cheese, and filling, placing four buns on each baking sheet. Cover the buns with plastic wrap and let rise until puffed, about 20 minutes.

5. Bake the buns until golden brown, about 20 minutes, switching and rotating the baking sheets halfway through the baking time. Brush the hot buns with the remaining melted butter and serve.

Notes from the Test Kitchen

This dough is incredibly easy to work with and the sweetened milk complements the savory filling. We liked these buns so much, in fact, that we wanted more runsa in our runsa—so we upped the amount of filling called for in the original recipe. Because we found making the buns to be a little tricky, we pulled out a cereal bowl and used it to cradle the dough and the filling. Be careful that you don't overcook the cabbage, as you want it to provide some crunch when you bite into these mouth-watering sandwiches.

SHAPING THE RUNSAS

1. Divide the dough into eight equal pieces and roll each piece into a 7-inch circle.

2. To form each runsa, place one dough round in a deep cereal bowl.

3. Top the dough circle with a slice of cheese and ³/4 cup of filling.

4. Stretch the dough over the filling, pinching the edges together to form a bun.

Gedempte Stuffed Cabbage

ANN ILTON | BOCA RATON, FLORIDA

Gedempte is Yiddish for "well-stewed" or, as Ann interprets it, "cooked long and lovingly to blend and meld the wonderful flavors." Stuffed cabbage has been made by Jews from around the world for generations, though the recipes vary from culture to culture. In general, it's common that the fillings pair both sweet and savory ingredients, though for Rosh Hashanah some recipes omit sour ingredients entirely for fear it will spoil the sweetness of the new year. The sweet/sour style of Ann's recipe is one common to Russia and Eastern Europe—except for her creative addition of cranberry sauce.

SERVES 4 TO 6

- 1   large head Savoy cabbage
- 1   tablespoon olive oil
- 1   small onion, chopped fine
- 1   (15-ounce) can tomato sauce
- 1½   pounds 85% lean ground beef
- ⅓   cup dried bread crumbs
- ¼   cup long-grain rice, boiled until just tender and drained
- 1   large egg
-     Salt and pepper
- 1   (16-ounce) can whole berry cranberry sauce
- 1   (14.5-ounce) can diced tomatoes
- ¼   cup golden raisins

1. Freeze the cabbage until very firm, at least 24 hours or up to 2 days.

2. Adjust an oven rack to the middle position and heat the oven to 375 degrees. Heat the oil in a large skillet over medium heat until shimmering. Cook the onion until golden, about 5 minutes. Add ½ cup of the tomato sauce and simmer until slightly thickened, about 2 minutes. Transfer the mixture to a medium bowl and let cool completely, about 20 minutes. Mix in the beef, bread crumbs, rice, egg, 1 teaspoon salt, and ½ teaspoon pepper.

3. Place the frozen cabbage under warm running water and gently pull off 12 of the large, outermost leaves. Pull off six more leaves and set aside. Divide the filling evenly among the 12 outer leaves. Roll the leaves around the filling and tuck in the ends to create a neat envelope. Set aside.

4. Combine the cranberry sauce, remaining tomato sauce, diced tomatoes, raisins, and ½ teaspoon salt in a large bowl. Reserve ½ cup. Pour the remaining sauce on the bottom of a 13 by 9-inch baking pan. Arrange the stuffed cabbage in a single layer on top of the sauce and spoon the reserved sauce over the top. Cover the cabbage rolls with the reserved cabbage leaves and wrap the pan tightly with aluminum foil.

5. Bake until the cabbage is completely tender and the filling is cooked through, about 1¼ hours. Remove the foil and continue to bake until the sauce reduces slightly, about 15 minutes. Remove and discard the cabbage leaves on top and serve.

Notes from the Test Kitchen
We've never been big fans of stuffed cabbage—it simply seemed like too much work. But this recipe, with its easy sauce and trick of freezing the cabbage leaves instead of boiling them, has made us a convert. Ann's recipe originally called for instant brown rice, but the brands we tried tasted stale and bland. Instead we chose to parboil white rice, which tasted fresher and allowed the flavors of the filling to come through.

Glazed Pork with Caramelized Pears and Sweet Potatoes

BRENDA BUEHLER | MONTICELLO, INDIANA

Here an old-fashioned picnic roast is dressed up and turned into a full meal with caramelized pears and sweet potatoes that cook alongside it part of the time. Brenda's father came up with this flavorful recipe. "Since there were 10 kids in our family, finances were always a challenge. But Dad discovered this inexpensive way to use a pork shoulder roast, a less expensive cut of pork. It quickly became our special event meal! Dad first made this for us over 30 years ago, and even though he is no longer with us, we can make it and feel like he is right here, asking us if we are enjoying our meal."

SERVES 6 TO 8

- ¹/₂ teaspoon salt
- ¹/₂ teaspoon pepper
- ¹/₂ teaspoon ground cinnamon
- 1 (6- to 7-pound) bone-in pork picnic shoulder roast (see note)
- 4 tablespoons unsalted butter
- ¹/₂ cup maple syrup
- ¹/₄ cup packed light brown sugar
- ¹/₈ teaspoon ground cloves
- ¹/₈ teaspoon ground nutmeg
- ¹/₄ cup water
- 2 pounds sweet potatoes, peeled and cut into large chunks
- 2 large, firm Anjou or Bartlett pears, peeled, cored, and quartered

1. Adjust an oven rack to the lower-middle position and heat the oven to 350 degrees. Mix the salt, pepper, and cinnamon together and rub all over the pork. Transfer the roast, fat-side up, to a large roasting pan and cook until the fat becomes golden, about 2 hours.

2. Meanwhile, melt the butter in a small saucepan over medium heat. Stir in the maple syrup, brown sugar, cloves, nutmeg, and water, and bring to a boil. As soon as the mixture comes to a boil, remove the pan from the heat and set aside.

3. Remove the roast from the oven and pour off the excess fat from the bottom of the pan.

Toss the sweet potatoes and pears with half of the maple mixture and then transfer them to the bottom of the roasting pan. Brush the top and sides of the roast with the remaining maple mixture. Return to the oven and cook until the top of the roast is golden brown, about 1 hour.

4. Increase the oven temperature to 425 degrees and continue to cook until the pork registers 180 degrees and the vegetables are completely softened, about 45 minutes. Transfer the pork to a cutting board, tent with foil, and let rest 20 minutes. (If the pears and potatoes are still not tender, return them to the oven to cook while the pork roast is resting.) Slice the pork and place on a serving platter. Arrange the pears and sweet potatoes around the roast, and pour the sauce from the roasting pan over the roast. Serve.

Notes from the Test Kitchen

We increased the cooking temperature at the end to further thicken the sauce and to help the pears and potatoes caramelize. Be sure to buy firm pears so that they do not become mushy during the long cooking time. Watch carefully in the last half hour of cooking to make sure that the sauce does not scorch. If the roast comes with the skin still on the meat, carefully remove it with a sharp knife but leave most of the fat cap intact. You can also use boneless pork shoulder roast (Boston butt) if you prefer.

Lamb Shanks with Barley Broth

MARCIA DIER | ESTACADA, OREGON

This is a very old traditional Scottish recipe, known the world over as Scotch Broth—essentially a thick stew made with lamb (or fowl or a cheap cut of beef), vegetables, and barley (and sometimes dried peas as well). Often, the lamb is served separately as an entrée, although here it remains in the pot as part of the stew. This particular recipe was handed down in Marcia's family from Scottish relatives.

SERVES 10

- 2 tablespoons olive oil
- 6 lamb shanks
- 1 large onion, chopped medium
- 1 pound carrots, peeled and chopped medium
- 4 celery ribs, chopped medium
- 4 garlic cloves, minced
- 1 tablespoon minced fresh thyme
- 9 cups water
- 2 bay leaves
- 1 tablespoon salt
- 1 teaspoon pepper
- 1½ cups pearl barley

1. Heat the oil in a large Dutch oven over medium-high heat until just smoking. Cook the lamb shanks until browned on all sides, 5 to 7 minutes, then transfer to a plate. Drain off all but 1 tablespoon fat from the pot. Add the onion, carrots, celery, garlic, and thyme to the fat in the now-empty pot and cook until the vegetables are softened, about 5 minutes. Transfer the vegetable mixture to a bowl.

2. Add the lamb shanks, any accumulated juices, water, bay leaves, salt, and pepper to the pot and bring to a simmer over medium-high heat. Reduce the heat to low and simmer, covered, until the lamb is just tender, about 3 hours. Remove the shanks from the pot and when cool remove the meat and return it to the pot.

3. Add the vegetables and barley to the pot, return to a simmer, and cook, covered, until the barley is soft, about 1½ hours. Discard the bay leaves. Serve.

Notes from the Test Kitchen

We loved the strong flavor from the lamb, the sweetness of the carrots, and the nuttiness of the barley, but the original mixture was a little stodgy. For herbal flavor, we added thyme to the ingredient list, and to make the dish a little less hearty we reduced the suggested amount of barley.

Beef Rouladen

JULIE NEVES | SUNBURY, PENNSYLVANIA

This savory dish of filled beef rolls is Germany's version of the French *roulade* and the Italian *braciole*. To make rouladen, you must cut bottom round roast into very thin slices, fill and roll them, then brown and bake them. Versions vary pretty widely with respect to the filling but many, like this one, include bacon (or ham) as well as pickles (though this recipe does not). Sometimes a red wine or tomato sauce is made on the side and spooned over the rolls, but here the beef is braised until tender in a mixture of red wine and water and then the liquid is reduced on the stovetop to a sauce-like consistency.

This particular dish has big nostalgia value for Julie: "My grandparents came from Germany, so I'm sure this recipe arrived with them. When my husband was courting me, I served this dish to him. (After all, the way to a man's heart . . .) He was so impressed with it that we ended up serving rouladen at our wedding for all of our friends and family to enjoy with us! It's a good thing rouladen freeze well, as my family did much of the cooking ahead of time for the wedding. (We still like to make a large quantity to freeze for later meals—far better than TV dinners!) There are many variations of rouladen, some more elaborate; but this simple method is how we enjoy it."

SERVES 6 TO 8

- 1 tablespoon vegetable oil
- 4 large onions, halved and sliced thin
- 1 (3-pound) bottom round roast
- 1/2 cup Dijon mustard
  Salt and pepper
- 20 slices bacon
- 2 cups low-sodium beef broth
- 1 cup dry red wine
- 2 tablespoons cornstarch

1. Adjust an oven rack to the middle position and heat the oven to 300 degrees. Heat the oil in a large skillet over medium heat until shimmering. Cook the onions until well browned, about 15 minutes. Transfer to a bowl.

2. Following the photos, slice the roast against the grain into sixteen 1/4-inch-thick slices. (The slices should measure roughly 7 by 4 inches in size.) Spread each slice of beef with 1 1/2 teaspoons mustard and season with salt and pepper. Place one slice of bacon, folded in half, in the center of each slice and top with 1 heaping tablespoon of the browned onions. Roll up each beef slice lengthwise, tucking in the ends as you go to form a roll. Using two 8-inch pieces of kitchen twine, tie up each roll securely.

3. Cook the remaining four slices of bacon in a large skillet over medium heat until crisp, about 8 minutes. Using a slotted spoon, transfer the bacon to a paper-towel-lined plate. Increase the heat to medium-high and working in two batches, cook the beef rolls in the bacon fat until browned on all sides, 5 to 7 minutes. Arrange the rolls in a single layer in a 13 by 9 inch baking dish.

4. Stir the broth and wine together, then pour over the beef rolls (add water as necessary to ensure the beef rolls are covered with liquid). Cover the baking dish with foil. Bake the beef rolls until the meat is very tender, about 2 hours. (Add more water as necessary to keep the rolls covered.)

5. Transfer the rolls to a cutting board and tent with foil. Strain the broth into a large saucepan and bring to a simmer over medium-high heat.

Mix the cornstarch with ¼ cup water and stir into the simmering broth. Simmer until the sauce thickens, about 1 minute. Meanwhile, remove the twine from the beef rolls and arrange the rolls on a deep serving platter. Pour the sauce over the rolls, crumble the remaining cooked bacon, and sprinkle on top. Serve.

Notes from the Test Kitchen

Filled with onions, mustard, and bacon, and simmered until fall-apart tender, this easy oven braise of beef rolls makes perfect sense for a weekend dinner. We felt that the original sauce needed a boost of flavor, so we doubled the amount of mustard, wine, and onions in the recipe. We also browned the onions until they were dark and soft. The result was a much bolder flavor. Try to buy an evenly-shaped roast; otherwise you may have trouble cutting 16 slices.

ROLLING ROULADEN

1. Slice the roast against the grain into sixteen ¼-inch-thick slices.

2. After spreading mustard over each slice of beef, place one bacon slice, folded in half, in the center.

3. Add a tablespoon of browned onion and roll up each filled piece of beef lengthwise, tucking in the ends as you go.

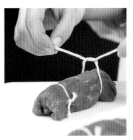

4. Use two 8-inch lengths of twine to secure each beef roll.

GRAM'S DOUGHNUTS

Breakfast and Breads

Fluffies

DAWN KARRINGTON | KISSIMMEE, FLORIDA

Truly light and fluffy, these little silver-dollar pancakes get a tangy kick from sour cream and their ethereal texture from beaten egg whites. Sure, they take a little more time to prepare than pancakes from a mix, but they are well worth the effort. Dawn's recipe was handed down to her from her grandmother, who used to make them when Dawn spent the night: "The best part of staying at her house was waking up early on Sunday mornings to the sound of her scurrying around her kitchen preparing my favorite breakfast of tiny Fluffies with butter and syrup. I would crawl out of bed with sleep in my eyes and run to the kitchen table. There she would place a plate heaping with tiny golden-brown, fluffy pancakes before me. Today, I make the same Fluffies for my step daughters when they're visiting for the weekend. I even use my grandmother's handwritten recipe card."

SERVES 4

- 1/4 cup all-purpose flour
- 1 teaspoon sugar
- 1/4 teaspoon salt
- 1/8 teaspoon ground nutmeg
- 3 large eggs, separated
- 1/2 cup sour cream
- 1–2 tablespoons vegetable oil

1. Whisk the flour, sugar, salt, and nutmeg in a large bowl. Beat the egg yolks and sour cream in a medium bowl until smooth. With an electric mixer or whisk, beat the egg whites in a large bowl to soft peaks. Stir the egg yolk mixture into the flour mixture until just combined. (The batter should be lumpy, with visible streaks of flour.) Using a spatula, carefully fold the whites into the batter until just combined. (Do not overmix—a few streaks of whites should be visible.)

2. Heat 2 teaspoons of the oil in a large nonstick skillet over medium-low heat for 5 minutes. Drop the batter by tablespoons into the pan. Cook until the pancakes are evenly browned on both sides, 3 to 4 minutes. Repeat with the remaining batter, using additional vegetable oil as needed to grease the pan. Serve.

Notes from the Test Kitchen

Although these pancakes are at their puffiest when served in batches, they can be kept warm on a cooling rack coated with cooking spray and placed over a rimmed baking sheet in a 200-degree oven for up to 20 minutes. Take care not to overbeat the egg whites. Beating the egg whites to soft peaks will produce the tallest and fluffiest pancakes.

Midwinter Buckwheat Pancakes

MICKEY STRANG | MCKINLEYVILLE, CALIFORNIA

Mickey's husband grew up in Wyoming, where "buckwheat cakes were a winter treasure—a way to send kids off to school and men off to work with a warm tummy full of a good breakfast." Old-fashioned buckwheat pancake recipes were two-day affairs and required a starter dough that rose overnight, tempering and softening the assertiveness of the buckwheat. Some included milk-soaked bread crumbs along with the buckwheat; many incorporated molasses or honey as the sweetener and also added one or more chemical leaveners on the second day. Mickey's modernized recipe is more straightforward, with a mere 1/2 cup buckwheat—just enough to flavor the batter. Mickey adds both cornmeal and all-purpose flour and lightens up the texture with beaten egg whites. She also includes diced apples for subtle sweetness. While not traditional, this recipe captures the rustic and hearty nature of these pancakes.

SERVES 4

- 1 cup all-purpose flour
- 1/2 cup buckwheat flour
- 1/2 cup cornmeal
- 4 teaspoons baking powder
- 1 teaspoon baking soda
- 1 teaspoon salt
- 4 large eggs, separated
- 2 cups buttermilk
- 1 tablespoon vegetable oil, plus extra for the pan
- 2 Golden Delicious apples, peeled and cut into 1/2-inch pieces

1. Whisk the flours, cornmeal, baking powder, baking soda, and salt in a large bowl. Beat the egg yolks, buttermilk, and vegetable oil in a medium bowl until incorporated. With an electric mixer or whisk, beat the egg whites in a large bowl to soft peaks. Stir the egg yolk mixture and apples into the flour mixture until just combined. (The batter should be lumpy, with visible streaks of flour.) Using a spatula, carefully fold the egg whites into the batter. (Do not overmix—a few streaks of whites should be visible.)

2. Heat 2 teaspoons oil in a large nonstick skillet over medium-low heat for 5 minutes. Using a 1/8-cup measure or a small ladle, drop the batter into the pan. Cook until the pancakes are evenly browned on both sides, about 5 minutes. Repeat with the remaining batter, using additional vegetable oil as needed to grease the pan. Serve.

Notes from the Test Kitchen

Hearty yet light, these apple-studded pancakes are lightened up thanks to fluffy beaten egg whites. Originally the chopped apples were sprinkled on top of each pancake as it cooked, but we found that inevitably some apples would fall out of the pancakes when they were flipped. Instead, we chose to incorporate the apples right into the batter—and this worked like a charm.

Bops

HARRIET LITTLE | SUMMERVILLE, SOUTH CAROLINA

A cross between a crêpe and a pancake, bops date back to the mid-1800s. In fact, we found them in the 1855 receipt book of a woman named Emily Sinkler, who lived just 40 miles from Harriet. Harriet calls these "breakfast breads," though they are pie-plate-sized pancakes made from a thin batter and baked, not cooked on the stovetop; each puffed and cooked layer is then slathered with butter and stacked one on top of the other and cut into wedges for serving. As to the origin of the curious name, bops, we suspect they are related to the bread known as baps used for sandwiches in Northern Ireland and England. This simple recipe came from Harriet's grandmother, and Harriet recorded it more than 50 years ago for her church's recipe collection.

SERVES 4

- 3 large eggs
- 1 cup all-purpose flour
- 2 cups milk
- 1 tablespoon vegetable oil
- ½ teaspoon salt
- 3 tablespoons unsalted butter, softened

1. Adjust two oven racks to the upper-middle and lower-middle positions and heat the oven to 375 degrees. Grease three 9-inch pie plates. With an electric mixer on high speed, beat the eggs in a large bowl until pale and thick, about 2 minutes. Add the flour and mix on the lowest speed until just combined. Add the milk, oil, and salt and mix until incorporated (the batter will be thin).

2. Add 1 cup batter to each of the prepared pie plates and bake, switching the plate positions halfway through baking, until puffed and browned, about 25 minutes.

3. Cool the pancakes until just warm (they will collapse as they cool). Place one pancake on a serving plate and spread with 1 tablespoon of the softened butter. Spread the remaining two pancakes with the remaining butter in the same manner, then stack the pancakes, butter-side up, on top of one another. Cut into wedges. Serve.

Notes from the Test Kitchen
We loved the warm, buttery layers of these crêpe-like pancakes. In addition, they provide a good excuse to buy a few more pie plates—we favor glass Pyrex pie plates for multiple reasons: They're cheap, durable, and see-through, so you can monitor how the bottom of a pie (or a bop) is browning. Serve with maple syrup or honey.

Orange Drop Doughnuts

THE EDITORS OF COOK'S COUNTRY

Though the history of American doughnuts dates back to the Dutch settlers in New Amsterdam (eventually New York), doughnuts gained widespread popularity because of their association with the Salvation Army and the women, called "lassies," who made and distributed them to soldiers during World War I. Dropping spoonfuls of cake batter into hot oil means that fresh doughnuts can be on the table in minutes, without the fuss of rolling and stamping. Drop doughnuts caught on like wildfire, and soon there were flavors of every kind—spiced, chocolate, and even orange. In the late 1940s and into the 1950s, the name Orange Drop Doughnuts started to appear in Betty Crocker cookbooks and magazines. Here's our take on this popular midcentury doughnut.

MAKES 24 TO 30

- 1   cup sugar
- 1   tablespoon plus 1 teaspoon grated orange zest
- 2   quarts vegetable oil
- 2   cups all-purpose flour
- 2   teaspoons baking powder
- 1/4   teaspoon salt
- 2   large eggs
- 1/2   cup orange juice
- 2   tablespoons unsalted butter, melted

1. Pulse 1/2 cup of the sugar and 1 teaspoon orange zest in a food processor until blended. Transfer to a bowl. (If making by hand, toss the zest and sugar in a bowl using a fork until evenly blended.)

2. Heat the oil in a large Dutch oven until the temperature reaches 350 degrees. Whisk the flour, baking powder, and salt in a medium bowl. Whisk the eggs, remaining 1/2 cup sugar, and 1 tablespoon orange zest in a large bowl. Whisk in the orange juice, then the butter, until well combined. Stir in the flour mixture until evenly moistened.

3. Use two dinner teaspoons to carefully drop heaping spoonfuls of batter into the hot oil. (You should be able to fit about six spoonfuls in the pot at one time. Do not overcrowd.) Fry, maintaining a temperature between 325 and 350 degrees, until the doughnuts are crisp and deeply browned on all sides, 3 to 6 minutes. Using a slotted spoon, transfer the doughnuts to a plate lined with paper towels and let drain for 5 minutes. Toss the doughnuts in the bowl with the orange sugar until well coated and transfer to a serving plate. Repeat with the remaining batter, sugaring the doughnuts as directed and regulating the oil temperature as necessary. Serve.

Notes from the Test Kitchen
Some recipes we uncovered in our research use nearly 3 cups of flour for two dozen doughnuts, but we thought these were too heavy. Two cups of flour paired with 2 teaspoons of baking powder worked much better. As for liquid ingredients, some recipes call for milk as well as orange juice. But diluting the orange flavor just seemed wrong, so we added only juice. For even more orange flavor, we added a whopping tablespoon of grated zest to the batter—far more than the teaspoon or so found in older recipes. Finally, taking a cue from a few recipes, we rolled the hot doughnuts in a batch of homemade orange-flavored sugar. You'll need three oranges for the zest and juice.

Naked Ladies with Their Legs Crossed (Spiced Crullers)

SHIRLEY SIERADZKI | MISHAWAKA, INDIANA

This recipe wins the prize for most creative title, but it was the taste of these spiced crullers (which disappeared as fast as we could make them) that really sold us. Although the exact origin of crullers is unclear, recipes similar to Shirley's can be found in late-19th-century cookbooks, when the advent of chemical leaveners meant that many doughnut recipes could be made with baking powder or baking soda rather than the traditional yeast. This recipe comes from Shirley's grandmother; Shirley speculates that her grandmother's German ancestry might have had something to do with her decision to add mashed potatoes to the dough. The dough is rolled like pie crust and cut into strips. Each strip is then slashed in the middle and twisted to look like crossed legs.

Shirley's favorite memory associated with this recipe involves one of her five grandchildren. "When our granddaughter was in the fourth or fifth grade, her teacher asked her what she did that weekend. Can you picture the look on the teacher's face when my granddaughter said, 'We made naked ladies with their legs crossed'?" Eventually, all was explained, and Shirley treated her granddaughter's class to a platter of these tasty doughnuts.

MAKES 24

- 1 russet potato, peeled and cut into 1-inch chunks
- 1 large egg
- 2 tablespoons milk
- 1¼ cups sugar
- ½ teaspoon vanilla extract
- 1½ cups all-purpose flour
- 1½ teaspoons baking powder
- ½ teaspoon salt
- ½ teaspoon ground cinnamon
- ⅛ teaspoon ground nutmeg
- 2 quarts vegetable oil

1. Bring the potato and water to cover to a boil in a small saucepan. Reduce the heat and simmer until the potato is tender, about 15 minutes. Drain the potato, then mash until smooth. Let cool completely, at least 30 minutes.

2. Transfer ½ cup mashed potato to a medium bowl (discard the remaining potato) and beat in the egg, milk, ½ cup of the sugar, and vanilla until combined. Whisk the flour, baking powder, salt, cinnamon, and nutmeg in a large bowl. Make a well in the center of the flour mixture and add the potato mixture. Stir to form a moist and sticky dough.

(Continued on page 70)

3. Following the photos and working on a heavily floured work surface, roll the dough into an 18 by 14-inch rectangle about ¼ inch thick. Cut the dough in half lengthwise, then cut each half crosswise into 1½-inch-wide strips; make a slit in each strip, and twist to shape the dough to resemble crossed legs. Transfer the crullers to a floured baking sheet and refrigerate until ready to fry. (The crullers may be covered with plastic wrap and refrigerated for up to 24 hours.)

4. Heat the oil in a large Dutch oven over medium heat until the temperature reaches 350 degrees. Carefully lower six crullers into the hot oil and fry, maintaining a temperature between 325 and 350 degrees, until crisp and deep brown on both sides, about 6 minutes. Using a slotted spoon, transfer the crullers to a plate lined with paper towels and drain for 3 minutes. Toss the crullers in a bowl with the remaining ¾ cup sugar and transfer to a serving plate. Repeat with the remaining crullers, regulating the oil temperature as necessary. Serve.

Notes from the Test Kitchen

Tasters commented on the crisp crust and soft, chewy interior of these crullers. That chew and texture comes from just a little mashed potato. But don't be tempted to use leftover mashed potatoes you may have on hand. We did and soon discovered that the butter and dairy we had added to them made the crullers too sticky.

SHAPING THE LADIES

1. Roll the dough into an 18 by 14-inch rectangle about ¼ inch thick.

2. Cut the dough in half lengthwise, then cut each half crosswise into 1½-inch-wide strips.

3. Cut each strip lengthwise three-quarters of the way to the top to make a pair of legs.

4. Twist the legs around each other twice to cross.

Gram's Doughnuts

JOANNE DOWNS | BELLPORT, NEW YORK

The recipe for these old-fashioned aromatic doughnuts, spiced with nutmeg and ginger, came from Joanne's grandmother, who used to make them during the Depression to raise extra cash for her family. "A Civilian Conservation Corps crew was working in the woods near my grandparents' New England farm, so Grandpa invited the men in for coffee and doughnuts—10 cents a man, all you can eat—and a seat in a warm kitchen. Robert Frost may have enjoyed his roadside view of the snowy woods, but it was another thing to work in those woods. The men were from Lowell, city men, and they didn't have proper boots for the woods. Grandpa took them to the barn and wrapped burlap bags around their shoes." Nearly 80 years after the end of the Depression, Joanne still makes these doughnuts and tells us "no one gets to eat one without hearing how the New Deal worked in real life."

MAKES 16

- 2 cups sugar
- 2 teaspoons ground cinnamon
- 4 cups all-purpose flour
- 1 tablespoon baking powder
- 1/2 teaspoon baking soda
- 1 teaspoon salt
- 1 teaspoon ground ginger
- 1 teaspoon ground nutmeg
- 2 large eggs
- 1 cup buttermilk
- 2 quarts vegetable oil

1. Mix 1 cup of the sugar and the cinnamon in a medium bowl until combined. Set aside. Whisk the flour, baking powder, baking soda, salt, ginger, and nutmeg in a large bowl. Beat the eggs, buttermilk, and remaining 1 cup sugar together in a medium bowl. Make a well in the center of the flour mixture and add the egg mixture. Stir together to form a moist and sticky dough.

2. On a heavily floured work surface, roll out the dough into a 14-inch circle about 1/2 inch thick. Cut out dough rings with a floured doughnut cutter, reflouring between cuts.

Transfer the doughnuts to a floured baking sheet. Gather the scraps and gently press into a disk; repeat the rolling and cutting process until all the dough is used. (The cut doughnuts can be covered with plastic wrap and stored at room temperature for up to 2 hours.)

3. Heat the oil in a large Dutch oven over medium heat until the temperature reaches 350 degrees. Carefully lower 6 doughnuts into the hot oil. Turn the doughnuts as they rise to the surface with tongs or a slotted spoon and fry, maintaining a temperature between 325 and 350 degrees, until the doughnuts are golden brown on both sides, about 4 minutes. Using a slotted spoon, transfer the doughnuts to a plate lined with paper towels and drain for 3 minutes. Toss the doughnuts in the bowl with the cinnamon sugar and transfer to a plate. Repeat with the remaining doughnuts, regulating the oil temperature as necessary. Serve.

Notes from the Test Kitchen

We loved these—but thought a toss in some cinnamon sugar would improve them even more, and it did. If you don't have a doughnut cutter, use a 2 1/2-inch cookie cutter to cut the dough rounds, and a 1-inch cutter to make the holes.

Kolaches (Sweet Czech Pastries)

JUANITA PERKINS | CALDWELL, TEXAS

Kolaches, which originated in Eastern Europe centuries ago, are sweet round pastries with an indentation that holds various sweet fillings, from jam and nuts to dried fruit or cream cheese. These pastries, which get their name from the old Slavonic word for wheel, *kolo,* made their U.S. debut in Texas, where many Czech immigrants established communities beginning in the 1840s. As with many recipes brought stateside by immigrants, kolaches changed a bit over time, with savory variations becoming popular—the dough was formed into buns and filled with a variety of meat fillings. Juanita's recipe, however, is in the true Czech tradition, perhaps because she comes from the heart of Texas Czech country—the triangle between Dallas, San Antonio, and Houston. Her hometown of Caldwell has an annual kolache festival each September. This recipe was handed down from Juanita's grandmother, Lena Dannhaus, an avid baker who passed away in 1953 when Juanita was 11 years old: "I think of her every time I smell, see, or make any kind of bread, because she made bread about three days a week and I learned to knead under her watchful eye, standing on a chair, when I was six. It was from her I got my love of the art of cooking, even though she used a wood-burning stove that took a lot of work."

MAKES 20

DOUGH

- ½ cup warm milk (110 degrees)
- 3 tablespoons sugar
- 2 tablespoons unsalted butter, melted
- 1 large egg yolk, beaten
- 1½ cups all-purpose flour
- 1 teaspoon rapid-rise or instant yeast
- ¼ teaspoon salt

FILLING

- ½ cup pitted prunes
- ⅓ cup water
- 2 tablespoons sugar
- ½ teaspoon ground cinnamon

1. FOR THE DOUGH: Lightly grease a large bowl with cooking spray. Mix the milk, sugar, butter, and egg yolk together in a large measuring cup. Stir the flour, yeast, and salt in the bowl of a standing mixer fitted with the dough hook. With the mixer on low, add the milk mixture. After the dough comes together, increase the speed to medium and mix until shiny and smooth, 5 to 7 minutes. Turn the dough out onto a heavily floured work surface, shape into a ball, and place in the greased bowl. (To make the dough by hand, see the instructions on page 74.) Cover the bowl with plastic wrap and let rest in a warm place until doubled in size, about 1 hour.

(Continued on page 74)

2. Spray two 9-inch cake pans with cooking spray. On a lightly floured work surface, roll out the dough to a 12-inch circle, about ¼ inch thick. Using a 2-inch round cutter, cut the dough into rounds and arrange in the greased cake pans with two in the center and eight around the perimeter of each pan. Cover the pans with plastic wrap and let rise until the dough is doubled in size, about 45 minutes.

3. FOR THE FILLING: Bring the prunes, water, sugar, and cinnamon to a boil in a small saucepan over medium-high heat. Simmer until the prunes soften, about 5 to 7 minutes. Transfer the mixture to a food processor and puree until smooth.

4. Adjust an oven rack to the middle position and heat the oven to 375 degrees. Using your fingers, make a 1-inch-wide indentation on the top of each dough round and press to form a small circle. Fill the center of each round with 1 teaspoon of the filling. Bake until golden brown, 15 to 20 minutes. Serve warm.

Notes from the Test Kitchen

Juanita's dough is soft and flavorful, and would work well with almost any filling. A cream cheese and jam filling is very popular in Texas bakeries. To make it, just mix 4 ounces softened cream cheese and 2 tablespoons sugar. Fill each dough round with about 1 teaspoon of the sweetened cream cheese and top it with ½ teaspoon apricot or seedless raspberry jam. Bake as directed.

MAKING YEAST DOUGH BY HAND

While it is easier to make yeast dough with a standing electric mixer, with few exceptions, most yeast doughs can also be made by hand. With a little elbow grease, these doughs will have the same texture and flavor as those made with a machine. Just follow the steps below, then proof and bake the dough according to the specific recipe.

1. Whisk the flour, yeast, salt, and other dry ingredients together in a large bowl.

2. Whisk all the wet and sweet ingredients, including milk, water, butter, eggs, vanilla, sugar, and honey, together in a large measuring cup.

3. Make a small well in the flour mixture. Pour the wet ingredients into the well and stir until the mixture is shaggy and becomes difficult to stir.

4. Turn the dough out onto a lightly floured work surface and knead by hand until the dough is smooth. Depending on the dough, this should take 5 to 10 minutes.

Monkey Bread

THE EDITORS OF COOK'S COUNTRY

There is a magic to monkey bread that's hard to describe, but if you've ever tasted this rich and yeasted pull-apart bread with its caramelized exterior, you'll understand why several of our readers asked us to re-create the recipe. Its origins date back at least a century, and the super-soft Parker House roll is surely a close relation. The name itself remains an enigma. Some say it comes from the bread's resemblance to the prickly monkey-puzzle tree while others, ourselves included, think it refers to the way we eat it—that is, using our hands to pull apart the sticky clumps of bread and stuff them in our mouths. And for those who think monkey bread lacks panache, consider that former First Lady Nancy Reagan served monkey bread at the White House.

SERVES 6 TO 8

DOUGH
- 2 tablespoons unsalted butter, softened, plus 2 tablespoons melted
- 1 cup warm milk (110 degrees)
- ½ cup warm water (110 degrees)
- ¼ cup granulated sugar
- 1 package rapid-rise or instant yeast
- 3¼ cups all-purpose flour
- 2 teaspoons salt

BROWN SUGAR COATING
- 1 cup packed light brown sugar
- 2 teaspoons ground cinnamon
- 8 tablespoons (1 stick) unsalted butter, melted

GLAZE
- 1 cup confectioners' sugar
- 2 tablespoons milk

1. FOR THE DOUGH: Adjust an oven rack to the medium-low position and heat the oven to 200 degrees. When the oven reaches 200 degrees, turn it off. Lightly grease a large bowl with cooking spray. Butter a Bundt pan with 2 tablespoons softened butter. Set the bowl and pan aside.

2. Mix the milk, water, melted butter, granulated sugar, and yeast together in a large measuring cup. Stir the flour and salt together in the bowl of a standing mixer fitted with the dough hook. With the mixer on low, slowly add the milk mixture. After the dough comes together, increase the speed to medium and mix until the dough is shiny and smooth, 6 to 7 minutes. Turn the dough onto a lightly floured work surface and knead briefly to form a smooth, round ball. Place the dough in the greased bowl and coat the surface of the dough with cooking spray. (To make the dough by hand, see the instructions on page 74.) Cover the bowl with plastic wrap and place in the warm turned-off oven until the dough is doubled in size, 50 to 60 minutes.

3. FOR THE SUGAR COATING: While the dough is rising, mix the brown sugar and cinnamon together in a bowl. Place the melted butter in a second bowl. Set aside.

4. TO FORM THE BREAD: Gently remove the dough from the bowl and pat into a rough 8-inch square. Following the photos on page 77 and using a bench scraper or knife, cut the dough into 64 pieces.

(Continued on page 77)

5. Roll each dough piece into a ball and, working one at a time, dip the balls in the melted butter, allowing the excess butter to drip back into the bowl. Roll in the brown sugar mixture, then layer the balls in the greased Bundt pan, staggering the seams where the dough balls meet as you build the layers.

6. Cover the Bundt pan tightly with plastic wrap and place in the turned-off oven until the dough balls are puffy and have risen 1 to 2 inches above the top rim of the pan, 50 to 70 minutes.

7. Remove the pan from the oven and heat the oven to 350 degrees. Remove the plastic wrap from the pan and bake until the top is deep brown and caramel begins to bubble around the edges, 30 to 35 minutes. Cool in the pan for 5 minutes, then turn out on a platter and let cool slightly, about 10 minutes.

8. **FOR THE GLAZE:** While the bread cools, whisk the confectioners' sugar and milk together in a small bowl until smooth and no lumps remain. Using a whisk, drizzle the glaze over the warm monkey bread, letting it run over the top and down the sides. Serve warm.

Notes from the Test Kitchen

The oldest monkey bread recipes we found were two-day affairs with the dough started the night before, refrigerated, and then shaped and baked the next day. Looking into contemporary recipes, we discovered that many of them used store-bought biscuit dough for convenience. We tried these super-quick recipes but soon realized that the time saved just wasn't worth it. The dough was too lean, too bland, and too dry. Our recipe stays the course in terms of richness and flavor but uses a whole package of rapid-rise yeast so that making monkey bread is a same-morning affair, with no need to plan ahead. The dough should be sticky, but if you find that it's too wet and not coming together in the mixer, add 2 tablespoons more flour and mix until the dough forms a cohesive mass. Be sure to use light brown sugar for the coating mix; dark brown sugar has a stronger molasses flavor that can be overwhelming. After baking, don't let the bread cool in the pan for more than 5 minutes or it will stick to the pan and come out in pieces. Monkey bread is at its best served warm.

HOW TO MAKE MONKEY BREAD

1. After patting the dough into a rough 8-inch square, cut the square into quarters.

2. Cut each quarter into 16 pieces.

3. Roll each piece of dough into a ball. Coat the balls with melted butter, then roll them in the brown sugar mixture.

4. Layer the coated balls in a buttered Bundt pan, staggering the seams where the balls meet.

Potica (Slovenian Sweet Bread)

PATRICIA ROY | MUSKEGON, MICHIGAN

This rolled ethnic yeast bread is so iconic of Slovenia that it even appears on their postage stamps. Sometimes it is baked in special molds, though here the dough is filled, rolled into two cylinders, and formed into simple spirals in two cake pans. The fillings vary endlessly, though a combination of dried fruit and nuts is very prevalent. Patricia recounts the legacy of this family recipe as being very long indeed: "My great-grandmother made it in her native Slovenia, and then the recipe was carried to this country during the 1800s. My great-grandmother and grandmother made it in their hometown of Ely, in northern Minnesota, and taught my mother to make it when she married into the family. The original recipe said to cool the cooked filling in the snow!"

MAKES 2 BREADS, EACH SERVING 6

DOUGH

8   tablespoons (1 stick) unsalted butter, melted
3/4 cup warm milk (110 degrees)
2   tablespoons sugar, plus 1 tablespoon for sprinkling on top
3   large egg yolks (save whites for filling), plus 1 large egg, beaten, for brushing on top
2 1/2–3 cups all-purpose flour
2   packages rapid-rise or instant yeast
1/4 teaspoon salt

FILLING

3/4 cup dried dates, chopped
1/4 cup milk
3   tablespoons plus 3/4 cup sugar
1   teaspoon ground cinnamon
3   large egg whites
1/2 cup walnuts, chopped

1. FOR THE DOUGH: Lightly grease a large bowl with cooking spray. Mix the butter, milk, sugar, and egg yolks together in a large measuring cup. Stir 2 1/2 cups flour, the yeast, and salt together in the bowl of a standing mixer fitted with the dough hook. With the mixer on low, add the milk mixture. After the dough comes together, increase the speed to medium and mix until shiny and smooth, 4 to 6 minutes. (If the dough is sticky after 3 minutes, add the remaining 1/2 cup flour, 2 tablespoons at a time.) Turn the dough out onto a heavily floured work surface and shape into a ball. Knead just until the dough becomes smooth, about 20 seconds. (To make the dough by hand, see the instructions on page 74.) Place the dough in the greased bowl, cover with plastic wrap, and let rest in a warm place until doubled in size, 1 1/2 to 2 hours.

2. FOR THE FILLING: While the dough is rising, bring the dates, milk, 3 tablespoons sugar, and cinnamon to a simmer in a small nonstick skillet over medium-high heat. Lower the heat to medium-low and cook until the milk is evaporated and the mixture becomes a thick paste, about 5 minutes. Cool to room temperature, at least 30 minutes.

3. With an electric mixer, beat the egg whites at medium-low speed until frothy, about 1 minute. Increase the speed to medium and gradually add the remaining 3/4 cup sugar until incorporated, about 1 minute. Increase the speed to high and beat until the whites hold soft peaks, about 2 minutes. Add the date mixture and beat on low speed until just incorporated, about 10 seconds.

(Continued on page 80)

4. Coat two 8-inch cake pans with cooking spray. Punch down the dough, remove it from the bowl, and divide it into two balls. Following the photos, roll each piece of dough into a 20-inch square on a lightly floured work surface. Spread each square with half the filling and top with half the walnuts. Roll each into a cylinder and arrange in the prepared pans in a spiral. Cover with plastic wrap coated with cooking spray and let rise 1 hour.

5. Adjust an oven rack to the middle position and heat the oven to 350 degrees. Brush the dough spirals with the beaten egg and sprinkle with the remaining 1 tablespoon sugar. Bake until golden brown, 25 to 30 minutes. Serve warm.

Notes from the Test Kitchen

Since the dough is rolled out thin, we experienced some difficulty spreading the filling without tearing the dough. We found that if we eliminated the walnuts from the filling and sprinkled them on top instead we solved this problem. These poticas are flaky and delicious, and well worth the effort it takes to make them—especially for a holiday treat.

HOW TO MAKE POTICA

1. Working on a lightly floured work surface, roll each ball of dough into a paper-thin 20-inch square.

2. Spread the surface of the square with half of the filling, leaving a ¹/₂-inch border around the edges. Sprinkle with half the walnuts.

3. Using both hands, roll up the dough into an even, but not too tight, cylinder and pinch the seam closed.

4. Starting at the center of the prepared cake pan, form the dough into a spiral by wrapping it around itself.

Hungarian Sweet Rolls

ERIN GLASPY | CAMANO ISLAND, WASHINGTON

With a buttery, flaky crust and sweet, crispy meringue center, these light-as-air rolls won us over in a flash. "My grandmother's rolls have been a staple of our Christmas celebrations since long before I was born," Erin tells us. "The recipe was given to my grandmother, Elsie Wietzke, by her sister-in-law, my great-aunt Lois. I can vividly remember the dough being rolled out to smooth perfection and the walnuts being diligently ground with a nut grinder. The rolls were cut and shaped with such precision that they appeared to be as perfect as the presents we unwrapped on Christmas Eve."

Erin's family has roots in Chicago. Both her grandfather and great-grandfather were Lutheran pastors, and this family recipe was printed in a church cookbook back in the 1930s. Erin, an elementary school teacher, loves to bake and is always looking for connections to the past. "To know that my ancestors smelled the same warm scents that fill the house as these rolls bake creates a unique kinship with the past."

MAKES 24

DOUGH

- 4 cups all-purpose flour
- 1 package rapid-rise or instant yeast
- 1/2 teaspoon salt
- 24 tablespoons (3 sticks) unsalted butter, cut into 1/2-inch pieces and chilled
- 3 large egg yolks (save whites for filling)
- 1 cup sour cream
- 1 teaspoon vanilla extract

FILLING

- 3 large egg whites
- 1 cup granulated sugar
- 1/4 teaspoon vanilla extract
- 1/2 cup walnuts, chopped fine
  Confectioners' sugar for rolling out dough

1. FOR THE DOUGH: Pulse the flour, yeast, and salt in a food processor until blended. Add the butter and pulse until the flour is pale yellow and resembles coarse cornmeal. Turn the mixture into a large bowl. (To do this by hand: Use the large holes on a box grater to grate frozen butter into a bowl with the flour mixture, then rub flour-coated pieces between your fingers until the flour mixture turns pale yellow and coarse.)

2. Beat the egg yolks, sour cream, and vanilla in a bowl. Using a wooden spoon, stir the yolk mixture into the flour mixture, pressing the mixture against the sides of the bowl to form a sticky dough. Divide the dough into two pieces, wrap tightly with plastic wrap, and refrigerate until well chilled, at least 2 hours and up to 24 hours.

(Continued on page 82)

3. FOR THE FILLING: Adjust two oven racks to the upper-middle and lower-middle positions and heat the oven to 400 degrees. Line two baking sheets with parchment paper. With an electric mixer at medium-low speed, beat the egg whites in a large bowl until frothy. Increase the speed to medium and gradually add the granulated sugar until incorporated. Add the vanilla, increase the speed to high, and beat until the whites hold soft peaks, about 2 minutes. Using a rubber spatula, fold in the walnuts.

4. Heavily sprinkle a work surface with confectioners' sugar. Working with one piece of dough at a time, form the rolls following the photos. Arrange 12 rolls on each lined baking sheet, spacing them about 2 inches apart. Bake until the tops are golden brown and puffed, 15 to 18 minutes, rotating and switching the baking sheets halfway through the baking. Serve warm or at room temperature.

Notes from the Test Kitchen
It's important to use plenty of confectioners' sugar to roll out the dough, as it is quite sticky. The confectioners' sugar also ensures that the dough tastes sweet.

FORMING HUNGARIAN SWEET ROLLS

1. Roll one piece of dough out into a 16-inch circle, about 1/8 inch thick.

2. Spread half the filling over the dough.

3. Using a knife or pizza cutter, cut the dough into 12 equal wedges.

4. Starting at the wider end of each wedge, gently roll up the dough, ending with the pointed end on the bottom.

Almond Crescents with Burnt Butter Icing

BARBARA ESTABROOK | RHINELANDER, WISCONSIN

These yeasted coffee cakes are similar to Danish, with their buttery crumb, rich filling, and flavorful icing. They are especially easy to put together since the dough requires no kneading, a plus for Barbara, who has had this recipe in her recipe box for more than 40 years: "As a young homemaker who loved to bake, it was my favorite because I could actually make a yeasted coffee cake without kneading the dough. In the early 1960s, almost all coffee cake recipes required kneading and because my mom did very little baking, I never learned how to knead."

MAKES 2 CRESCENTS, EACH SERVING 6

DOUGH

- 2¼ cups all-purpose flour
- 1 package rapid-rise or instant yeast
- 1 teaspoon salt
- 8 tablespoons (1 stick) unsalted butter, cut into ½-inch pieces and chilled
- ¼ cup warm evaporated milk (110 degrees)
- ¼ cup warm water (110 degrees)
- 2 tablespoons granulated sugar
- 1 large egg

FILLING

- ½ cup packed light brown sugar
- ½ cup sliced almonds, toasted
- 3 tablespoons unsalted butter, melted

BURNT BUTTER ICING

- 2 tablespoons unsalted butter
- 1 cup confectioners' sugar
- 2 tablespoons milk

1. FOR THE DOUGH: Pulse the flour, yeast, and salt in a food processor until blended. Add the butter and pulse until the flour is pale yellow and resembles coarse cornmeal. Turn the mixture into a large bowl. (To do this by hand: Use the large holes on a box grater to grate frozen butter into a bowl with the flour mixture, then rub flour-coated pieces between your fingers until the flour mixture turns pale yellow and coarse.)

2. Beat the milk, water, sugar, and egg in a medium bowl. Using a rubber spatula, fold the milk mixture into the flour mixture, then press against the side of the bowl. (The dough will be sticky.) Divide the dough into two pieces, wrap tightly in plastic wrap, and refrigerate until well chilled, at least 2 hours and up to 24 hours.

3. FOR THE FILLING: Line two baking sheets with parchment paper. Stir the brown sugar and almonds together in a small bowl.

4. Following the photos on page 86 and working with one piece of dough at a time on a lightly floured surface, roll the dough out to a 14 by 9-inch rectangle. Brush the dough with half the melted butter, then sprinkle with half the almond mixture, leaving a ¼-inch border around the edges. Starting at the long end, roll the dough into an even cylinder and pinch the dough to seal. Form the cylinder into a crescent shape on a prepared baking sheet and shape and slice the dough following the photos. Repeat with the remaining dough and filling. Cover with plastic wrap coated with cooking spray and let rise until the dough is almost doubled in size, about 1 hour.

(Continued on page 86)

5. Adjust two oven racks to the upper-middle and lower-middle positions and heat the oven to 350 degrees. Bake until the crescents are golden brown, about 20 minutes, rotating and switching the baking sheets halfway through baking. Cool on a rack until just warm, at least 40 minutes.

6. FOR THE ICING: While the crescents are cooling, heat the butter in a small saucepan over medium heat, swirling the pan constantly, until the butter is golden brown, 3 to 5 minutes. Transfer the butter to a bowl and whisk in the confectioners' sugar and milk. Drizzle the icing over the crescents. Serve.

Notes from the Test Kitchen

We were won over by the taste of these crescents and how easy they were to prepare. Because the crescents are meant to be flaky and not bready in texture, they don't require kneading. We only made a few minor adjustments to the recipe. First, we substituted milk for the water in the icing, which increased its flavor; we also eliminated the vanilla since it overpowered the wonderful nutty flavor of the burnt butter. It's easiest to "burn" the butter in a light-colored pan; not surprisingly, it's very difficult to judge the progress of the butter in a dark pan, especially one with a nonstick surface.

HOW TO MAKE ALMOND CRESCENTS

1. Roll the dough into a 14 by 9-inch rectangle, brush with half the melted butter, and sprinkle with half the almond mixture.

2. Place the cylinder of dough, seam-side down, on the prepared baking sheet and form into a crescent shape.

3. With a paring knife, make cuts around the outside of the ring, spacing them about 1 inch apart.

4. Rotate each piece of dough cut-side up.

Quaker Bonnet Biscuits

FROM THE EDITORS OF COOK'S COUNTRY

These old-fashioned biscuits, tiny replicas of a woman's bonnet viewed from the back, combine the convenience of a biscuit with the soft texture and yeasty flavor of good dinner rolls. Clues to the origin of this recipe proved elusive—that is, until we started searching through old Quaker journals and recipe collections. We found our most promising lead in a book written nearly a century ago entitled *Mary at the Farm and Book of Recipes Compiled during Her Visit among the Pennsylvania Germans* by Edith M. Thomas. With a lot of guesswork (this recipe was short on details, as well as calling for lard and cake yeast), we reproduced a pretty good biscuit from Mary's recipe but, hoping to bring it into this century, we spent some time updating it and streamlining it (Mary's biscuit required two risings). Taking our cue from existing recipes for super-quick Southern yeast biscuits, including Alabama biscuits and angel biscuits, we rolled out the dough, cut it, allowed it to rise, then baked it. This worked like a charm and we found that if we let the biscuits rise in a warm oven, the rising time was just half an hour. Here's a recipe that belongs in any modern kitchen.

MAKES 18 BISCUITS

1	cup milk
1	large egg
1	package rapid-rise or instant yeast
4	cups all-purpose flour
2	tablespoons sugar
1 1/2	teaspoons salt
8	tablespoons (1 stick) unsalted butter, cut into 1/2-inch pieces and chilled, plus 1 tablespoon melted (for assembling biscuits)

1. Adjust the oven racks to the upper-middle and lower-middle positions and heat the oven to 200 degrees. Once the oven reaches 200 degrees, maintain the temperature for 10 minutes, then turn off the oven.

2. Stir the milk, egg, and yeast together in a large measuring cup until combined.

3. Process the flour, sugar, and salt in a food processor until combined. Add the chilled butter and pulse until the mixture looks like coarse cornmeal, about fifteen 1-second pulses. Transfer to a large bowl.

(Continued on page 88)

4. Stir in the milk mixture until the dough comes together. Turn the dough out onto a lightly floured work surface. Briefly knead to bring the dough together, about 1 minute, adding more flour if necessary. Following the photos, roll, cut, and assemble the biscuits on parchment-lined baking sheets. Cover with kitchen towels and place in the warm oven. Let rise until doubled in size, 25 to 35 minutes.

5. Remove the baking sheets with the biscuits from the oven and heat the oven to 375 degrees; return the baking sheets to the oven once it is fully preheated. Bake the biscuits until golden brown, about 15 minutes, rotating and switching the baking sheets halfway through baking. Serve hot or warm.

Notes from the Test Kitchen

During our testing process for this recipe, we turned to rapid-rise yeast to speed up the rising time and found that after an hour, the dough doubled in size. We also recommend that you let the dough rise in a warm oven so you can cut the rising time even further.

To make these biscuits without a food processor, freeze the stick of butter until hard and then grate it into the dry ingredients using the large holes of a box grater. Toss gently with your hands to evenly distribute the butter, and proceed with the recipe.

HOW TO MAKE QUAKER BONNET BISCUITS

1. Roll the dough into a 12-inch round. Cut out eighteen 2½-inch circles, ¾ inch thick, and place them on parchment-lined baking sheets.

2. Re-roll the remaining dough out to a thickness of ½ inch, then cut out eighteen 1¼-inch rounds.

3. Lightly brush the larger dough rounds with melted butter.

4. Place one smaller round slightly off center on top of each larger round.

Pioneer Bread

MEMORY BLODGETT | SPOKANE, WASHINGTON

Between 1820 and 1880, the promise of free land (and sometimes gold) tempted settlers to make the perilous journey westward by covered wagon. It's easy to imagine how comforting this dense quick bread was for the migrating settlers. Original recipes were made with both cornmeal and rye and wheat flour, since wheat was hard to come by during this time period. And they relied on either saleratus (sodium bicarbonate) as the leavening agent, or a sourdough sponge.

This bread is a bit more refined than true Pioneer Bread, but it still has the same hearty spirit of earlier recipes. Memory recalls the interesting legacy of this particular version: "When waves of covered wagons crossed the Great Prairie from Minnesota headed toward the open land and riches of the West, this recipe came with my husband's great-grandparents. Later, their daughter Nellie (who lived until the age of 99) told us the history. She recalled that her mother made this bread at Thanksgiving and Christmas, and that the recipe was never written down until her own daughter asked for it for a school project. I was given the recipe (slightly modified by my mother-in-law) upon my marriage, thus continuing a long line of family cooks who never had a holiday without Pioneer Bread."

MAKES 2 LOAVES

- 3 cups whole-wheat flour
- 1 cup all-purpose flour
- 1/2 cup sugar
- 1 teaspoon baking powder
- 1 teaspoon baking soda
- 1 teaspoon salt
- 1 large egg
- 2 cups buttermilk
- 1/2 cup corn syrup
- 1 cup walnuts, chopped
- 1/2 cup raisins
- 1/2 cup dried dates, chopped

1. Adjust an oven rack to the middle position and heat the oven to 300 degrees. Grease two 9 by 5-inch loaf pans. Whisk the flours, sugar, baking powder, baking soda, and salt together in a large bowl. Beat the egg in a medium bowl, then stir in the buttermilk and corn syrup. Stir the egg mixture into the flour mixture until just combined (a few streaks of flour should remain), then stir in the walnuts, raisins, and dates until just incorporated.

2. Divide the batter evenly between the prepared loaf pans and bake until a toothpick inserted into the center of the bread comes out clean, about 1 hour. Cool on a rack for 10 minutes, then turn out onto the rack to cool completely, at least 45 minutes. Serve. (The bread will keep at room temperature wrapped in plastic wrap for up to 4 days. The bread can also be wrapped in two layers of aluminum foil and frozen for up to 2 months.)

Notes from the Test Kitchen
This bread fit the bill for everything from morning toast to an afternoon snack. An equal amount of pecans can be substituted for the walnuts.

Butter Horn Rolls

STACI WHITE | ROCKY HILL, CONNECTICUT

These old-fashioned buttery rolls look as though they might be hard to make but are actually quite easy. We weren't surprised to hear that this recipe had a special place on Staci's family's Thanksgiving table. With the horns' curled shape and buttery taste, they definitely seem special. Staci says, "This bread recipe has been in my family at least as far back as my great-grandmother, Alice Banister. A Kansas mother of 10, Great-Grandma Alice's recipes have been widely praised and reproduced amongst all branches of the family throughout Texas, Colorado, and Kansas. This is a favorite of ours at special meals, but we can always count on having them at Thanksgiving."

MAKES 24 ROLLS

12	tablespoons (1$\frac{1}{2}$ sticks) unsalted butter
1	cup warm milk (110 degrees)
$\frac{1}{2}$	cup sugar
3	large eggs
4$\frac{1}{2}$–5	cups all-purpose flour
1	package rapid-rise or instant yeast
1$\frac{1}{2}$	teaspoons salt

1. Lightly grease a large bowl with cooking spray. Melt 8 tablespoons of the butter in a small saucepan over medium heat; let cool. Mix the melted butter, milk, sugar, and eggs in a large measuring cup. Mix 4$\frac{1}{2}$ cups flour, the yeast, and salt together in the bowl of a standing mixer fitted with the dough hook. With the mixer on low, add the milk mixture. After the dough comes together, increase the speed to medium and mix until shiny and smooth, 4 to 6 minutes. (If the dough is sticky after 3 minutes, add the remaining $\frac{1}{2}$ cup flour, 2 tablespoons at a time.) Turn the dough out onto a heavily floured work surface, shape into a ball, and place in the greased bowl. (To make the dough by hand, see the instructions on page 74.) Cover the bowl with plastic wrap and let rest in a warm place until the dough is doubled in size, about 1 hour.

2. Spray two baking sheets with cooking spray. Melt the remaining 4 tablespoons butter over medium heat; let cool. Divide the dough into three equal pieces. Working on a lightly floured work surface, roll each piece of dough into a 10-inch circle; brush with melted butter. Using a knife or pizza cutter, cut each circle into eight equal wedges. Starting at the wide end, roll up the dough, ending with the pointed tip on the bottom. Place 2 inches apart on the prepared baking sheets and curl in the ends slightly to form a crescent shape. Cover the rolls with plastic wrap coated with cooking spray and let rise until the rolls are doubled in size, about 45 minutes.

3. Adjust two oven racks to the upper-middle and lower-middle positions and heat the oven to 325 degrees. Bake the rolls until golden brown, 25 to 30 minutes, switching and rotating the baking sheets halfway through baking. Serve hot or warm.

Notes from the Test Kitchen
These soft and buttery rolls are the perfect accompaniment for any meal. The only change we made to Staci's recipe was to use butter instead of margarine. Just be sure to start rolling from the wide end of the wedge of dough and end with the pointed tip facing down.

Corn Dodgers

THE EDITORS OF COOK'S COUNTRY

Abraham Lincoln was raised on these little oval cornmeal cakes, George Washington Carver took them to school, and John Wayne used them for target practice in the movie *True Grit*. Dating back to the 1800s, the first corn dodgers were made from "hot water corn bread," a mixture of cornmeal, pork fat, salt, and boiling water that was formed into small oblong loaves and baked. Similar recipes were given different names depending on how the dough was shaped and cooked. Corn pone have the same oblong shape as dodgers, but are pan-fried in lots of oil. Johnnycakes are flattened into small pancakes, then griddle-fried. Ashcakes are rounds of dough wrapped in cabbage leaves, then placed in the ashes of the campfire to cook. Hoecakes are formed into small pancakes, then placed on the flat side of a garden hoe (really!) and cooked over the campfire.

MAKES 22

- 2 tablespoons corn or vegetable oil
- 2 cups yellow cornmeal
- 1½ tablespoons sugar
- ½ teaspoon baking soda
- ½ teaspoon salt
- 2 cups water
- 1 cup buttermilk
- 1 tablespoon unsalted butter
- 2 teaspoons baking powder
- 1 large egg

1. Adjust an oven rack to the middle position and heat the oven to 450 degrees. Brush 1 tablespoon of the oil on a rimmed baking sheet.

2. Whisk the cornmeal, sugar, baking soda, and salt in a medium bowl. Combine the water, buttermilk, and butter in a large saucepan. In a slow, steady stream, whisk the cornmeal mixture into the liquid. Cook the mixture over medium-high heat, whisking constantly, until the water is absorbed and the mixture is very thick, about 6 minutes. Remove from the heat and cool until warm, about 10 minutes.

3. Whisk the baking powder and egg in a small bowl, then stir into the cornmeal mixture. Fill a medium bowl with tap water. Scoop out a generous 2 tablespoons of the mixture and, using wet hands, form into a 4 by 1½-inch loaf shape. Place on the prepared baking sheet and repeat with the remaining mixture, spacing the dodgers about ½ inch apart. Brush with the remaining 1 tablespoon oil. Bake until deep brown on the bottom and golden brown on top, rotating the pan halfway through baking, 25 to 30 minutes. Transfer the corn dodgers to a rack to cool slightly. Serve warm. (The corn dodgers can be refrigerated for up to 2 days; reheat on a baking sheet in a 350-degree oven.)

Notes from the Test Kitchen

Most 19th-century recipes we tried yielded corn dodgers that were dense, gritty, and hard as a brick. Starting with the base recipe of cornmeal, salt, butter, and hot water, we added a bit of sugar (just 1½ tablespoons) to bring out the cornmeal's sweet side. Replacing some of the water with buttermilk gave the dodgers a tangy flavor that tasters loved. Baking soda (which reacts with the buttermilk) and baking powder helped to lighten the dodgers considerably, and a single egg provided richness and gave the dodgers a creamy interior.

7UP CAKE

Cakes

Nana's Gingerbread

KEITH NICHOLS | WILLIAMSBURG, MASSACHUSETTS

The history of gingerbread goes back centuries and has roots in the medieval fairs of England and the Christmas celebrations of Germany and other countries. This treasured family recipe (Nana was from East Concord, Vermont, and was born in 1893) is typical of many gingerbreads and includes blackstrap molasses, baking soda, and boiling water. Says Keith: "Nana Boutwell always made this rich, moist, spicy delicacy for us when we were visiting from our home in Connecticut. And her stove was a wood burner. I know that probably added something to the essence of this gingerbread, but it works wonderfully in today's kitchen. When my wife bakes Nana's Gingerbread, the spicy scent of molasses and cinnamon fills my home and takes me back to my childhood. The only thing missing is the mix of wood and cinnamon." Keith recommends serving his grandmother's gingerbread with applesauce, whipped cream, or vanilla ice cream, and we agree.

SERVES 12

- 2   cups all-purpose flour
- 1/2 cup sugar
- 2   teaspoons ground ginger
- 1/4 teaspoon ground allspice
- 1   teaspoon ground cinnamon
- 1   cup blackstrap molasses (see note)
- 8   tablespoons (1 stick) unsalted butter, cut into 1/2-inch pieces and softened
- 2   large eggs, room temperature
- 2   teaspoons baking soda
- 1   cup boiling water

1. Adjust an oven rack to the middle position and heat the oven to 350 degrees. Grease and flour a 9-inch square baking pan. Whisk the flour, sugar, ginger, allspice, and cinnamon in a large bowl. Stir the molasses, butter, and eggs together in a medium bowl (some pieces of butter will remain).

2. Make a well in the center of the flour mixture. Add the molasses mixture to the well and stir until well blended. Stir the baking soda and boiling water together in a medium liquid measuring cup, pour over the batter, and stir until the butter is completely melted. Scrape the batter into the prepared pan and bake until a toothpick inserted in the center of the cake comes out clean, 30 to 40 minutes. Cool completely in the pan, at least 1 hour. Serve. (The cake can be stored at room temperature for up to 4 days.)

Notes from the Test Kitchen

We were very curious about this recipe since it called for blackstrap molasses, which we generally shy away from as it is so strongly flavored that any spices are completely overpowered by it. Its potency comes as a result of a third round of boiling during the cane sugar refining process—the two earlier rounds yielding mild (light) and robust (dark) molasses. With each successive boiling the molasses grows more bitter or pronounced in flavor as more sugar is extracted. Much to our surprise, we found that the hearty blackstrap molasses stood up to the spices and gave this cake a distinctively smoky note we liked. That said, you can certainly use robust molasses (which is easier to find) and this cake will still be delicious.

Mama Honey's Strawberry Bread

LESLIE GELLERMAN | RESEDA, CALIFORNIA

This simple and sweet "bread" is really more like a tea cake. The strawberries infuse the bread with their aroma and melt into it, making tasty, moist pockets throughout. This simple bread recipe had been in Mama Honey's family for generations and it took years for Leslie to work up the nerve to ask for it: "Mama Honey was famous for her Southern hospitality and her magnificent Strawberry Bread. The first time (and every time) I visited Dallas to see my in-laws, my visit would always include paying a call on Mama Honey. With each and every visit, Strawberry Bread, coffee, and good conversation would be on the agenda. As the years passed and Mama Honey aged, I wanted to request her recipe as a memento. I was a bit apprehensive about asking, as some people take offense at divulging family recipes. Luckily for me, this was not the case with Mama Honey."

MAKES 2 LOAVES

3	cups all-purpose flour
1	tablespoon ground cinnamon
1	teaspoon baking soda
1	teaspoon salt
4	large eggs
1½	cups sugar
1	cup vegetable oil
2	cups strawberries, hulled and chopped
1¼	cups pecans, toasted and chopped

1. Adjust an oven rack to the middle position and heat the oven to 325 degrees. Grease and flour two 9 by 5-inch loaf pans. Whisk the flour, cinnamon, baking soda, and salt in a large bowl. Whisk the eggs, sugar, and oil in a medium bowl.

2. Make a well in the center of the flour mixture. Add the egg mixture to the well and stir until well blended. Stir in the strawberries and pecans. Scrape the batter into the prepared pans and bake until a toothpick inserted in the center of the loaves comes out clean, 60 to 70 minutes. Cool in the pans for 10 minutes, then turn out onto a rack to cool completely, at least 1 hour. Serve. (The bread can be stored in the refrigerator for up to 3 days.)

Notes from the Test Kitchen

In an effort to streamline the recipe, we tried using frozen strawberries instead of fresh (just in case we craved this bread in January). It was a no-go, as the frozen strawberries leached water into the batter, making for soggy, unappealing bread that was a strange purple color.

Wacky Cake

THE EDITORS OF COOK'S COUNTRY

During both world wars, butter, sugar, milk, and eggs were often in short supply, leading American women to devise a variety of "make-do" cakes like this one. We couldn't understand how this recipe earned its name until we found it in *The Time Reader's Book of Recipes,* a collection of reader recipes compiled by the editors of *Time* magazine in 1949. Mrs. Donald Adam of Detroit, Michigan, submitted this strange recipe, which called for mixing the dry ingredients—flour, cocoa powder, sugar, salt, and baking soda—right in the baking pan. If that wasn't strange enough, three holes—two small and one large—were made in the dry mix. Into the large hole went melted vegetable shortening, while vanilla and vinegar were destined for the smaller holes. Cold water was poured over everything, then the whole mess was stirred and popped into the oven. How does this strange recipe work? Without eggs, this cake depends on the last-minute reaction of vinegar and baking soda to lift the thick batter. The three holes ensure that the dry ingredients (including the baking soda) remain dry until the last possible second. The lift provided by the baking soda and vinegar reaction is fleeting, and the recipe's odd mixing method ensures that the batter gets into the oven quickly.

SERVES 6 TO 8

- 1 1/2 cups all-purpose flour
- 3/4 cup sugar
- 1/4 cup natural cocoa powder
- 3/4 teaspoon baking soda
- 1/2 teaspoon salt
- 5 tablespoons vegetable oil
- 1 tablespoon white vinegar
- 1 teaspoon vanilla extract
- 1 cup water
- Confectioners' sugar for dusting

1. Adjust an oven rack to the middle position and heat the oven to 350 degrees. Grease an 8-inch square baking pan.

2. Whisk the flour, sugar, cocoa powder, baking soda, and salt in the prepared pan. Following the photos, make one large and two small craters in the dry ingredients. Add the oil to the large crater and vinegar and vanilla separately to the small craters. Pour the water into the pan and mix until just a few streaks of flour remain.

Immediately put the pan in the oven.

3. Bake until a toothpick inserted in the center of the cake comes out with a few moist crumbs attached, about 30 minutes. Cool in the pan, then dust with confectioners' sugar. (The cake can be stored at room temperature for up to 3 days.)

A WACKY MIXING METHOD

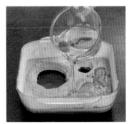 

1. Make one large and two small craters in the dry mix. Pour oil into the large crater, then vinegar and vanilla into the smaller craters. Pour the water over everything.

2. Using a wooden spoon or spatula, mix the batter, taking care not to over-mix; the batter should still contain a few streaks of flour.

Real Carrot Cake

CONNEE SHECKLER | MARRIOTTSVILLE, MARYLAND

Legend has it that in 1783, George Washington was served carrot cake in a tavern in lower Manhattan to mark British Evacuation Day. Molly O'Neill, in her *New York Cookbook*, printed the recipe for the cake, a simple spiced oil cake with no frosting. Since then, the history of carrot cakes in America has seen lots of twists and turns, disappearing from cookbooks for a while and then re-emerging with a vengeance in the 1960s, when the popularity of easy oil cakes coincided with the health food craze. This interesting cake is closer in spirit to earlier carrot (and other spice) cakes and forgoes the gooey cream cheese frosting of modern times for a simple rum-infused glaze.

SERVES 12

CAKE

- 3 cups plus 2 teaspoons all-purpose flour
- 2 teaspoons baking powder
- 2 teaspoons baking soda
- 2 teaspoons ground cinnamon
- 1/2 teaspoon salt
- 1 cup walnuts, chopped
- 1 cup raisins
- 5 large eggs, room temperature
- 1 3/4 cups granulated sugar
- 1 cup vegetable oil
- 1 pound carrots, peeled and grated

TOPPING

- 1/2 cup dry white wine or dry vermouth
- 1 cup confectioners' sugar
- 2 tablespoons buttermilk
- 1 teaspoon dark rum

1. FOR THE CAKE: Adjust an oven rack to the middle position and heat the oven to 325 degrees. Grease and flour a 12-cup Bundt pan. Whisk 3 cups flour, baking powder, baking soda, cinnamon, and salt in a medium bowl. Toss the walnuts, raisins, and 2 teaspoons flour in a small bowl until well coated.

2. With an electric mixer at medium-high speed, beat the eggs and granulated sugar until combined. Reduce the speed to medium and slowly add the oil until incorporated. Increase the speed to high and beat until the mixture is light and creamy. Using a rubber spatula, stir in the flour mixture, the walnuts and raisins, and carrots until combined. Scrape the batter into the prepared pan and bake until a toothpick inserted in the center comes out clean, 50 to 60 minutes. Cool the cake in the pan for 30 minutes, then turn out onto a rack to cool completely, at least 1 hour.

3. FOR THE TOPPING: Brush the vermouth over the cake until it is absorbed. Whisk the confectioners' sugar, buttermilk, and rum in a medium bowl. Drizzle over the cake. Serve. (The cake can be stored at room temperature for up to 5 days.)

Notes from the Test Kitchen

Originally the recipe called for covering the cake in cheesecloth, then pouring the wine over it. This step was burdensome, so we tried brushing the wine on instead. This gave the cake just as much flavor. As for the carrots, grating a whole pound of them on a box grater is enough to keep you from making this cake to begin with. We recommend, therefore, using your food processor fitted with the shredding disk, which makes mercifully quick work of the task.

World War II Chocolate Mayonnaise Cake

ALAN CAVALLARO | PLAINFIELD, NEW JERSEY

Carolyn Wyman, in her book *The Kitchen Sink Cookbook: Offbeat Recipes from Unusual Ingredients,* writes that this recipe was developed in 1937 by Mrs. Paul Prince, the wife of a Hellmann's sales distributor, though the *New York Times* attributed the recipe to a grocer's wife. Regardless of its actual origin, there is no disputing what Alan says: "It was a way for people to have cake at a time when eggs, butter, and shortening were rationed. On one occasion my mother made this cake to take to my parents' weekend house. As they prepared to leave the weekend house and return home, they forgot the cake. Covered with aluminum foil, it was left on the kitchen counter. My parents returned the following weekend and the cake was as moist and delicious as it was the previous weekend."

SERVES 12

CAKE
- 2 cups all-purpose flour
- 1/4 cup Dutch-processed cocoa powder
- 1 1/2 teaspoons baking powder
- 1 teaspoon baking soda
- 1 cup mayonnaise
- 1 cup granulated sugar
- 1 teaspoon vanilla extract
- 1 cup water

FROSTING
- 4 tablespoons unsalted butter
- 1/2 cup packed light brown sugar
- 2 tablespoons milk
- 1 cup confectioners' sugar

1. FOR THE CAKE: Adjust an oven rack to the middle position and heat the oven to 350 degrees. Grease and flour a 9-inch square baking pan. Whisk the flour, cocoa, baking powder, and baking soda in a medium bowl.

2. Stir the mayonnaise, granulated sugar, and vanilla together in a large bowl until smooth. Add the water and stir until combined. Whisk in the flour mixture until incorporated. Scrape the batter into the prepared pan and bake until a toothpick inserted in the center comes out clean, 30 to 35 minutes. Cool completely in the pan, at least 45 minutes.

3. FOR THE FROSTING: Melt the butter in small saucepan over medium-high heat. Stir in the brown sugar and bring to a boil. Boil until the mixture begins to thicken, about 2 minutes, then, off the heat, carefully stir in the milk. Return to a boil, then remove from the heat to cool until just warm, about 30 minutes. Stir in the confectioners' sugar and spread the icing evenly over the cake. Serve. (The cake can be stored at room temperature for up to 3 days.)

Notes from the Test Kitchen
This homey cake is very rich and makes a great snack cake. Many of us were familiar with the concept of a mayonnaise cake, but the toffee-like icing gave it an interesting twist. Do not add extra salt to the cake, as the mayonnaise has plenty of seasoning. In an attempt to slim things down, the test kitchen tried substituting both low-fat and fat-free mayonnaise. We had mixed results. The low-fat mayo worked just as well as the full-fat kind—no change in texture or flavor at all. The fat-free mayonnaise cake was another story. Rubbery and strangely salty, this cake was an experiment we'd rather not repeat.

Prunella Cake

SHAREN DOWNEN | SPARTA, MISSOURI

Recipes for prune cake can be found in cookbooks beginning in the early 20th century. Most are spice cakes like this one, rich and moist with softened or stewed prunes; they often include buttermilk or sour cream in the batter. This recipe comes from Sharen's grandmother, Grace Light, born in 1908. "Each Christmas Granny made her famous cake for each family in our family. Each cake was about 4 by 9 inches because she baked it in a 13 by 9-inch cake pan and cut three cakes from each pan."

SERVES 16

CAKE
- 1 cup pitted prunes
- 1 cup water
- 1½ cups all-purpose flour
- ½ teaspoon baking powder
- ½ teaspoon baking soda
- ½ teaspoon salt
- ¼ teaspoon ground cinnamon
- ¼ teaspoon ground nutmeg
- ¼ teaspoon ground allspice
- ⅔ cup buttermilk
- 2 large eggs, room temperature
- 8 tablespoons (1 stick) unsalted butter, softened
- 1 cup granulated sugar

FROSTING
- 2 cups confectioners' sugar
- 2 tablespoons unsalted butter, melted
- 1 teaspoon lemon juice
- ½ teaspoon salt

1. FOR THE CAKE: Adjust an oven rack to the middle position and heat the oven to 350 degrees. Grease and flour a 13 by 9-inch baking pan. Place the prunes and water in a small saucepan and cook over medium heat until the prunes soften, 6 to 8 minutes. Drain the prunes, reserving 3 tablespoons of the liquid. When the prunes are completely cool, chop them fine. Whisk the flour, baking powder, baking soda, salt, cinnamon, nutmeg, and allspice in a medium bowl. Whisk the buttermilk, eggs, and prunes in a large measuring cup.

2. With an electric mixer on medium-high speed, beat the butter and granulated sugar until fluffy, about 2 minutes. Add the flour mixture and the buttermilk mixture alternately in two batches, beating after each addition until combined. Scrape the batter into the prepared pan and bake until a toothpick inserted in the center comes out clean, 25 to 30 minutes. Cool completely in the pan, at least 1 hour.

3. FOR THE FROSTING: Whisk the reserved prune liquid, confectioners' sugar, butter, lemon juice, and salt in a medium bowl until smooth. Spread evenly over the cake and allow the frosting to set, about 30 minutes. Serve. (The cake can be stored at room temperature for up to 4 days.)

Notes from the Test Kitchen
While we admit the name of this cake did scare us at first, we were instantly won over by its remarkably moist texture—thanks to the prunes. Do not forget to reserve the 3 tablespoons of prune soaking liquid. Its fruity tang really adds great flavor to the frosting.

Scotch Cake

MELINDA HARVEY | LUBBOCK, TEXAS

The origin of the name for this simple sheet cake, with its unique pecan and coconut topping, was a mystery to Melinda and her mother, whose recipe card for it included a note that said: "I don't understand the name of this cake. I just call it my 'boil it' cake." We did, however, find a nearly identical recipe in a Vernon, Texas, newspaper from 1965, which noted that it was a very convenient recipe and would keep moist "indefinitely."

SERVES 12

CAKE

- 2 cups all-purpose flour
- 2 cups granulated sugar
- 16 tablespoons (2 sticks) unsalted butter
- 1 cup water
- 4 teaspoons Dutch-processed cocoa powder
- 1/2 cup buttermilk
- 3 large eggs
- 1 teaspoon baking soda
- 1 teaspoon vanilla extract
- 1/8 teaspoon salt

TOPPING

- 8 tablespoons (1 stick) unsalted butter
- 6 tablespoons whole milk
- 4 teaspoons Dutch-processed cocoa powder
- 4 cups confectioners' sugar
- 1 teaspoon vanilla extract
- 1 cup sweetened, shredded coconut
- 1 cup chopped pecans

1. FOR THE CAKE: Adjust an oven rack to the middle position and heat the oven to 350 degrees. Grease and flour a 13 by 9-inch baking pan. Whisk the flour and granulated sugar in a large bowl. Heat the butter, water, and cocoa in a medium saucepan over medium heat until the butter melts and the mixture comes to a boil. Pour over the flour mixture and mix until just combined. Stir in the buttermilk, eggs, baking soda, vanilla, and salt until incorporated. Scrape the batter into the prepared pan and bake until a toothpick inserted in the center comes out clean, 35 to 40 minutes.

2. FOR THE TOPPING: Meanwhile heat the butter, milk, and cocoa powder in a large saucepan over medium heat until the butter melts. Off the heat, stir in the confectioners' sugar, vanilla, coconut, and pecans until combined. Spread over the warm cake and let cool completely, at least 45 minutes. Serve. (The cake can be refrigerated for up to 3 days. Bring the cake to room temperature before serving.)

Notes from the Test Kitchen
We loved the fact that this cake was a snap to put together (no mixer required!) and we had a hard time not snacking on it before it was cool. One thing that surprised us about the cake was the noticeable chocolate flavor that came from only 4 teaspoons cocoa powder. We attribute this to the fact that the cocoa is heated with the butter and water, thereby allowing its flavors to bloom.

Oatmeal Cake

ANNE O'BRIEN | SILVERDALE, WASHINGTON

With its old-fashioned broiled and caramel-like topping, this cake is like a chewy oatmeal bar, but much better. Turns out that Anne and her family misplaced the recipe card for this cake for many years, during which time they tried to duplicate it, with mixed results. We're glad this truly "lost" recipe, which came from Anne's great-aunt Stella, finally turned up again. While we suspect that oatmeal cakes are old in origin, recipes for them only started appearing around the 1960s, along with the release into the market of Quaker's quick-cooking oats.

SERVES 12

CAKE
1½ cups all-purpose flour
1 teaspoon baking soda
1 teaspoon ground cinnamon
½ teaspoon ground nutmeg
½ teaspoon salt
1 cup quick-cooking oats (see note)
1 cup hot water
8 tablespoons (1 stick) unsalted butter, softened
1 cup granulated sugar
1 cup packed light brown sugar
2 teaspoons vanilla extract
2 large eggs, room temperature

TOPPING
4 tablespoons unsalted butter
¾ cup packed light brown sugar
¼ cup milk
1⅓ cups sweetened, shredded coconut

1. **FOR THE CAKE:** Adjust an oven rack to the middle position and heat the oven to 350 degrees. Grease and flour a 13 by 9-inch broiler-safe baking pan. Whisk the flour, baking soda, cinnamon, nutmeg, and salt in a large bowl. Combine the oats and water in a medium bowl and let sit until the water is absorbed, about 5 minutes.

2. With an electric mixer at medium-high speed, beat the butter, sugars, and vanilla until fluffy, about 2 minutes. Reduce the speed to medium and add the eggs one at a time, mixing until incorporated. Add the flour mixture in two batches, beating after each addition until combined. Add the oatmeal mixture and beat until incorporated. Scrape the batter into the prepared pan and bake until a toothpick inserted in the center comes out clean, 30 to 35 minutes. Let cool slightly in the pan (the cake should be warm but not hot), about 10 minutes. Heat the broiler.

3. **FOR THE TOPPING:** Meanwhile, bring the butter, sugar, and milk to a boil in a medium saucepan over medium-high heat. Off the heat, stir in the coconut. Spread the topping evenly over the cake and broil until the topping bubbles and just begins to brown, 2 to 3 minutes. Serve warm. (The cake can be stored at room temperature for up to 4 days. Reheat individual slices in the microwave on the highest power for 30 seconds.)

Notes from the Test Kitchen
Be sure to use a metal pan for this cake, as a Pyrex pan is not broiler safe. As for the cake itself, we wondered if the texture would change if we used the longer-cooking rolled oats. So, we tried them, and the texture did change for the worse. The oats retained much of their chewy texture, making the cake really dense. The quick-cooking oats were the winner.

Lazy Daisy Cake

LINDSAY WEISS | OVERLAND PARK, KANSAS

This easy cake with its broiled icing borrows a technique from the classic Hot Milk Cake (see page 110), where the butter and milk are heated together and then all the wet and dry ingredients are simply combined to make the batter. What could be easier? This is not a fine-textured cake, but the simple broiled icing with coconut caramelizes, making it seem more complex. Cakes such as this proliferated in the 1930s and 1940s and sometimes had other names, but Lazy Daisy is the one that has survived the test of time. This recipe came from Lindsay's grandmother.

SERVES 12

CAKE

- 2 cups all-purpose flour
- 2 teaspoons baking powder
- 1/2 teaspoon salt
- 4 tablespoons unsalted butter
- 1 cup milk
- 1 teaspoon vanilla extract
- 4 large eggs, room temperature
- 2 cups granulated sugar

TOPPING

- 9 tablespoons unsalted butter, melted
- 3/4 cup packed light brown sugar
- 6 tablespoons evaporated milk
- 1 1/2 cups sweetened, shredded coconut

1. FOR THE CAKE: Adjust an oven rack to the middle position and heat the oven to 350 degrees. Grease and flour a 13 by 9-inch broiler-safe baking pan. Whisk the flour, baking powder, and salt in a large bowl. Heat the butter and milk in a medium saucepan over medium heat until the butter melts. Stir in the vanilla.

2. With an electric mixer on medium-high speed, beat the eggs and granulated sugar until pale and thick, about 6 minutes. Using a rubber spatula, fold in the flour mixture and milk mixture alternately in two batches until just incorporated. Scrape the batter into the prepared pan and bake until a toothpick inserted in the center comes out clean, 30 to 35 minutes. Let cool slightly in the pan, about 10 minutes. Heat the broiler.

3. FOR THE TOPPING: Meanwhile, combine the butter, brown sugar, evaporated milk, and coconut in a medium bowl. Spread the topping evenly over the cake. Broil until the topping bubbles and just begins to brown, 2 to 3 minutes. Serve warm. (The cake can be stored at room temperature for up to 4 days. Reheat individual slices in the microwave on the highest power for 30 seconds.)

Notes from the Test Kitchen

We loved the caramelized flavor that the broiled icing gave the cake. You will need to use a metal pan for this recipe, as a Pyrex pan is not broiler safe. Do not be tempted to move this cake closer to the broiler during the last few minutes in the oven. Keeping the cake on the middle rack allows the topping to crisp and bubble at a safe distance.

Hot Milk Cake

ELSIE REAMY | RICHMOND, VIRGINIA

Hot milk cakes, popular during the Depression, usually require just a few tablespoons of butter, because heating the milk and the eggs gives the resulting cake a surprising richness. Some think that this richness comes from the method—the eggs begin to cook in the batter. This cake, which calls for a full stick of butter, departs from the norm (maybe the butter amount was adjusted upward after rationing ended), but yields a moist and rich cake with a tender crumb (plus it's easy to make). This recipe came from Elsie's mother, who was born in rural Virginia in 1913.

SERVES 12

- 2 cups all-purpose flour
- 2 teaspoons baking powder
- 1 teaspoon salt
- 8 tablespoons (1 stick) unsalted butter
- 1 cup milk
- 2 teaspoons vanilla extract
- 4 large eggs, room temperature
- 2 cups sugar

1. Adjust an oven rack to the middle position and heat the oven to 325 degrees. Grease and flour a 12-cup tube pan. Whisk the flour, baking powder, and salt in a large bowl. Heat the butter and milk in a medium saucepan until the butter melts and the mixture is very hot, but not boiling. Stir in the vanilla.

2. With an electric mixer on medium-high speed, beat the eggs and sugar until tripled in volume, about 6 minutes. Reduce the speed to medium and slowly beat in the hot milk mixture until incorporated. Add the flour mixture in two batches, beating after each addition until just incorporated. Pour the batter into the prepared pan and bake until a toothpick inserted in the center comes out clean, 50 to 60 minutes. Cool the cake in the pan for 10 minutes, then turn out onto a rack to cool completely, at least 1 hour. Serve. (The cake can be stored at room temperature for up to 3 days.)

Notes from the Test Kitchen

This is a versatile and easy golden cake with good flavor and texture. Because this cake is so plain, and is usually served plain, it is essential that you don't overbake it. Be sure to check the cake a few minutes before the recommended baking time is up.

Blueberry Boy Bait

THE EDITORS OF COOK'S COUNTRY

Forget the funny name—after one bite of this moist and simple blueberry coffee cake, you'll be hooked, too. Much more than a moist yellow sheet cake topped with a layer of blueberries and crisp cinnamon sugar, it is possibly the best coffee cake we've ever eaten. We found the source of this recipe in the *Chicago Tribune* in 1954. A 15-year-old girl named Adrienne (AKA Renny) Powell of Chicago entered her dessert—Blueberry Boy Bait—in the junior division of the 1954 Pillsbury Grand National Baking Contest. She won second place, which included a $2,000 cash prize plus a promise to print her recipe in *Pillsbury's 5th Grand National Recipes Cookbook*. Renny named the cake (a family recipe) for the effect it had on teenage boys—one bite and they were hooked.

SERVES 12

CAKE
- 2 cups plus 1 teaspoon all-purpose flour
- 1 tablespoon baking powder
- 1 teaspoon salt
- 16 tablespoons (2 sticks) unsalted butter, softened
- ¾ cup packed light brown sugar
- ½ cup granulated sugar
- 3 large eggs
- 1 cup milk
- ½ cup blueberries, fresh or frozen (see note)

TOPPING
- ½ cup blueberries, fresh or frozen (see note)
- ¼ cup granulated sugar
- ½ teaspoon ground cinnamon

1. FOR THE CAKE: Adjust an oven rack to the middle position and heat the oven to 350 degrees. Grease and flour a 13 by 9-inch baking pan.

2. Whisk 2 cups flour, baking powder, and salt in a medium bowl. With an electric mixer on medium-high speed, beat the butter and sugars until fluffy, about 2 minutes. Add the eggs, one at a time, beating until just incorporated. Reduce the speed to medium and beat in the flour mixture and the milk alternately in two batches until incorporated. Toss the blueberries with the remaining 1 teaspoon flour. Using a rubber spatula, gently fold in the blueberries. Scrape the batter into the prepared pan.

3. FOR THE TOPPING: Scatter the blueberries over the top of the batter. Stir the sugar and cinnamon together in a small bowl and sprinkle over the batter. Bake until a toothpick inserted in the center of the cake comes out clean, 45 to 50 minutes. Cool the cake in the pan for 20 minutes, then turn out and place on serving platter (topping side up). Serve warm or at room temperature. (The cake can be stored at room temperature for up to 3 days.)

Notes from the Test Kitchen
For deeper flavor, we exchanged the shortening in the original recipe for butter and about half of the granulated sugar for brown sugar. For more structure, we added an extra egg. And since this cake has "blueberry" in its name, we doubled the amount. If using frozen blueberries, do not let them thaw, as they will turn the batter a blue-green color.

Crumb Cake

BETTY HILL | SWAINSBORO, GEORGIA

If you're like us, when you hear the name "crumb cake" you're apt to think of a rich and dense coffee cake with buttery sweet "crumbs" adorning the top. This cake is something else altogether. First, it's made in a tube pan, so it really is a cake. And here graham cracker crumbs stand in for flour, giving it an unusual flavor and appealing texture. Packed with nuts and coconut and topped off with a glaze and crushed pineapple, this cake is one of a kind. The recipe came from Betty's grandmother.

SERVES 12

CAKE

- 4½ cups finely ground graham cracker crumbs, 27 to 30 whole graham crackers
- 2 teaspoons baking powder
- 5 large eggs, room temperature
- 1 teaspoon vanilla extract
- 16 tablespoons (2 sticks) unsalted butter, softened
- 2 cups granulated sugar
- 2⅔ cups sweetened, shredded coconut
- 1½ cups pecans, toasted and chopped

GLAZE

- 1 cup confectioners' sugar
- 1 teaspoon lemon juice
- 1 (6-ounce) can crushed pineapple packed in juice, drained, 2 tablespoons juice reserved

1. FOR THE CAKE: Adjust an oven rack to the middle position and heat the oven to 325 degrees. Grease and flour a 12-cup tube pan. Whisk the graham cracker crumbs and baking powder in a large bowl. Whisk the eggs and vanilla in a medium bowl.

2. With an electric mixer on medium-high speed, beat the butter and granulated sugar until fluffy, about 2 minutes. Add the crumb mixture and the egg mixture alternately in two batches, beating after each addition until combined. Using a rubber spatula, fold in the coconut and pecans. Scrape the batter into the prepared pan, leveling it with a spatula, and bake until a toothpick inserted in the center comes out clean, 60 to 75 minutes. Cool the cake in the pan for 10 minutes, then turn out onto a rack to cool completely, at least 1 hour.

3. FOR THE GLAZE: Stir the confectioners' sugar, lemon juice, and reserved pineapple juice in a small bowl until smooth. Drizzle over the cooled cake and then top with the crushed pineapple. Cover and refrigerate until ready to serve. (The cake can be refrigerated for up to 3 days.)

Notes from the Test Kitchen

It's very important to finely grind the graham crackers. Crushing graham crackers by hand can take awhile, but a food processor makes quick work of the job. Don't be tempted to skirt the cracker-grinding process altogether by buying a box of crumbs; we found that the ready-made crumbs often taste stale.

7UP Cake

MICHELE BAILEY | VERONA, NEW JERSEY

The first appearance of 7UP on the marketplace was in 1929 (though it was called Bib-Label Lithiated Lemon-Lime Soda until it was renamed 7UP in 1936). Cake recipes using 7UP didn't start appearing in newspapers until around 1950, but most of these involved a cake mix. Made-from-scratch recipes like this one from Michele's grandmother became popular a decade later. It was a particular family favorite: "My sister and I both had this cake at our weddings and both of the bakers asked to keep the recipe. It was also the first birthday cake for both of my children."

SERVES 12

CAKE
- 3 cups all-purpose flour
- 1/2 teaspoon salt
- 3/4 cup 7UP
- 5 large eggs, room temperature
- 2 teaspoons grated lemon zest
- 1 teaspoon vanilla extract
- 16 tablespoons (2 sticks) unsalted butter, softened
- 1/2 cup vegetable shortening
- 3 cups granulated sugar

GLAZE
- 1 cup confectioners' sugar
- 4 teaspoons lemon juice
- 1 teaspoon water

1. FOR THE CAKE: Adjust an oven rack to the middle position and heat the oven to 325 degrees. Grease and flour a 12-cup tube or Bundt pan. Whisk the flour and salt in a medium bowl. Whisk the 7UP, eggs, lemon zest, and vanilla in a large measuring cup.

2. With an electric mixer on medium-high speed, beat the butter, shortening, and granulated sugar together until fluffy, about 2 minutes. Reduce the speed to low and add the flour mixture and the 7UP mixture alternately in two batches, beating after each addition until combined. Scrape the batter into the prepared pan and bake until a toothpick inserted in the center comes out clean, about 1 hour. Cool the cake in the pan for 10 minutes, then turn out onto a rack to cool completely, at least 1 hour.

3. FOR THE GLAZE: Whisk all the ingredients in a small bowl. Drizzle over the cooled cake. Serve. (The cake can be stored at room temperature for up to 5 days.)

Notes from the Test Kitchen
Although it doesn't taste like a can of 7UP, this cake has great citrus flavor. We wanted still more of that sprightly flavor, though, so we added a lemon glaze. The amazing thing about this cake is that it contains neither baking powder nor baking soda: It is the 7UP that provides the lift. As for the texture, it is that of a moist pound cake. And if you're wondering (we did) if you can substitute Sprite or Mountain Dew for the 7UP, go ahead and use either of them. We noticed no difference in the cake when we made it with those sodas.

Chocolate Blackout Cake

THE EDITORS OF COOK'S COUNTRY

Mention Ebinger's to most Brooklynites over the age of 40 and you'll see a sparkle of nostalgia in their eyes. Bring up Chocolate Blackout Cake and you might actually see a tear or two. When the Brooklyn-based chain of bakeries closed its doors, the borough went into mourning. On that fateful day, August 27, 1972, the *New York Times* ran a story titled "Tears Replace the Coffee Cakes." Of all the lost Ebinger's recipes, none has received more attention in the past 35 years than its Chocolate Blackout Cake. A forerunner of "death by chocolate" confections, Chocolate Blackout Cake is decidedly decadent, marrying fudgy, dark chocolate layers with a rich, creamy chocolate pudding that acts as both filling and frosting. But what really sets this cake apart is its signature shaggy coating of chocolate cake crumbs. Blackout Cake got its name from the blackout drills performed by the Civilian Defense Corps during World War II. When the Navy sent its ships to sea from the Brooklyn Navy Yard, the streets of the borough were "blacked out" to avoid silhouetting the battleships against the cityscapes of Brooklyn and Manhattan. The cake was so named because of its darkly chocolate—practically black—appearance. According to some, the crumbled cake crumbs on top are reminiscent of a city skyline. Ebinger's original recipe was never published, leaving cookbook authors and Brooklyn grandmothers to rely on their taste buds to reproduce "authentic" versions. After much testing and streamlining, here is our version.

SERVES 10 TO 12

PUDDING

- 1 1/4 cups granulated sugar
- 1/4 cup cornstarch
- 1/2 teaspoon salt
- 2 cups half-and-half
- 1 cup milk
- 6 ounces unsweetened chocolate, chopped
- 2 teaspoons vanilla extract

CAKE

- 1 1/2 cups all-purpose flour
- 2 teaspoons baking powder
- 1/2 teaspoon baking soda
- 1/2 teaspoon salt

- 8 tablespoons (1 stick) unsalted butter
- 3/4 cup Dutch-processed cocoa powder
- 1 cup brewed coffee, room temperature
- 1 cup buttermilk
- 1 cup packed light brown sugar
- 1 cup granulated sugar
- 2 large eggs
- 1 teaspoon vanilla extract

1. FOR THE PUDDING: Whisk the granulated sugar, cornstarch, salt, half-and-half, and milk in a large saucepan. Set the pan over medium heat. Add the chocolate and whisk constantly until the chocolate melts and the mixture begins to bubble, 2 to 4 minutes. Stir in the vanilla and

(Continued on page 116)

transfer the pudding to a large bowl. Place plastic wrap directly on the surface of the pudding and refrigerate until cold, at least 4 hours or up to 1 day.

2. FOR THE CAKE: Adjust an oven rack to the middle position and heat the oven to 325 degrees. Grease and flour two 8-inch cake pans. Whisk the flour, baking powder, baking soda, and salt in a medium bowl.

3. Melt the butter in a large saucepan over medium heat. Stir in the cocoa powder and cook until fragrant, about 1 minute. Off the heat, whisk in the coffee, buttermilk, and sugars until dissolved. Whisk in the eggs and vanilla, then slowly whisk in the flour mixture.

4. Divide the batter evenly between the prepared pans and bake until a toothpick inserted in the center comes out clean, 30 to 35 minutes. Cool the cakes in the pans 15 minutes, then invert onto a wire rack to cool completely, at least 1 hour.

5. TO ASSEMBLE THE CAKE: Cut each cake in half horizontally. Crumble one cake layer into medium crumbs and set aside. Place one cake layer on a serving platter or cardboard round. Spread 1 cup pudding over the cake layer and top with another layer. Repeat with 1 cup pudding and the last cake layer. Following the photos, spread the remaining pudding evenly over the top and sides of the cake. Sprinkle the cake crumbs evenly over the top and sides of the cake, pressing lightly to adhere the crumbs. Serve. (The cake can be refrigerated for up to 2 days.)

Notes from the Test Kitchen

We focused our testing on creating a simple cake with big chocolate flavor. We found the best results by using Dutch-processed cocoa powder bloomed in melted butter and combined with buttermilk, which carried its flavor through the cake; brewed coffee further enhanced the nuances of the cocoa. We did try adding melted chocolate to the batter but that made the cake dense and gummy. We also found that we could make the batter entirely in a saucepan on the stovetop, avoiding dirtying all the dishes usually required when making a layer cake. Be sure to give the pudding and the cake enough time to cool or you'll end up with runny pudding and gummy cake.

ASSEMBLING BLACKOUT CAKE

1. Spread the pudding all over the top and sides of the cake.

2. Sprinkle the reserved cake crumbs over the entire cake, pressing the crumbs lightly into the pudding.

Chocolate Sauerkraut Cake

TRACEY DUBLE | ARDMORE, PENNSYLVANIA

Popular as an April Fool's Day recipe in the 1960s, Chocolate Sauerkraut Cake actually makes a lot of sense, since vinegar was often added to early chocolate cakes to make them moist and tender. Sauerkraut has the same effect, plus it adds a coconut-like texture that is very appealing. This cake didn't seem at all unusual to Tracey, who came from a German/Polish background. "My mother used to make sauerkraut cake for us when we were kids. I didn't realize how strange it was until I took this cake into school one day when I was in sixth grade. Everyone loved it until I said that it had sauerkraut in it."

SERVES 12

CAKE

- 2 cups all-purpose flour
- ³/₄ cup Dutch-processed cocoa powder
- 1 teaspoon baking powder
- 1 teaspoon baking soda
- ¹/₄ teaspoon salt
- 1 cup water
- 3 large eggs, room temperature
- 1 teaspoon vanilla extract
- 12 tablespoons (1¹/₂ sticks) unsalted butter, softened
- 1¹/₂ cups sugar
- 1¹/₂ cups sauerkraut, rinsed and drained
- ¹/₂ cup chopped pecans

FROSTING AND FILLING

- 2 cups semisweet chocolate chips, melted
- ²/₃ cup mayonnaise
- ²/₃ cup sweetened, shredded coconut
- ²/₃ cup chopped pecans

1. FOR THE CAKE: Adjust two oven racks to the upper-middle and lower-middle positions and heat the oven to 350 degrees. Grease and flour three 9-inch cake pans. Whisk the flour, cocoa, baking powder, baking soda, and salt in a medium bowl. Whisk the water, eggs, and vanilla in a large measuring cup.

2. With an electric mixer on medium-high speed, beat the butter and sugar together until fluffy, about 2 minutes. Add the flour mixture and the water mixture alternately in two batches, beating after each addition until combined. Using a rubber spatula, fold in the sauerkraut and pecans. Divide the batter evenly among the prepared pans and bake until a toothpick inserted in the center comes out clean, 25 to 30 minutes, rotating and switching the pan positions halfway through baking. Cool the cakes in the pans for 10 minutes, then turn out onto racks to cool completely, at least 30 minutes.

3. FOR THE FROSTING AND FILLING: Whisk the melted chocolate chips and mayonnaise in a medium bowl and reserve 2 cups. To the frosting remaining in the bowl, add ¹/₃ cup coconut and ¹/₃ cup chopped pecans (this is the filling).

4. Spread half the filling on one cake layer. Repeat with the second layer and the remaining filling. Top with the final layer and spread the top and sides of the cake with the reserved frosting. Press the remaining coconut and pecans into the sides of the cake. Cover and refrigerate until ready to serve. (The cake can be refrigerated for up to 3 days.)

Hummingbird Cake

MONA WRIGHT | VILLA RICA, GEORGIA

This rich three-layer cake with cream cheese frosting is a Southern favorite—in fact, it has the honor of being one of *Southern Living*'s most requested recipes, first appearing in its pages in 1978 (submitted by Mrs. L.H. Wiggins of Greensboro, North Carolina) and then again in its Silver Jubilee issue in 1990. Although we could not confirm the origin of this cake, we suspect that it (and other cakes like it) became more popular once canned pineapple was widely available in the early 1900s. Our research revealed no clear reason for the bird connection (though we found multiple theories). But according to an interesting article about the cake in 1985 in the *Arkansas Democrat-Gazette,* it is also known as the Cake That Won't Last, Nothing Left Cake, and Never Ending Cake.

SERVES 12

CAKE

- 3 cups all-purpose flour
- 2 cups granulated sugar
- 1 teaspoon baking soda
- 1 teaspoon salt
- 1 teaspoon ground cinnamon
- 1 cup vegetable oil
- 3 large eggs
- 1 tablespoon vanilla extract
- 1 (6-ounce) can crushed pineapple packed in juice
- 1½ cups pecans, toasted and chopped, plus extra for garnishing if desired
- 2 ripe bananas, peeled and chopped

FROSTING

- 16 tablespoons (2 sticks) unsalted butter, softened
- 4 cups confectioners' sugar
- 16 ounces cream cheese, cut into 8 pieces, softened
- 1½ teaspoons vanilla extract
  Pinch salt

1. FOR THE CAKE: Adjust two oven racks to the upper-middle and lower-middle positions and heat the oven to 350 degrees. Grease and flour three 9-inch cake pans. Whisk the flour, granulated sugar, baking soda, salt, and cinnamon in a large bowl. Whisk the oil, eggs, and vanilla in a medium bowl, add to the flour mixture, and whisk until combined. Using a rubber spatula, fold in the pineapple (with the juice), pecans, and bananas. Divide the batter evenly among the prepared pans and bake until a toothpick inserted in the center comes out clean, 25 to 30 minutes, rotating and switching the pan positions halfway through baking. Cool the cakes in the pans for 10 minutes, then turn out onto racks to cool completely, at least 30 minutes.

2. FOR THE FROSTING: With an electric mixer on medium-high speed, beat the butter and confectioners' sugar until fluffy, about 2 minutes. Add the cream cheese, one piece at a time, and beat until incorporated. Beat in the vanilla and salt. Refrigerate until ready to use.

3. Spread about 1½ cups of the frosting on one cake layer. Top with a second cake layer and another 1½ cups frosting. Top with the final cake layer and spread the top and sides of the cake with the remaining frosting. Cover and refrigerate until ready to serve. (The cake can be refrigerated for up to 3 days.)

My Mother's Family Bourbon Cake

ALICE L. EVERITT | PETERSBURG, VIRGINIA

It's no surprise to see an old-fashioned cake like this coming from the South, where bourbon still reigns supreme. Moist and dense like pound cake, this recipe gets its rich orange flavor from a triple hit of orange oil, orange peel ground with sugar, and orange juice. A sweet bourbon glaze is the finishing touch. Alice found the handwritten recipe on a faded piece of paper in one of her grandmother Cora's old cookbooks from the turn of the century and took it upon herself to make it and modernize it, finding that a food processor made it a snap to prepare.

SERVES 12

CAKE

2³/₄	cups all-purpose flour
1	tablespoon baking powder
¹/₂	teaspoon salt
4	oranges, outer peel removed with a vegetable peeler and reserved, and ³/₄ cup juice reserved
2	teaspoons orange oil or orange extract
2	cups sugar
16	tablespoons (2 sticks) unsalted butter, softened
5	large eggs, room temperature

GLAZE

8	tablespoons (1 stick) unsalted butter
²/₃	cup sugar
¹/₂	cup bourbon

1. FOR THE CAKE: Adjust an oven rack to the middle position and heat the oven to 350 degrees. Grease and flour a 12-cup tube pan. Whisk the flour, baking powder, and salt in a medium bowl. Whisk the orange juice and orange oil in a medium bowl.

2. Process ²/₃ cup of the sugar and the orange peel in a food processor until finely ground. Add the remaining sugar and the butter and process until smooth. With the machine running, add the eggs, one at a time, and process until light in color. Transfer the mixture to a large bowl.

3. Using a rubber spatula, fold in the flour mixture and orange juice mixture alternately in two batches until combined. Scrape the batter into the prepared pan and bake until a toothpick inserted in the center comes out clean, 45 to 55 minutes.

4. FOR THE GLAZE: Meanwhile, melt the butter in a small saucepan. Stir in the sugar and bring to a boil. Off the heat, add the bourbon. Remove the cake from the oven and let rest 10 minutes. Using a wooden skewer, poke several deep holes all over the top of the cake. Slowly spoon the glaze over the cake, giving it time to soak in; allow the cake to cool completely in the pan, at least 2 hours. Turn the cake out onto a serving platter. Serve. (The cake can be stored at room temperature for up to 5 days.)

Notes from the Test Kitchen

We liked that this cake was easy to whip up in a food processor, and we loved the orange and bourbon flavor combination. As it is, the cake packs a powerful bourbon punch (it is definitely not one for the kiddies), but you can make it without the bourbon. For the glaze, simply substitute ¹/₂ cup orange juice for the bourbon and proceed with the recipe as directed. When using orange peel, be sure to take a paring knife and remove any bitter white pith that may cling to the peel. Garnish with strips of zest if desired.

Tennessee Stack Cake

ANDREA HALL | PUYALLUP, WASHINGTON

This eight-layer cake, an Appalachian specialty, is known by various names, including Apple Stack Cake, Pioneer Stack Cake, and Washday Stack Cake. The last name refers to how the cookie-like layers were often baked on washday and then layered with apple butter and left to sit for a day or two before being served. As the cake sits, the cookie-like layers soak up moisture from the apple butter and soften, becoming tender and cake-like in the process.

Andrea's recipe certainly won us over, but so did the story that accompanied her entry. "I remember my grandmother—'Mom-Mom'—saying that there was always stack cake on the dining room table when she was growing up. She was born in 1917 into a family of 10 in Lone Mountain, Tennessee, a very beautiful rural area south of Cumberland Gap. Baking day was Saturday, and dried apple rings were brought down from the attic where they were hung every fall, reserved mainly for use in this special cake. Once baked, everything was placed on the dining room table to cool, then covered with a clean tablecloth to keep the flies off until items were put away Sunday morning. Mom-Mom remembers how they loved to go downstairs in the morning and see the large hump under the cloth where the stack cake lay! The anticipation was heightened by the fact that the cake could not be eaten until after Sunday dinner, and all day the scent of spiced apples and baked sugar cookies lingered throughout the house."

SERVES 10 TO 12

FILLING
- 3 (6-ounce) bags dried apples
- 1 cup packed light brown sugar
- 1½ teaspoons ground cinnamon
- ½ teaspoon ground cloves
- ½ teaspoon ground allspice

LAYERS
- 6 cups all-purpose flour
- 1 tablespoon baking powder
- 1 teaspoon baking soda
- ¼ teaspoon salt
- ½ cup buttermilk
- 2 large eggs
- 1 teaspoon vanilla extract
- 16 tablespoons (2 sticks) unsalted butter, softened
- 2 cups granulated sugar

Confectioners' sugar for dusting

1. FOR THE FILLING: Bring the apples and water to cover to a boil in a large saucepan. Reduce the heat and simmer until the apples are completely softened, about 10 minutes. Drain the apples and let cool until just warm, about 15 minutes. Puree the apples in a food processor until smooth. Transfer to a bowl and stir in the brown sugar, cinnamon, cloves, and allspice. (The filling can be refrigerated for up to 2 days.)

(Continued on page 124)

2. FOR THE LAYERS: Adjust two oven racks to the upper-middle and lower-middle positions and heat the oven to 350 degrees. Coat two baking sheets with cooking spray. Whisk the flour, baking powder, baking soda, and salt in a medium bowl. Whisk the buttermilk, eggs, and vanilla in a large measuring cup.

3. With an electric mixer at medium-high speed, beat the butter and granulated sugar in a large bowl until fluffy, about 2 minutes. Add the flour mixture and buttermilk mixture alternately in two batches, beating after each addition until combined. (The dough will be thick.)

4. Divide the dough into eight equal portions. Following the photos, work with two portions at a time on a lightly floured surface, rolling each out into a 10-inch circle about 1/8 inch thick. Using a 9-inch cake pan as a template, trim away the excess dough to form two perfectly round 9-inch disks. Transfer the disks to the prepared baking sheets and bake until golden brown, 10 to 12 minutes, rotating

and switching the baking sheets halfway through baking. Transfer the disks to racks and cool completely, at least 1 hour. Repeat with the remaining dough. (The layers can be wrapped tightly in plastic wrap and stored at room temperature for up to 2 days.)

5. TO ASSEMBLE THE CAKE: Place one layer on a serving plate and spread with 3/4 cup filling. Repeat six times. Top with the final layer, wrap tightly in plastic wrap, and refrigerate until the layers soften, at least 24 hours or up to 2 days. Dust with confectioners' sugar and serve.

Notes from the Test Kitchen

Be sure to let the cake sit at least 24 hours, as the moisture from the filling transforms the texture of the cookie-like layers into a tender apple-flavored cake. This cake takes a while to create but each step is simple and the dough rounds that form each layer are sturdy and easy to handle. Using a cake pan as a template will make this part of the process easy and foolproof.

HOW TO MAKE TENNESSEE STACK CAKE

1. After dividing the dough into eighths, roll out one piece of the dough into a 10-inch circle.

2. Using a 9-inch cake pan as a template, cut out a neat circle from the dough.

3. Gently slide the dough round onto a removable tart pan bottom, flat plate, or cardboard cake round, and transfer to one of the prepared baking sheets.

4. Place one layer on a serving plate. Spread 3/4 cup filling over the layer. Repeat, leaving the final layer plain.

Czardas Cake

JULIE DEMATTEO | CLEMENTON, NEW JERSEY

Czardas is a traditional Hungarian/Slovakian dance that begins slowly and increases in speed. What does this have to do with this rich-tasting nut torte? We were not sure, though there is a connection to Hungary here. As Julie says, "This recipe was brought to the U.S. by my grandmother in the early 20th century from Hungary. Mostly she would make it with black walnuts from the tree in her backyard, and sometimes with hazelnuts, a very traditional Hungarian ingredient or, as in this recipe, regular walnuts. She also used raw egg yolks in her frosting, which I have eliminated for safety reasons. Usually she would make this cake for holidays and special occasions."

SERVES 12

CAKE

- ¼ cup semisweet chocolate chips
- 3½ cups walnuts
- ¼ cup all-purpose flour
- 4 teaspoons instant coffee granules
- ¼ teaspoon salt
- 8 large eggs, room temperature
- 1 cup granulated sugar

FROSTING

- 3 tablespoons heavy cream
- 4½ teaspoons instant coffee granules
- 1½ teaspoons vanilla extract
- 1 pound (4 sticks) unsalted butter, softened
- 3¾ cups confectioners' sugar
- ⅛ teaspoon salt

1. FOR THE CAKE: Adjust an oven rack to the middle position and heat the oven to 350 degrees. Grease three 8-inch cake pans, line them with parchment paper, then grease the paper. Process the chocolate chips in a food processor until finely ground. Add 3 cups walnuts and pulse until finely ground. Transfer to a medium bowl and whisk in the flour, coffee granules, and salt.

2. With an electric mixer on medium-high speed, beat the eggs and granulated sugar until pale and thick, about 6 minutes. Using a rubber spatula, fold in the flour mixture in two batches. Divide the batter evenly among the prepared pans and bake until a toothpick inserted in the center comes out clean, about 20 minutes, rotating and switching the pan positions halfway through baking. Cool the cakes in the pans for 10 minutes, then turn out onto racks to cool completely, at least 30 minutes.

3. FOR THE FROSTING: Stir the cream, coffee granules, and vanilla together in a small bowl until the coffee dissolves. Set aside. With an electric mixer on medium-high speed, beat the butter until smooth. Add the confectioners' sugar and salt and beat at medium-low speed until incorporated. Add the cream mixture and beat until light and fluffy, about 4 minutes.

4. Spread about ⅔ cup frosting on one cake layer. Repeat with the second cake layer and ⅔ cup more frosting. Top with the final cake layer and spread the top and sides of the cake with the remaining frosting. Press the remaining ½ cup walnuts around the bottom of the cake. Serve. (The cake can be refrigerated for up to 3 days.)

Notes from the Test Kitchen

This is essentially a walnut torte. The coffee frosting gives it a nice twist. For a deeper coffee flavor in the cake, try substituting instant espresso powder for the instant coffee granules.

Red Velvet Cake

THE EDITORS OF COOK'S COUNTRY

With its shockingly red layers and billowy white frosting, this cake is a real looker. Plus it's extraordinarily moist and tender. Red cakes—with names like Red Devil Cake and Oxblood Cake—date back to the late 19th century. Over time, the naturally occurring faint red color—the by-product of a chemical reaction between vinegar and/or buttermilk and cocoa powder—was augmented, first by beets (a common ingredient during the sugar rationing of World War II) and then by red food coloring.

SERVES 12

CAKE

2¼ cups all-purpose flour
1½ teaspoons baking soda
    Pinch salt
1   cup buttermilk
1   tablespoon white vinegar
1   teaspoon vanilla extract
2   large eggs
2   tablespoons natural cocoa powder (see note)
2   tablespoons (one 1-ounce bottle) red food coloring
12 tablespoons (1½ sticks) unsalted butter, softened
1½ cups granulated sugar

FROSTING

16 tablespoons (2 sticks) unsalted butter, softened
4   cups confectioners' sugar
16 ounces cream cheese, cut into 8 pieces, softened
1½ teaspoons vanilla extract
    Pinch salt

1. FOR THE CAKE: Adjust an oven rack to the middle position and heat the oven to 350 degrees. Grease and flour two 9-inch cake pans. Whisk the flour, baking soda, and salt in a medium bowl. Whisk the buttermilk, vinegar, vanilla, and eggs in a large measuring cup. Mix the cocoa with the food coloring in a small bowl until a smooth paste forms.

2. With an electric mixer on medium-high speed, beat the butter and granulated sugar together until fluffy, about 2 minutes. Add the flour mixture and the buttermilk mixture alternately in two batches, beating after each addition until combined. Add the cocoa mixture and beat on medium speed until completely incorporated. Divide the batter evenly between the prepared pans and bake until a toothpick inserted in the center comes out clean, about 25 minutes. Cool the cakes in the pans 10 minutes, then turn out onto a rack to cool completely, at least 30 minutes.

3. FOR THE FROSTING: With an electric mixer on medium-high speed, beat the butter and confectioners' sugar until fluffy, about 2 minutes. Add the cream cheese, one piece at a time, and beat until incorporated. Beat in the vanilla and salt.

4. Spread about 2 cups frosting on one cake layer. Top with the second cake layer and spread the top and sides of the cake with the remaining frosting. Serve. (The cake can be refrigerated for up to 3 days.)

Notes from the Test Kitchen

After trying beets (which gave the cake a vegetal flavor), it was clear that food coloring was a must; any less than 2 tablespoons yielded a cake that was more pink than red. To make the color uniform throughout the cake, we found it best to make a paste with the food coloring and 2 tablespoons cocoa powder before adding it to the batter. This recipe must be prepared with natural cocoa powder. Dutch-processed cocoa will not yield the proper color or rise.

Daisy Mae's Delight

SUZANNE FONTAN | JEFFERSON, LOUISIANA

The recipe for this unusual cake, in which graham cracker crumbs take the place of flour, was nearly lost during Hurricane Katrina. Suzanne's house was flooded with nearly four feet of water, but fortunately she had stored her recipe collection on the top shelf of a heavily anchored bookcase. This recipe came from Suzanne's husband's grandmother and was his birthday cake every year. Now she carries on the tradition.

SERVES 12

CAKE

3½	cups finely-ground graham cracker crumbs, 21 to 24 whole graham crackers
1½	cups milk
1	teaspoon ground cinnamon
5	large eggs, separated
1½	teaspoons vanilla extract
12	tablespoons (1½ sticks) unsalted butter, softened
1½	cups granulated sugar
1	tablespoon baking powder
1½	cups walnuts, chopped

FROSTING

16	tablespoons (2 sticks) unsalted butter, softened
4	cups confectioners' sugar
16	ounces cream cheese, cut into 8 pieces, softened
1½	teaspoon vanilla extract
	Pinch salt

1. FOR THE CAKE: Adjust an oven rack to the middle position and heat the oven to 350 degrees. Grease and flour two 9-inch cake pans. Combine the graham cracker crumbs, milk, and cinnamon in a medium bowl and let sit until the milk is absorbed, about 15 minutes. Whisk the egg yolks and vanilla in a small bowl.

2. With an electric mixer on medium-high speed, beat the egg whites to soft peaks. Transfer to a bowl and set aside. Beat the butter and granulated sugar together on medium-high speed until fluffy, about 2 minutes. Reduce the speed to medium and add the egg yolk mixture, mixing until incorporated, about 30 seconds. Add the crumb mixture and baking powder and beat until combined. Using a rubber spatula, fold in the walnuts and egg whites. Divide the batter evenly between the prepared pans and bake until a toothpick inserted in the center comes out clean, 30 to 40 minutes. Cool the cakes in the pans for 10 minutes, then turn out onto a rack to cool completely, at least 30 minutes.

3. FOR THE FROSTING: With an electric mixer on medium-high speed, beat the butter and confectioners' sugar together until fluffy, about 2 minutes. Add the cream cheese, one piece at a time, and beat until incorporated. Beat in the vanilla and salt.

4. Spread about 2 cups frosting on one cake layer. Top with the second cake layer and spread the top and sides of the cake with the remaining frosting. Serve. (The cake can be refrigerated for up to 3 days.)

Notes from the Test Kitchen
We liked the hearty texture of this cake, but thought that the flavor could use a boost. So we added a teaspoon of cinnamon, which complemented the graham flavor nicely. The author of this recipe was not sure what the original frosting was—she suggested either a buttercream or cream cheese frosting. We tried it with cream cheese frosting and enjoyed the tang of the cream cheese against the cinnamon-graham flavor of the cake.

Huguenot Torte with Cinnamon Chantilly Crème

JANICE ELDER | CHARLOTTE, NORTH CAROLINA

This simple torte, studded with pecans and apples, has long been identified with the Carolinas, most especially with Charleston, South Carolina. In fact, we found a recipe similar to this one in *Charleston Receipts* (1950). And while you might think that it gets its name from the Huguenots, the French Protestant refugees who settled in the Carolinas in the late 17th century, the truth is that this recipe is an adaptation of a dish called Ozark Pudding, a cake-like pudding made famous by association with Harry Truman. We think this cake may have gotten its name because it was served at the Huguenot Tavern in Charleston.

SERVES 8

TORTE
- ¼ cup all-purpose flour
- 2 teaspoons baking powder
- ¼ teaspoon salt
- 1 tablespoon dark rum
- 2 teaspoons vanilla extract
- 2 teaspoons grated zest plus 2 teaspoons juice from 1 lemon
- 2 large eggs, room temperature
- ¾ cup granulated sugar
- 1 Granny Smith apple, peeled and chopped coarse
- ½ cup pecans, toasted and chopped

CHANTILLY CRÈME
- 1 cup heavy cream, chilled
- 3 tablespoons confectioners' sugar
- ½ teaspoon vanilla extract
- ½ teaspoon ground cinnamon

1. FOR THE TORTE: Adjust an oven rack to the middle position and heat the oven to 325 degrees. Grease and flour an 8-inch square pan. Whisk the flour, baking powder, and salt in a large bowl. Stir the rum, vanilla, lemon zest, and juice together in a small bowl.

2. With an electric mixer on medium-high speed, beat the eggs and granulated sugar until thick and pale, about 5 minutes. Reduce the speed to low and beat in the flour mixture in two additions until incorporated. Add the rum mixture and beat until combined. Using a rubber spatula, gently fold in the apple and pecans. Scrape the batter into the prepared pan and bake until a toothpick inserted in the center comes out clean, 40 to 45 minutes. Cool in the pan for 10 minutes, then turn out onto a rack to cool until just warm, about 20 minutes.

3. FOR THE CHANTILLY CRÈME: With an electric mixer on medium-high speed, beat the cream to soft peaks. Reduce the speed to low, add the confectioners' sugar, vanilla, and cinnamon and beat until incorporated. Cut the warm torte into squares and serve with a dollop of the cream. (The cake can be stored at room temperature for up to 2 days. Make the cream just before serving.)

Notes from the Test Kitchen
This plain-looking cake is certainly not short on flavor. Rum, vanilla, and lemon all permeate the cake, which is topped with a dollop of whipped cream flavored with cinnamon and vanilla. Often when whipping cream in the test kitchen, we've had trouble getting the cream to whip to full puffed peaks. We've found it helps to put the mixing bowl and the whisk attachment in the freezer until they are both very cold.

Sophie's Cherry Cake

LOIS AARONSON | BOERNE, TEXAS

This unusual cake—perfect when you are looking for a simple, homey dessert or an alternative to a traditional coffee cake—traveled (with Sophie) from Russia to the United States in the mid-1800s and has been passed down through the generations of her family. Infused with the flavors of sour cherries and almond, it is sweet without being cloying.

SERVES 8

CAKE

- 1   cup all-purpose flour
- 1½   teaspoons baking powder
- ¼   teaspoon salt
- 2   large eggs, room temperature
- 1   teaspoon vanilla extract
- 4   tablespoons unsalted butter, softened
- ¾   cup sugar
- 1   (14.5-ounce) can tart cherries, drained, juice reserved for topping

TOPPING

- 2½   tablespoons cornstarch
- ¾   cup sugar
- 1   teaspoon almond extract
- ½   cup pecans, toasted (see note)

1. FOR THE CAKE: Adjust an oven rack to the middle position and heat the oven to 350 degrees. Grease and flour a 9-inch cake pan. Whisk the flour, baking powder, and salt in a medium bowl. Whisk the eggs and vanilla in a small bowl.

2. With an electric mixer on medium-high speed, beat the butter and sugar together until fluffy, about 2 minutes. Reduce the speed to low and add the flour mixture and egg mixture alternately in two batches, beating on low speed until combined. Using a rubber spatula, gently fold in the cherries. Scrape the batter into the prepared pan and bake until a toothpick inserted in the center comes out clean, 30 to 35 minutes. Cool completely in the pan.

3. FOR THE TOPPING: Combine the reserved cherry juice, cornstarch, sugar, and almond extract in a small saucepan over medium heat until it just begins to bubble, about 4 minutes. Let cool completely, at least 30 minutes. Spread the topping over the cooled cake and arrange the pecans decoratively on the top. Serve. (The cake can be stored at room temperature for up to 2 days.)

Notes from the Test Kitchen

Everyone in the test kitchen liked the pleasingly tart flavor of this cake as well as the shiny red topping. The original recipe was a little complicated, requiring the folding of beaten egg whites into a very stiff batter. In order to fully incorporate the whites, they ended up deflating (and defeating the whole purpose to begin with). We eliminated this fussy step and added the eggs whole; the cake was exactly the same, just easier. We also decided to leave the nuts whole rather than chopping them. This made the preparation easier too, plus the chopped nuts covered up the pretty glaze.

Nell's White Fruitcake

M.J. MARRS | HONDO, TEXAS

Recipes for white fruitcakes, which lack the trademark molasses and spices of dark fruitcakes, first appeared in print in 1877, in *Buckeye Cookery* by Estelle Woods Wilcox and *The White House Cookbook* by Fanny Lemura Gillette. Some were baked traditionally, while others were baked over a pan of water, like a pudding. In fact, a pressure cooker was originally used to make this recipe, which would date it no earlier than the 1930s. M.J. writes in her letter, "The cake was originally cooked in an old-fashioned canner (pressure cooker). Everyone used them to preserve meat, chicken, vegetables, and fruits. The pressure cooker was as important to the kitchen then as the microwave is today."

SERVES 16

- 2 cups golden raisins
- 2 cups candied cherries, quartered
- 2 cups candied pineapple, chopped coarse
- 2 cups pecans, chopped coarse
- 16 tablespoons (2 sticks) unsalted butter, softened
- 1 cup sugar
- 3 large eggs, room temperature
- 1½ tablespoons lemon extract
- ½ teaspoon salt
- 2 cups all-purpose flour

1. Grease a 12-cup tube pan and line the bottom with parchment or waxed paper. Grease the paper. Toss the raisins, cherries, pineapple, and pecans together in a large bowl until combined.

2. Bring 1 inch of water to a boil in a large Dutch oven over medium-high heat. Meanwhile, with an electric mixer at medium-high speed, beat the butter and sugar together until fluffy, about 2 minutes. Reduce the speed to medium and add the eggs, lemon extract, and salt and mix until incorporated. Add the flour and beat until just combined. Using a rubber spatula, fold in the fruit and nut mixture. Scrape the batter into the prepared pan and lower the pan into the simmering water. Cover the pot, reduce the heat to low, and cook until the cake is firm to the touch, about 1½ hours, adding water as needed. Remove the pot from the heat, remove the lid, and leave the cake pan in the water until it is cool enough to handle, about 20 minutes.

3. Meanwhile, adjust an oven rack to the middle position and heat the oven to 250 degrees. Remove the tube pan from the pot and invert the cake onto a rack. Place the rack on a rimmed baking sheet and bake until the exterior of the cake is no longer wet, about 20 minutes. Cool the cake completely, at least 2 hours. Serve. (The cake can be stored at room temperature for up to 2 weeks.)

Notes from the Test Kitchen

Sweet and fruity without being cloying, this cake is very appealing. The first time we made it, we cooked it in a pressure cooker as directed. But we didn't notice any difference between cakes made this way and cakes that were steamed in a covered Dutch oven. So we omitted the pressure cooker altogether, which made the process easier. And we opted to use a standard tube pan rather than coffee cans (Nell's recipe mentioned both as options). It is essential to give this cake a chance to dry out in the oven or you'll end up with a cake that is unappealingly sticky. Be sure to use lemon extract rather than lemon flavoring, which will over-power all the other flavors in this delicate fruitcake.

Mincemeat Cake

RHEBA TURPIN | OLIVE BRANCH, MISSISSIPPI

In her book *North Carolina and Old Salem Cookery* (1955), Elizabeth Hedgecock Sparks makes the observation that "in the days after the Christmas fruit cakes are baked but are not yet ready to cut, it is customary in many households to whip up a mincemeat cake so the children won't run you ragged trying to get a slice of fruit cake." Mincemeat cake recipes began appearing in newspapers in the 1930s with many of them promoting it as an easier alternative to mincemeat pie or fruitcake. In the 1950s, a recipe for mincemeat cake was included in one of Pillsbury's collections of prize-winning recipes, but by the 1990s newspaper readers were writing in requesting copies of this "lost" recipe. Rheba's recipe came from her grandmother, who made this cake every Christmas. "Grandmother baked the cake at least one week before she planned to serve it as she said the flavors blended better after it had set a while. She would wrap it in several layers of waxed paper and then wrapped it in a tea towel. The fragrance was wonderful and you could hardly wait until it was finally opened and eaten."

SERVES 12

- 2 cups all-purpose flour
- 1 teaspoon baking soda
- 1/2 teaspoon salt
- 2 large eggs, separated, room temperature
- 2 tablespoons bourbon
- 8 tablespoons (1 stick) unsalted butter, softened
- 1 cup sugar
- 2 cups canned or jarred mincemeat
- 1 1/2 cups pecans, chopped
- 1 cup raisins

1. Adjust an oven rack to the middle position and heat the oven to 325 degrees. Grease and flour a 12-cup tube pan. Whisk the flour, baking soda, and salt in a medium bowl. Whisk the egg yolks and bourbon in a small bowl.

2. With an electric mixer on medium-high speed, beat the egg whites to soft peaks. Transfer to a bowl and set aside. Beat the butter and sugar together on medium-high speed until fluffy, about 2 minutes. Reduce the speed to medium and add the egg yolk mixture, mixing until incorporated. Add the mincemeat and mix until combined. Reduce the speed to low, add the flour mixture, and mix until combined. Using a rubber spatula, fold in the pecans, raisins, and egg whites.

3. Scrape the batter into the prepared pan and bake until a toothpick inserted in the center comes out clean, 50 to 60 minutes. Cool in the pan for 10 minutes, then turn out onto a rack to cool completely, at least 1 hour. (The cake can be stored at room temperature for up to 1 week.)

Notes from the Test Kitchen
This cake is full of fruit flavor and spice without feeling too much like a fruitcake. Be sure to beat the mincemeat into the cake batter rather than fold it in by hand. Beating the sticky mincemeat into the batter ensures that it is well distributed throughout the cake and will not cling together in pockets. If desired, you can substitute water for the bourbon in this recipe.

Mrs. Ashmead's Cake

LEOTA CHURCH | PORTLAND, OREGON

Judging by the story submitted with this simple spice cake, we would bet that it is a 19th-century recipe. Says Leota: "I am 92 years old, and have made this cake countless times. It has no strange or exotic ingredients; in fact, it might be considered a 'Depression cake,' as most people had all these things in their pantry. I call it 'Mrs. Ashmead's Cake' because Mrs. Ashmead was (with Mr. Ashmead) a friend of my grandparents. When we were invited to their home for Sunday dinner, Mrs. Ashmead invariably served this cake, usually along with fruit Jell-O and sweetened whipped cream. Depression and pre-Depression times make little impression on the present generation, but simple recipes from the past might be considered of value."

SERVES 12

- 2 cups sugar
- 2 cups water
- 1 1/2 cups raisins
- 2/3 cup vegetable shortening
- 1/3 cup Dutch-processed cocoa powder (see note)
- 1 teaspoon ground cinnamon
- 1/4 teaspoon ground cloves
- 1/4 teaspoon ground nutmeg
- 3 cups all-purpose flour
- 2 teaspoons baking powder
- 1 teaspoon baking soda
- 1/2 teaspoon salt
- 1 teaspoon vanilla extract
- 1 cup walnuts, chopped

1. Heat the sugar, water, raisins, shortening, cocoa, cinnamon, cloves, and nutmeg in a medium saucepan over medium heat until the shortening melts, about 5 minutes. Transfer to a medium bowl and cool to room temperature, about 1 hour.

2. Adjust an oven rack to the middle position and heat the oven to 350 degrees. Grease and flour a 12-cup tube pan. Whisk the flour, baking powder, baking soda, and salt in a large bowl. Add the raisin mixture and the vanilla to the flour mixture and whisk until incorporated. Stir in the walnuts.

3. Scrape the batter into the prepared pan and bake until a toothpick inserted in the center comes out clean, 45 to 50 minutes. Cool in the pan for 10 minutes, then turn out onto a rack to cool completely, at least 1 hour. Serve. (The cake can be stored at room temperature for up to 4 days.)

Notes from the Test Kitchen

This simple cake is very moist, with a lightly spiced flavor. The hint of cocoa powder is a nice twist on an otherwise plain spice cake. Be sure to use Dutch-processed cocoa for the cake. Dutch-processed or "Dutched" cocoa has been treated with an alkaline solution that reduces the choc-olate's natural acidity. It also deepens the color of the cocoa, mellows its flavor, and improves its solubility in liquid. Our attempts at using regular or "natural" cocoa powder resulted in a sour-tasting cake.

Cold Oven Pound Cake

MURRAY JOHNSTON | BIRMINGHAM, ALABAMA

This recipe came with very emphatic instructions. Says Murray, "My grandmother was adamant about putting the batter-filled tube pan in a COLD oven, saying over and over to me '. . . and THEN you turn the oven on.' You were not supposed to have used the oven at all since the night prior to putting the cake in to bake or it would not be a 'cold' oven and the cake would then not rise and create such a wonderful crust." We were curious about the origin of this unusual technique, which goes against the most fundamental principle of baking: Make sure your oven is properly preheated. We learned that cooking demonstrations and gas range advertisements in the first two decades of the 20th century focused on gas economy, and the apparently unthinkable notion that cakes could be baked successfully starting with a cold oven. One expert, quoted in a 1905 syndicated newspaper column called "Household Matters," gave this rule of thumb: "Loaf cake in a cold oven, layer cake in a warm oven, and no cake in a hot oven." We can't recommend this advice, though we can recommend this cake.

SERVES 12

- 3 cups all-purpose flour
- 1/2 teaspoon salt
- 1 cup skim or 1 percent milk (see note)
- 1 teaspoon vanilla extract
- 5 large eggs, separated, room temperature
- 16 tablespoons (2 sticks) unsalted butter, softened
- 1/2 cup vegetable shortening
- 3 cups sugar

1. Adjust an oven rack to the middle position. (Do not heat the oven.) Grease and flour a 12-cup tube pan. Whisk the flour and salt in a medium bowl. Whisk the milk, vanilla, and egg yolks in a large measuring cup.

2. With an electric mixer on medium-high speed, beat the egg whites to soft peaks. Transfer to a bowl and set aside. Beat the butter, shortening, and sugar together on medium-high speed until fluffy, about 2 minutes. Reduce the speed to low, and add the flour mixture and the milk mixture alternately in two batches, beating after each addition until combined. Using a rubber spatula, gently fold in the egg whites. Scrape the batter into the prepared pan and place in the cold oven.

3. Heat the oven to 300 degrees and bake the cake for 45 minutes. Increase the oven temperature to 325 and bake until a toothpick inserted in the center comes out clean, about 45 minutes. Cool the cake in the pan for 20 minutes, run a knife around the edge of the cake, then turn out onto a rack to cool completely, at least 1 hour. Serve. (The cake can be stored at room temperature for up to 3 days.)

Notes from the Test Kitchen

Starting the cake in a cold oven sounds like a recipe for disaster, but instead it helps the cake develop a nice crust and delicate crumb. We tried baking the cake in both a slightly warm oven (the oven had been used for a previous recipe) and a preheated oven. The truly cold oven cake had the sturdiest crust of all. It is important to use skim or 1 percent milk for this recipe. Using 2 percent or whole milk will result in a heavier cake, with less height.

Great-Aunt Ellen's Upside-Down Lemon Pudding Cake

SUSAN GILLUM | LOS GATOS, CALIFORNIA

Pudding cakes are much like egg custards but, because they include a little flour and beaten egg whites, during baking the egg whites float to the top, creating a delicate spongy cake, while the rest of the batter settles to the bottom, making a pudding-like layer. As Susan says, "When inverted on a plate, the bottom is cake-like with the sauce flowing over the top. The appearance is that of a dessert that took hours to make when in fact it is very quick and easy."

Recipes such as these date back to the 18th century, when a simple dish called "flour pudding" appeared in Amelia Simmons's *American Cookery* (1798). These puddings were sometimes flavored with wine or rose water and usually served with a sweet sauce. Over time, beaten egg whites were added, causing the batter to separate, like this one, into distinct pudding and cake layers.

SERVES 6

- 2 large eggs, separated, room temperature
- 2 tablespoons unsalted butter, softened
- ²/₃ cup sugar
- 2 tablespoons grated zest plus ¼ cup juice from 2 lemons
- 2 tablespoons all-purpose flour
- ⅛ teaspoon salt
- 1 cup milk

1. Adjust an oven rack to the middle position and heat the oven to 350 degrees. Grease a 2-quart baking dish or six 6-ounce ramekins.

2. With an electric mixer on medium-high speed, beat the egg whites to soft peaks. Transfer to a bowl and set aside. Beat the butter, sugar, and zest together on medium-high speed until fluffy, about 2 minutes. Reduce the speed to medium and add the egg yolks, mixing until incorporated. Add the flour and salt and beat until combined. Add the lemon juice and milk and beat until incorporated. Using a rubber spatula, fold in the egg whites. Pour the batter into the prepared dish or ramekins. Place the dishes in a large baking pan and add enough boiling water to the pan so that it reaches halfway up the sides of the dish or ramekins.

3. Bake until the top is golden and the center springs back when gently pressed, 35 to 45 minutes for a large baking dish or 25 to 35 minutes for the individual ramekins. Transfer the dishes to a rack to cool completely, at least 1½ hours. (The pudding cakes can be refrigerated for up to 2 days. Allow to sit at room temperature for 30 minutes before serving.) To serve, run a paring knife around the edges of the dish and invert onto a plate.

Notes from the Test Kitchen

Every time we tested this recipe, we were pleased with its light texture and delicious flavor. Although Susan suggested serving it either hot or cold, we actually we found that neither option was optimal. When served hot, the pudding did not invert well onto a serving dish, leaving us with an unattractive blob. When served cold, the cake looked great but the flavor was almost too harsh. Serving the cake at room temperature was best: It unmolded perfectly and the flavor was lemony but not too harsh. If making individual pudding cakes, it's best to ladle rather than pour the batter into the ramekins; otherwise the first cups get all the froth and the later cups get all the batter. Garnish with thin strips of lemon zest.

Clara's Chocolate Torte

BEVERLY CORNELIUS | LODI, CALIFORNIA

This appealing dessert is a snack cake—it isn't a true torte, as it includes flour. But all the elements of a fancy torte are here—the nuts, the cocoa, the butter, and the chocolate. It's just that the nuts and chocolate chips are sprinkled on top of the cake right before it goes into the oven. And the chopped dates give this cake its depth of flavor and its moistness. Says Beverly about the origins of this recipe: "I was a teacher in Bellflower, California, in the mid '50s. Our custodian, Clara, made so many special treats for us. One that I've continued to make for more than 50 years is her Chocolate Torte. It was the cake my son always requested for a birthday cake. And it is so easy to make and yummy to eat."

SERVES 16

1¼   cup dates, chopped
1   teaspoon baking soda
1   cup boiling water
1¾   cups all-purpose flour
2   tablespoons Dutch-processed cocoa powder
½   teaspoon salt
8   tablespoons (1 stick) unsalted butter, softened
½   cup vegetable shortening
1   cup sugar
1   teaspoon vanilla extract
2   large eggs, room temperature
1½   cup walnuts, chopped
1   cup semisweet chocolate chips

1. Adjust an oven rack to the middle position and heat the oven to 350 degrees. Grease and flour a 13 by 9-inch baking pan. Stir the dates, baking soda, and boiling water together in a medium bowl. Let stand until room temperature, about 20 minutes. Whisk the flour, cocoa, and salt in a medium bowl.

2. With an electric mixer on medium-high speed, beat the butter, shortening, sugar, and vanilla together until fluffy, about 2 minutes. Reduce the speed to medium and add the eggs one at a time, mixing until incorporated. Reduce the speed to low and add the flour mixture and date mixture alternately in two batches, beating on low speed after each addition until combined. Scrape the batter into the prepared pan and sprinkle the walnuts and chocolate chips evenly over the top. Bake until a toothpick inserted in the center comes out clean, 40 to 45 minutes. Cool completely in the pan, at least 1 hour. Serve. (The cake can be stored at room temperature for up to 4 days.)

Notes from the Test Kitchen
This hearty snack cake is decadently moist thanks to plumped dates and plenty of butter and shortening. The batter is incredibly easy to make and, thanks to a sprinkling of chocolate chips and walnuts, the final cake has a gooey topping that requires almost no work. When you are testing for doneness, be sure to avoid the chocolate chips or else you may think the cake is underdone.

Orange Kiss Me Cake

SUZANNE SEBASTE | LAKE WYLIE, SOUTH CAROLINA

This flavorful glazed orange, nut, and raisin sheetcake was popularized after winning the grand prize in the 1952 Pillsbury Bake-Off Contest. Suzanne's mother was a huge fan of the contest: "My mother was one of the original entrants in the Pillsbury Bake-Off Contest. We were so excited when a Pillsbury representative came to the house to interview her, but alas, she was not a winner. We always wondered if it was because she told them she used Crisco instead of Spry, since that appeared to be the shortening of choice. She collected all the prize-winning cookbooks (25 cents each), which I have inherited. And, many of these recipes became her favorites. This cake was one of them and is always taken to any family gathering."

SERVES 12

CAKE

- 2 cups all-purpose flour
- 1 teaspoon baking soda
- 1 teaspoon salt
- 1 cup raisins
- 1/3 cup walnuts
- 2 teaspoons grated zest plus 1/4 cup juice from 1 orange
- 1 cup milk
- 8 tablespoons (1 stick) unsalted butter, softened
- 1 cup granulated sugar
- 2 large eggs, room temperature

GLAZE

- 2 cups confectioners' sugar
- 1/4 cup juice from 1 orange
- 1 teaspoon lemon juice

1. FOR THE CAKE: Adjust an oven rack to the middle position and heat the oven to 350 degrees. Grease and flour a 13 by 9-inch baking pan. Whisk the flour, baking soda, and salt in a medium bowl. Process the raisins, walnuts, and orange zest in a food processor until finely chopped. Whisk the orange juice and milk in a small bowl.

2. With an electric mixer on medium-high speed, beat the butter and granulated sugar together until fluffy, about 2 minutes. Reduce the speed to medium and add the eggs one at a time, mixing until incorporated. Scrape down the sides of the bowl. Add the flour mixture and juice mixture alternately in two batches, beating after each addition until just combined. Using a rubber spatula, gently fold in the raisin mixture. Scrape the batter into the prepared pan and bake until a toothpick inserted in the center comes out clean, about 25 minutes. Cool in the pan completely, at least 2 hours.

3. FOR THE GLAZE: Whisk all the ingredients in a medium bowl until smooth. Spread all over the cake and let sit until hardened, about 30 minutes. Serve. (The cake can be stored at room temperature for up to 4 days.)

Notes from the Test Kitchen

This cake grabbed our attention not only for its cute name, but also for the fact that it called for a whole orange to be ground with the raisins and the nuts. While the concept was intriguing, we all had our doubts about it. Initial testing led to a moist cake, but its flavor was off-putting, overpowered by bitter white pith. We had much better luck achieving the right flavor by using orange juice and zest and eliminating the grinding up of an entire orange altogether.

Tipsy Squire

THE EDITORS OF COOK'S COUNTRY

Tipsy Squire, an old-fashioned American dessert, takes its inspiration from classic British trifles with layers of sherry-infused sponge cake, a rich custard, fruit, and sometimes nuts and whipped cream. Looking for its origins, we scoured cookbooks from Great Britain, home of the trifle. Books from the 19th century were packed with concoctions, from the straightforward Tipsy Cake (a sherry-soaked sponge cake filled with cream) to the more whimsical Tipsy Hedgehog (a booze-laden sponge cake covered with cream and studded with sliced almond "spikes"). Turning to early American cookbooks, we found an array of Tipsy Cakes and Puddings, but we did not find a Tipsy Squire (the name referring to the effect this dessert might have on a teetotaling man of importance) until 1928, when it appeared in *Southern Cooking* by Mrs. S.R. Dull. This Southern specialty was well known in Georgia, and it was definitely a trifle. It carried all of the tipsy traits: lots of sherry, layers of custard, and sponge cake. Taking some liberties with this recipe, we found a few tricks to modernize it and make it sturdier, including making "jam sandwiches" and incorporating almond macaroons.

SERVES 10 TO 12

CUSTARD
- 2 **cups heavy cream**
- ½ **cup sugar**
- **Pinch salt**
- 5 **large egg yolks**
- 3 **tablespoons cornstarch**
- 4 **tablespoons unsalted butter, cut into 4 pieces and chilled**
- 1½ **teaspoons vanilla extract**

TRIFLE
- 2 **(8-inch) round stale sponge cakes (each about 1½ inches thick), homemade or store-bought (see note)**
- 1½ **cups cream sherry**
- 1 **cup seedless raspberry jam**
- 2 **cups heavy cream**
- 40 **small almond macaroons or amaretti cookies, homemade or store-bought**
- 1 **cup fresh raspberries**

1. FOR THE CUSTARD: Heat the cream, 6 tablespoons sugar, and salt in a heavy saucepan over medium heat until simmering, stirring occasionally to dissolve the sugar. Meanwhile, whisk the egg yolks in a medium bowl until thoroughly combined. Whisk in the remaining 2 tablespoons sugar until the sugar begins to dissolve. Whisk in the cornstarch until the mixture is pale yellow and thick.

2. When the cream mixture reaches a full simmer, gradually whisk half into the yolk mixture to temper. Return the mixture to the saucepan, scraping the bowl with a rubber spatula; return to a simmer over medium heat, whisking constantly, until 3 or 4 bubbles burst on the surface and the mixture is thickened, about 1 minute. Off the heat, whisk in the butter and vanilla. Transfer the mixture to a bowl, press plastic wrap directly on the surface, and refrigerate until set, at least 3 hours or up to 2 days.

(Continued on page 144)

3. FOR THE TRIFLE: Slice each cake round in half horizontally. Brush each cut side of one cake with ¼ cup sherry, then spread with ¼ cup jam. Stack two cut sides together (resulting in a jam sandwich). Repeat with the second cake to make a second jam sandwich. Cut each cake into five long slices, then cut five more slices crosswise. (Reserve the small jam cakes for nibbling; you will need 30 to 40 of the larger jam cakes for step 5.)

4. With an electric mixer on medium-high speed, beat the cream and ¼ cup of the remaining sherry to soft peaks. Reduce the speed to low, gradually add the custard, and mix well, about 1 minute. Toss the macaroons with the remaining ¼ cup sherry in a large bowl.

5. Following the photos, arrange 12 to 14 (depending on size) macaroons in a single layer to cover the bottom of a 3-quart trifle bowl. Spoon 2 cups of the custard mixture evenly over the macaroons. Arrange 15 to 20 jam cakes in a single layer on the custard. Top with 2 cups custard mixture. Repeat the layering of macaroons, custard mixture, jam cakes, and custard mixture once more. Arrange the remaining 12 to 14 macaroons in a circle midway between the rim of the bowl and the center of the trifle, so that they stick up slightly like a crown. Cover tightly with plastic wrap and refrigerate at least 12 hours or up to 2 days. When ready to serve, pile raspberries inside the macaroons.

Notes from the Test Kitchen
The key to a trifle that didn't turn soggy was simple: stale sponge cake. We recommend that you buy sponge cake from a bakery and let it sit on the counter unwrapped overnight to become stale (or put it in 200-degree oven for 3 hours). No matter how soaked with sherry (very soaked) or buried beneath layers of custard (deeply), the cake retained some of its texture, and the custard was fresh and fluffy. Once assembled, Tipsy Squire actually improves after an overnight stay in the fridge. You'll need a 3-quart trifle dish to make this impressive dessert.

ASSEMBLING TIPSY SQUIRE

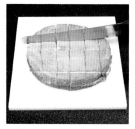

1. To make the raspberry jam sandwiches, cut the filled cake rounds into five long slices, then cut five more slices crosswise; you will need 30 to 40 jam cakes for the trifle.

2. Arrange one layer of soaked macaroons in the bottom of a trifle bowl.

3. Using the back of a serving spoon, spread 2 cups of the custard mixture over the macaroons in an even layer.

4. Place squares of jam-filled cake around the perimeter of the dish, making sure that the stripe of jam is visible. Fill in the center with more pieces of cake. Then spread 2 more cups custard on top. Repeat layers once more.

BLACKBERRY COBBLER

Pies, Puddings, and Fruit Desserts

Sweet Potato Pie

THE EDITORS OF COOK'S COUNTRY

This earthy cousin to pumpkin pie is rich and creamy with a taste all its own. Its origins and ingredients are humble, but made well, it's both filling and ethereal. We learned that the early colonists in Virginia were cultivating sweet potatoes by 1648 and that, because they grew so quickly (and underground where they could not be trodden upon), they became very popular during the Revolutionary and Civil Wars. No doubt their wide availability inspired cooks to experiment with them, though we don't know when this tuber first made its way into a pie shell. We did find a recipe remarkably similar to ours in *What Mrs. Fisher Knows About Southern Cooking*, a book published in 1881 by Abby Fisher, a former slave.

SERVES 8 TO 10

- 1 recipe Single-Crust Pie Dough, **partially baked and still hot (see page 174)**
- 2 **pounds sweet potatoes (about 5 small to medium)**
- 2 **tablespoons unsalted butter, softened**
- 3 **large eggs plus 2 yolks**
- 1 **cup granulated sugar**
- 1/2 **teaspoon ground nutmeg**
- 1/4 **teaspoon salt**
- 2–3 **tablespoons bourbon**
- 1 **tablespoon mild molasses (optional)**
- 1 **teaspoon vanilla extract**
- 2/3 **cup milk**
- 1/4 **cup packed dark brown sugar**

1. After removing the partially baked pie crust from the oven, reduce the oven temperature to 350 degrees.

2. While the crust bakes, prick the sweet potatoes several times with a fork and arrange over several layers of paper towels on a microwave-safe plate and microwave at full power for 5 minutes. Turn each potato over and cook until tender but not mushy, about 5 minutes longer. Remove the potatoes and let stand until cool enough to handle.

3. Slice each potato in half and scrape the flesh out into a large bowl. Mash the butter into the potatoes until just a few small potato lumps remain.

4. Whisk the eggs, yolks, granulated sugar, nutmeg, and salt together in a medium bowl. Stir in the bourbon, molasses (if using), and vanilla, then whisk in the milk. Gradually stir the egg mixture into the mashed sweet potatoes until smooth.

5. Sprinkle the bottom of the hot pie crust with the brown sugar. Spread the sweet potato mixture evenly over the brown sugar. Bake until the filling is set around the edges but the center wiggles slightly when jiggled, about 45 minutes. Transfer the pie to a wire rack and cool to room temperature before serving. (The pie can be refrigerated for up to 2 days.)

Notes from the Test Kitchen

Many recipes for sweet potato pie bury the delicate flavor of the potato under heavy spices and lots of sweetener. We opted to add a minimal number of spices to the sweet potatoes and keep some of the sugar in a distinct layer separate from the sweet potatoes. We found that by sprinkling a mere 1/4 cup of brown sugar over the bottom of the still-hot baked crust, we could sweeten the pie without masking the flavor of the earthy sweet potatoes. To avoid a soggy crust, be sure to add the warm filling to the hot crust.

Pecan Crunch Pie

JERRIE LEE WILMORE | PORTLAND, OREGON

This family recipe, handed down by Jerrie's grandmother, who died in 1933, is the essence of simplicity. This is the pie to make when what you really want is pecan pie but don't have the inclination or time to make the pastry. Here graham cracker crumbs and toasted pecans form the base not of a crust, but of a filling that also includes eggs and sugar.

SERVES 8 TO 10

- 3 large eggs
- 3/4 cup sugar
- 1/2 teaspoon baking powder
- 1 teaspoon vanilla extract
- 1 3/4 cups finely ground graham cracker crumbs, 11 to 14 whole graham crackers
- 1 1/4 cups pecans, toasted and chopped

1. Adjust an oven rack to the middle position and heat the oven to 350 degrees. Grease a 9-inch pie plate.

2. With an electric mixer at high speed, beat the eggs, sugar, baking powder, and vanilla until thickened and tripled in volume, about 5 minutes. Using a rubber spatula, fold in the graham cracker crumbs and pecans. Spoon the filling into the prepared pie plate and bake until well browned on top and a toothpick inserted in the center comes out with a few sticky crumbs attached, about 30 minutes. Transfer the pie to a wire rack and cool completely, about 1 hour. Serve. (The pie can be refrigerated for up to 3 days. Bring to room temperature before serving.)

Notes from the Test Kitchen
Our first instinct was to use prepackaged graham cracker crumbs, but this gave the pie a very stale flavor. It's much better to grind your own in a food processor. Another discovery we made with this easy recipe was that it was better to remove the pie from the oven while it was slightly underdone, when a few sticky crumbs were still attached to the toothpick. When baked until the tester came out clean, the pie became tough; the residual heat had continued to bake the pie as it cooled. Although Jerrie recommends serving this cold with whipped cream, we liked it better at room temperature, with a big scoop of vanilla ice cream.

Raisin Pie

LOIS BLUMENTHAL | YORK, PENNSYLVANIA

"My family settled in Maryland in the 1600s and were what is called Pennsylvania Dutch, though they weren't Dutch and it wasn't Pennsylvania," writes Lois. Recipes for pies like this one appeared as early as 1667 in the Dutch cookbook *The Sensible Cook*, a book that had a significant influence on Pennsylvania Dutch cooking in the New World. Lois's cache of heirloom recipes dates back to 1863 and to her great-great-grandmother, from whom she has handwritten recipes. Raisin pie has a reputation as funeral food among the Amish because it could be made virtually any time of year from ingredients everyone had on hand in their pantry, plus it traveled well without refrigeration. Most recipes, however, did not include apples, the ingredient that makes Lois's recipe so distinct.

SERVES 8 TO 10

- 1½ cups raisins
- 2 cups water
- 1½ cups sugar
- 2 tablespoons all-purpose flour
- ¼ teaspoon ground cinnamon
- ¼ teaspoon ground cloves
- 4 tablespoons unsalted butter, melted
- 1 large egg, lightly beaten
- 2 Granny Smith apples, peeled and sliced thin
- 1 recipe Double-Crust Pie Dough, bottom crust fit into a 9-inch pie plate, top crust rolled to a 12-inch circle and refrigerated (see page 175)

1. Adjust an oven rack to the middle position and heat the oven to 350 degrees. Bring the raisins and water to a boil in a small saucepan over medium-high heat. Drain the raisins, reserving 1 cup of the liquid.

2. Combine the sugar, flour, cinnamon, and cloves in a large bowl. Add the butter and egg and stir to combine. Add the reserved raisin liquid and mix until well combined. Toss the apples and raisins together in a medium bowl and spread them over the bottom of the pie crust. Pour the sugar mixture over the fruit and top with the remaining chilled circle of dough. Trim all but ½ inch of the dough overhanging the edge of the pie plate. Press the top and bottom crusts together, then tuck the edges underneath. Crimp the dough evenly around the edge of the pie, using your fingers. Cut four 2-inch slits in the top of the dough.

3. Bake until the top crust is well browned and the filling begins to bubble, 55 to 60 minutes. Transfer the pie to a wire rack and cool slightly before serving. (The pie can be refrigerated for up to 2 days.)

Notes from the Test Kitchen

Originally this pie called for precooking the apples before baking them in the pie, but we found that this produced an applesauce-raisin pie, and we wanted more texture. After testing various types of apples, we realized that we liked the tart flavor and firm texture of Granny Smith apples. Instead of precooking the apples, we simply tossed them with the raisins and baked them in the pie. This yielded sturdy yet tender apples, with a clean, bright flavor.

Slipped Custard Pie

THE EDITORS OF COOK'S COUNTRY

Made with ingredients most everyone has on hand—eggs, milk, cream, vanilla, and nutmeg—custard pies are thrifty and decidedly old-fashioned. But don't let that fool you into thinking they are a second-class dessert. Made well, a custard pie is as soul satisfyingly rich as the best chocolate cake or the creamiest cheesecake. That said, this is one pie where experience counts. Although it is deceptively simple to make, custard pie has its pitfalls, and they are major—namely, a custard that is overly eggy instead of silky and sweet and a pie shell that is soggy, not crispy, after it has baked with its custard filling.

Enter the old-fashioned "slipped" custard pie. Here the custard and the pie shell don't meet until each is cooked to perfection. Intrigued by the name (and the sleight of hand required to slip the custard intact into the shell), we started looking into the pie's origins. While custard pies are very old (we found a recipe in Lydia Maria Child's *The Frugal Housewife* from 1830), we could not find slipped custard pie recipes earlier than those that appeared in regional newspapers (and in a cookbook from shortening maker Spry) in 1949. Slipped custard pie recipes also appear in *The Fannie Farmer Baking Book* and early editions of *Joy of Cooking* (where the editors say you can also spoon the precooked filling into the cooled shell and that if you add a topping, no one will be the wiser). Recipes for making the custard seem to vary a good bit in terms of the ratio of eggs to milk or cream; plus, some suggest cooking the custard over a double boiler, some require a water bath, and some simply combine the ingredients and bake them. We think our method is easier and foolproof. And all you need to bring the perfect custard pie to the table is a little last-minute dexterity.

SERVES 8

2 cups whole milk
1 cup heavy cream
3 large eggs
2/3 cup sugar
3 tablespoons cornstarch
2 teaspoons vanilla extract
1/4 teaspoon ground nutmeg
1/8 teaspoon salt
1 recipe Single-Crust Pie Dough, fully baked and cooled (see page 174)

1. Adjust an oven rack to the lower-middle position and heat the oven to 375 degrees. Grease an 8-inch pie plate. Heat the milk and cream in a medium saucepan over medium-low heat until steaming. Meanwhile, whisk the eggs, sugar, cornstarch, vanilla, nutmeg, and salt in a medium bowl.

2. Slowly whisk the steaming milk mixture into the egg mixture. Return the mixture to the saucepan and cook, stirring constantly, until the custard begins to thicken and forms a ridge on the tip of the spoon when the bottom of the pan is scraped and the spoon is lifted, 6 to 8 minutes. (If using a thermometer, stir occasionally until the custard reaches 160 degrees.) Pour the custard into the pie plate and bake until the custard is set around the edges but jiggles slightly in the center when shaken, 12 to 15 minutes. Cool to room temperature, at least 2 hours, then refrigerate until well chilled, at least 2 hours or overnight.

3. Run a paring knife around the edges of the pie plate to loosen the custard. Hold the pie plate with the custard over the baked and cooled pie shell. In one, slow, steady motion, tip the pie plate so that the custard slips into the baked shell. Serve. (The pie can be refrigerated for up to 3 days.)

Notes from the Test Kitchen

To prevent overbaking and curdling of the custard, we added cornstarch and started cooking the custard on the stovetop, which speeds up the process. Second, we underbaked the custard just slightly. When the custard looks set around the very edges of the pie plate, but still wobbles in the center when the plate is jiggled, it's time to remove the pie from the oven. The center of the custard will continue to cook and set as it cools, while the outer set edges of the custard are the first to cool down. Be sure to butter the pie plate very well, and give the baked custard time to chill thoroughly—a firmer custard is a sturdier custard.

HOW TO "SLIP" THE CUSTARD

To be successful at "slipping" the pie, you must bake the custard in a pie plate that is smaller than the size of the pie crust. Slip the custard into the crust in one motion. Any hesitation, or moving of the pie plate, and our custard filling broke in half.

Hold the pie plate with the custard over the baked and cooled pie shell. In one slow, steady motion, tip the pie plate so that the custard slips into the baked shell.

Grandpa Boyen's Famous Belgian Rice Custard Pie

LINDA ROSE THOMSETT | PORT TOWNSEND, WASHINGTON

This creamy rice custard pie, with its layer of prune puree spread on the crust, has long been the star of Belgian harvest festivals (the Kermiss)—a tradition going back to 1300s and brought to America by Belgian immigrants in the 1850s. Says Linda about the origin of this recipe, "My grandpa was a boulanger-pâtissier in Belgium at the beginning of the 20th century. After World War I, he brought his recipes with him and settled in Great Falls, Montana, where he opened a general store and bakery. This pie was extraordinarily popular. To keep up with the demand, my granny and aunt learned to make it as well, and taught me how to make it when I was eight years old."

SERVES 8 TO 10

- 1 cup pitted prunes
- 1½ cups sugar
- 3 tablespoons brandy
- ½ cup medium-grain or Arborio rice (see note)
- ½ teaspoon salt
- 4 cups whole milk
- 1 teaspoon ground cinnamon
- 4 large eggs
- 2 teaspoons vanilla extract
- 1 recipe Single-Crust Pie Dough, fit into a deep-dish pie plate (see page 174)

1. Place the prunes, ½ cup sugar, 1 tablespoon brandy, and 3 tablespoons water in a small saucepan. Bring to a simmer over medium-low heat and cook until the prunes are fully softened and the syrup is thick and golden, 20 to 25 minutes. Transfer the mixture to a food processor, add the remaining 2 tablespoons brandy, and process until smooth.

2. Bring 1½ cups water to a boil in a medium saucepan over medium-high heat. Stir in the rice and salt, reduce the heat to medium-low, and cook, covered, until the rice is tender and the water has evaporated, about 20 minutes. Stir in the milk, remaining 1 cup sugar, and cinnamon, return to a simmer, and cook, stirring frequently, until the rice is thickened and very soft, 40 to 50 minutes.

3. Meanwhile, adjust an oven rack to the middle position and heat the oven to 350 degrees. Beat the eggs and vanilla in a medium bowl until blended. Add 1 cup of the hot rice mixture to the eggs and stir vigorously until incorporated. Add the egg and rice mixture back to the saucepan and cook, stirring constantly, until the mixture thickens, about 1 minute.

4. Spread the prune puree in an even layer over the bottom and sides of the unbaked pie shell. Pour the custard over the prune mixture and bake until the center of the custard has set, about 1 hour. Transfer the pie to a wire rack, cool slightly, then refrigerate until fully chilled, at least 2 hours. Serve. (The pie can be refrigerated for up to 2 days.)

Notes from the Test Kitchen

Linda's original recipe called for cooking the rice completely in the milk, but we found that it literally took hours to get the rice softened, and even then we still came across some crunchy grains. Instead, we chose to boil the rice in water until tender (which shaved hours off the recipe), and this gave us exactly what we hoped for—evenly cooked rice. We also concluded that it was necessary to use the starchier medium-grain, not long-grain, rice. We tried the recipe with long-grain rice, and the resulting filling was not nearly as rich and creamy. If you can't find medium-grain rice, Arborio rice works well too.

Nesselrode Pie

JAMIE SHANE | BAYSIDE, NEW YORK

This old New York dessert, a rich and creamy pie usually made up of a custard, meringue, whipped cream, and assorted dried and cognac-soaked fruits, is a relic of the past, and we bet that few people today really know what it is. In fact, in 1988, the *New York Times* featured it in their food section under the headline "The Culinary Mystery of Nesselrode Pie," interviewing many prominent chefs to find out if they knew what it was. Turns out not one of them could identify its defining ingredient: chestnuts.

Nesselrode Pie is named after a 19th-century Russian count who negotiated the Treaty of Paris after the Crimean War (and it seems that he had a passion for chestnuts, since many other dishes with chestnuts are named after him). This pie was the hallmark of a wholesale pie bakery run by Hortense Spier on New York's Upper West Side. Mrs. Spier baked Nesselrode and other cream pies for many of the city's restaurants throughout the 1940s and '50s.

Jamie's great-grandmother served this pie at her soirées. Apparently, she was so fond of sweets that she had parties where dessert was the only course served. According to Jamie, although her great-grandmother made this pie herself, she also "often brought over a store-bought version purchased from an enterprising woman who ran a neighborhood bakery—a small shop which supplied New York restaurants with excellent pies in the mid–20th century." Perhaps she bought them from Mrs. Spier? As a child, Jamie thought of the pie as "Nessel Rode Pie" and pictured a knight named Nessel riding on a pie. Regardless, as she wrote to us, this is "a very dreamy, creamy pie."

- ⅓ cup dried cherries
- ⅓ cup golden raisins
- ½ cup cognac or rum
- 1 (10-ounce) can chestnuts, drained and chopped
- 1 cup whole milk
- 1 tablespoon unflavored gelatin
- 2 large eggs, separated
- ½ cup plus 1 tablespoon sugar
  Salt
- 1 teaspoon vanilla extract
- ½ teaspoon cream of tartar
- ½ cup heavy cream
- 1 recipe Single-Crust Pie Dough, fit into a deep-dish pie plate and fully baked and cooled (see page 174)

  Shaved bittersweet or semisweet chocolate for garnish

1. Place the cherries and raisins in a medium bowl. Bring the cognac to a simmer in a small saucepan over medium-low heat; pour over the cherries and raisins and let sit until plump, about 20 minutes. Stir in the chestnuts and set aside.

2. Meanwhile, place ¼ cup milk in a small bowl and sprinkle the gelatin over the milk. Let stand 5 minutes. Heat the remaining ¾ cup milk in a medium saucepan until simmering. Meanwhile, whisk the egg yolks, 3 tablespoons sugar, and ¼ teaspoon salt in a medium bowl until pale yellow. When the milk reaches a full simmer, slowly whisk it into the yolk mixture. Return the mixture to the saucepan and cook over medium heat, whisking constantly, until the mixture is thickened and coats the back of a spoon, 1 to 2 minutes. Off the heat, whisk in the vanilla and softened gelatin mixture until smooth. Transfer to a large bowl and cool to room temperature, about 30 minutes, stirring every 10 minutes.

3. Combine the remaining 6 tablespoons sugar and 2 tablespoons water in a small saucepan. Cook over medium-high heat for about 4 minutes (the mixture will become slightly thickened and syrupy). Remove from the heat and set aside.

4. With an electric mixer at medium-low speed, beat the egg whites until frothy, about 1 minute. Add a pinch of salt and the cream of tartar and beat, gradually increasing the speed to medium-high, until the whites hold soft peaks, about 2 minutes. With the mixer running, slowly pour the hot sugar syrup into the beaten egg whites. Beat until the mixture (the meringue) has cooled and becomes very thick and shiny, 5 to 9 minutes.

5. Using a rubber spatula, fold the meringue into the cooled custard. With the electric mixer at medium-high speed, beat the heavy cream to soft peaks. Fold the whipped cream and fruit mixture into the custard-meringue mixture. Spoon into the prepared pie shell and refrigerate until thoroughly chilled, at least 2 hours and up to 2 days. Sprinkle with shaved chocolate just before serving.

Notes from the Test Kitchen

Nesselrode Pie is a notoriously involved recipe, so our first order of business was to find ways to shorten it. Jamie's recipe used a double boiler to make the custard base, and the process took a good 20 minutes. We simplified the procedure, using just a saucepan. The other intimidating part of this recipe, the making of the meringue, requires boiling sugar syrup to a precise temperature, then beating it into whipped egg whites. After much testing, we found that after exactly 4 minutes, the syrup was just the right consistency and temperature to add to the egg whites.

Grasshopper Pie

THE EDITORS OF COOK'S COUNTRY

This pie takes its name from a cocktail, the grasshopper, which was invented at Tujague's Restaurant in New Orleans near the end of Prohibition. This bright green drink is a mix of heavy cream, white crème de cacao (a clear version of the dark chocolate cordial), and green crème de menthe (a mint cordial) that is shaken with ice and strained into a cocktail glass. Grasshopper Pie was born during the 1950s, when chiffon pies were the rage.

SERVES 8

CRUST

- 16 Mint 'n Creme Oreo cookies, broken into rough pieces
- 3 tablespoons unsalted butter, melted and cooled

FILLING

- 3 large egg yolks
- 1 envelope unflavored gelatin
- 1/2 cup sugar
- 2 cups heavy cream
  Pinch salt
- 1/4 cup green crème de menthe
- 1/4 cup white crème de cacao

  Shaved bittersweet or semisweet chocolate for garnish (optional)

1. FOR THE CRUST: Adjust an oven rack to the middle position and heat the oven to 350 degrees. Grind the cookies in a food processor to fine crumbs. Transfer to a bowl, drizzle with the melted butter, and toss well. Press the crumbs evenly into the bottom and sides of a 9-inch pie plate and refrigerate until firm, about 20 minutes. Bake until set, 8 to 10 minutes. Transfer the pie plate to a wire rack and cool completely.

2. FOR THE FILLING: Beat the egg yolks in a medium bowl. Combine the gelatin, sugar, 1/2 cup cream, and salt in a medium saucepan and let sit until the gelatin softens, about 5 minutes. Cook over medium heat until the gelatin dissolves and the mixture is very hot but not boiling, about 2 minutes. Whisking vigorously, slowly add the gelatin mixture to the egg yolks. Return the mixture to the saucepan and cook, stirring constantly, until slightly thickened, about 2 minutes. Remove from the heat and add the crème de menthe and crème de cacao. Pour into a clean bowl and refrigerate, stirring occasionally, until wobbly but not set, about 20 minutes.

3. Beat the remaining 1 1/2 cups cream with an electric mixer at medium-high speed until stiff peaks form. Whisk 1 cup whipped cream into the gelatin mixture until completely incorporated. Using a rubber spatula, fold the gelatin mixture into the remaining whipped cream until no streaks of white remain. Scrape the mixture into the cooled pie shell, smooth the top, and refrigerate until firm, at least 6 hours or preferably overnight. (The pie will keep tightly wrapped in the refrigerator for up to 2 days.) Serve, topped with chocolate curls, if desired.

Notes from the Test Kitchen

Most recipes for this pie start with a flavored gelatin base and then fold in whipped egg whites and/or whipped cream. We found that whipped egg whites made this pie a little less creamy than we had hoped. We had better luck softening the gelatin in heavy cream, then combining that mixture with egg yolks and the requisite liqueurs, and lastly folding in whipped cream (no egg whites). For the crust, rather than using the traditional ground chocolate wafers, we tried Mint 'n Creme Oreo cookies, basically a "double stuffed" Oreo flavored with mint. Now, both the filling and the crust were flavored with both chocolate and mint.

Pumpkin Ice Cream Pie

HEIDI FREETAGE | MILLERSBURG, OHIO

This rich-tasting pie captures all the flavors of pumpkin pie à la mode—but is easier to make and, of course, must be made ahead. Heidi's family made this pie their traditional dessert for Thanksgiving and Christmas. "Growing up, I lived 2,500 miles away from my grandmother. It was rare that I was able to spend holidays with her and the rest of the family. However, on the few holidays that I did get to spend with Grandma, there was always one special dessert on the table . . . Pumpkin Ice Cream Pie. This has been a family tradition ever since my cousin and I can remember. And every year, the first bite brings a smile to my face . . . not only because it is so good, but because the first bite brings memories of holidays spent with my grandparents."

SERVES 8 TO 10

CRUST
- 8 whole graham crackers
- 2 tablespoons granulated sugar
- 5 tablespoons unsalted butter, melted and cooled

FILLING
- 1 cup canned pumpkin (see note)
- 1/2 cup packed light brown sugar
- 1/2 teaspoon salt
- 1/2 teaspoon ground cinnamon
- 1/4 teaspoon ground ginger
- 1/4 teaspoon ground allspice
- 1 quart vanilla ice cream, softened

1. FOR THE CRUST: Adjust an oven rack to the lower-middle position and heat the oven to 325 degrees. Pulse the graham crackers and granulated sugar in a food processor until finely ground. Add the melted butter, pulsing until the crumbs are evenly moistened and resemble damp sand. Press the crumbs evenly into the bottom and sides of a 9-inch pie plate. Bake until fragrant and browned around the edges, 15 to 18 minutes. Transfer the pie plate to a wire rack and let cool completely, at least 20 minutes.

2. FOR THE FILLING: Wipe out the food processor bowl. Process the pumpkin, brown sugar, salt, and spices until smooth, about 1 minute. Transfer to a large bowl and stir in the ice cream. Spoon into the prepared crust and freeze until firm, at least 2 hours. (The pie can be frozen for up to 1 month.) Serve.

Notes from the Test Kitchen
We loved the flavor of this pie and how easy it was to assemble, but discovered that some brands of canned pumpkin can be stringy, which will make the filling grainy. To avoid this, we added the extra step of blending the canned pumpkin with the spices until the pumpkin was completely smooth. Be sure to use canned pumpkin, not pumpkin pie filling, which already contains spices and doesn't taste as good.

Cranberry Pot Pie

MICHELLE MELLON | ST. PETERSBURG, FLORIDA

This early-20th-century recipe is sometimes called a pot pie, and at other times cranberry dumplings. Either way, the concept is simple: Cranberries are cooked down with sugar to a saucy consistency. Then they are either married with dumplings and baked or, as we do here, they are topped with a biscuit-like dough, covered, and steam-cooked. Be it biscuit wedges or dumplings, the bright berry sauce is always spooned over the top. Humble but delicious, this recipe makes the most of the cranberry harvest.

SERVES 8

FILLING

1	pound fresh or frozen thawed cranberries (4 cups)
1	cup granulated sugar
1	cup packed light brown sugar
1	teaspoon ground cinnamon
1/4	teaspoon salt
1 1/2	cups water

TOPPING

1 1/2	cups all-purpose flour
1/4	cup granulated sugar
1	teaspoon baking powder
1/2	teaspoon baking soda
1/2	teaspoon salt
4	tablespoons unsalted butter, cut into 1/2-inch pieces and chilled
1/2	cup buttermilk

1. FOR THE FILLING: Combine all the ingredients in a 12-inch skillet and bring to a simmer over medium heat. Cook until the cranberries break down and the mixture begins to thicken, about 15 minutes.

2. FOR THE TOPPING: Meanwhile, combine the flour, granulated sugar, baking powder, baking soda, and salt in a food processor. Add the butter and pulse until the mixture is the texture of coarse meal. Transfer to a medium bowl and fold in the buttermilk until a shaggy dough forms. Turn the dough out onto a sheet of parchment paper and roll it into a 12-inch round.

3. Place the dough over the thickened filling. Reduce the heat to low, cover, and cook until the dough is puffed and doubled in size, about 15 minutes. To serve, cut the dough top into eight wedges. Transfer each wedge to a serving bowl and spoon the filling over the top. Serve hot or warm. (The pot pie is best eaten on the day it is made.)

Notes from the Test Kitchen

This recipe looks like a cobbler, but the difference is that the biscuit-like topping is cooked covered on the stovetop, more like dumplings. The filling tasted great—all we did was add a little cinnamon to liven things up. We found the original dough too savory and a little tough. We added sugar for sweetness, and lightened it with a combination of baking soda and buttermilk, which gave it plenty of lift. To render the dough even more tender, we used the food processor to cut the butter into the flour mixture. Finally, to avoid overmixing, we transferred the mixture to a bowl and folded in the buttermilk just until the dough came together.

Peach Puzzle

LOIS SCHLADEMAN | STOW, OHIO

This recipe (which won the grand prize in the *Cook's Country* lost recipe contest) has all the abracadabra of a magic trick as well as beautiful presentation and great taste. Lois tells us the name refers to the "puzzling" cooking method. Her recipe begins by placing a custard cup upside down in the center of a pie plate. Seven peaches (peeled but still whole) are arranged around the cup and then drizzled with a mixture of brown sugar, butter, and vanilla. A buttery biscuit dough is then domed over the peaches and the custard cup. As the peaches bake under the crust, a vacuum forms inside the custard cup and the juices in the pie plate are pulled up inside the cup. Once cooled, the pie plate is flipped over to reveal the peaches nestled into the flaky biscuit. So where's the butterscotch-like syrup? It's all in the cup!

As you might imagine, Lois's recipe is pretty unique—in our research, we failed to come across a single recipe like it. Lois tells us that her mother made Peach Puzzle back in the 1940s or 1950s and that it has been a family favorite ever since.

How good does this recipe taste? Lois's description answers that question better than we could: "When you pour a spoonful of syrup over the warm peach and it soaks into the biscuit crust, you will think you've died and gone to heaven—where, when meeting my mom, she would be pleased that it was her recipe that made you come visit!"

SERVES 7

PEACHES AND SYRUP

- 7 medium peaches, peeled (see note)
- 3/4 cup packed light brown sugar
- 6 tablespoons water
- 2 tablespoons unsalted butter
- 1/2 teaspoon vanilla extract
- 1/8 teaspoon salt

DOUGH

- 1 1/4 cups all-purpose flour
- 2 tablespoons granulated sugar
- 1 tablespoon baking powder
- 1/4 teaspoon salt
- 5 tablespoons unsalted butter, cut into 1/4-inch pieces and chilled
- 6 tablespoons milk

1. FOR THE PEACHES AND SYRUP: Adjust an oven rack to the middle position and heat the oven to 400 degrees. Following the photos on page 164, place a 6-ounce custard cup or ramekin upside down in the center of a 9-inch pie plate and arrange the peaches around the custard cup. Combine the brown sugar, water, butter, vanilla, and salt in a medium saucepan and stir over medium heat until the sugar dissolves and the butter melts, about 5 minutes. Pour the syrup over the peaches.

(Continued on page 164)

2. FOR THE DOUGH: Pulse the flour, granulated sugar, baking powder, and salt in a food processor until blended. Add the butter and pulse until the flour mixture is pale yellow and resembles coarse cornmeal. Turn the mixture into a medium bowl. (To make the dough by hand: Use the large holes on a box grater to grate frozen butter into the bowl with the flour mixture, then rub flour-coated pieces between your fingers until the flour mixture turns pale yellow and coarse.)

3. Using a rubber spatula, fold the milk into the flour mixture, pressing the mixture against the sides of the bowl to form the dough. Squeeze the dough together and flatten into a disk. On a lightly floured work surface, roll the dough into a 9-inch circle. Lay the dough directly over the peaches and press and fit the dough so that it fits snugly around the peaches.

(The dough will stretch as you fit it around the peaches, but do not attach the dough to the pie plate.) Bake until the top is golden brown, 25 to 30 minutes. Transfer the pie plate to a rack and let cool for 30 minutes.

4. Place a large rimmed serving plate over the top of the pie plate and quickly invert the puzzle onto the plate. Cut into wedges around each peach and serve, pouring syrup over each portion.

Notes from the Test Kitchen
Since this dish is all about the peaches, save it for when fresh local peaches are in season. And it is important to choose peaches that are neither very ripe nor rock-hard—they should give a little when squeezed. Be sure to invert the pie plate quickly to avoid losing any of the syrup. Serve with vanilla ice cream or sweetened whipped cream.

HOW TO MAKE PEACH PUZZLE

1. Place a custard cup or ramekin upside down in the center of a 9-inch pie plate. Arrange the peeled peaches around the cup.

2. Fit the dough snugly around the peaches without attaching the dough to the pie plate. Bake as directed.

3. Place a serving plate over the cooked Peach Puzzle and quickly invert the pie plate.

4. Cut into wedges and pour the syrup in the custard cup over each portion.

Blackberry Cobbler

BOBBI DREYER | EL CERRITO, CALIFORNIA

This is an unusual cobbler—in fact we'd say it's closer to a pudding cake than a cobbler. Once the batter is made and topped with the fresh blackberries, sugar, and cubes of butter, hot water is poured all over the top before the dish goes into the oven. With baking, what looks to be a mistake is transformed into a dessert. The cake rises to the surtace, and the liquid that started out on top sinks to the bottom, taking the berries and sugar with it, creating a "sauce" in the bottom of the pan. Bobbi describes how she came to have this heirloom recipe in her collection: "Summer in my family has always meant Blackberry Cobbler. My aunt, Margaret, raised on a prune ranch in Morgan Hill, California, would pick wild blackberries and take a bucketful home for her Swedish mother to use and make what we call a cobbler. When her mother died in 1908, my aunt acquired the recipe. As time went by, her sister, who is my mother, also learned to make this cobbler. When my turn came, I found this recipe in Mother's collection."

SERVES 12

BATTER
- 1 1/2 cups all-purpose flour
- 2 teaspoons baking powder
- 1/2 teaspoon salt
- 1 cup milk
- 2 teaspoons vanilla extract
- 4 tablespoons unsalted butter, softened
- 1 cup sugar

FILLING
- 4 cups fresh blackberries
- 3/4 cup sugar
- 4 tablespoons unsalted butter, cut into 1/2-inch pieces
- 1 cup boiling water

1. FOR THE BATTER: Adjust an oven rack to the middle position and heat the oven to 350 degrees. Grease a 13 by 9-inch baking pan. Whisk the flour, baking powder, and salt in a medium bowl. Whisk the milk and vanilla in a small bowl.

2. With an electric mixer at medium-high speed, beat the butter and sugar together until fluffy, about 2 minutes, scraping down the bowl as necessary. Reduce the speed to medium and add the flour mixture and milk mixture alternately in two batches, beating after each addition until combined. Spread the batter into the prepared pan.

3. FOR THE FILLING: Scatter the blackberries evenly over the batter and sprinkle with the sugar. Dot the surface with the butter and slowly pour the water evenly over the top. Bake until the mixture is bubbling and the top is golden brown, about 45 minutes. Cool 10 minutes before serving. (The cobbler can be refrigerated for up to 2 days; reheat briefly before serving.)

Notes from the Test Kitchen
After pouring boiling water over the cobbler, we had grave doubts about whether the recipe would work, but the resulting cobbler was great. We felt it could use more berry flavor, so we doubled the amount of blackberries. We also wondered what would happen if we used frozen blackberries, but they simply turned to mush in the oven. This cobbler works just as well using an equal amount of raspberries.

Waukau (Berry Pancake)

JEFF HOFFMAN | CLINTONVILLE, WISCONSIN

A cross between a pancake and a cobbler, this interesting recipe comes from the farmland of Wisconsin. Most likely related to a German or Finnish pancake (*pfannkuchen* or *pannukakku*, respectively), it calls for the simplest of batters topped with berries and sugar and then baked (we made it in a skillet); the batter puffs up bowl-like all around the edges, while the sweet berry center sinks down in the moist middle. Berry picking was a summer pastime for Jeff and his 12 siblings and this recipe, a family favorite, was a great way to use them up. Says Jeff: "We had a couple names for it and my German-speaking grandmother didn't know how these came about. One was 'Waukau,' which happened to be a popular Indian name on a nearby reservation, and the other was 'Botch.' I don't know if the recipe is American Indian or German in its origins."

SERVES 8

- 1 cup all-purpose flour
- 1/2 teaspoon salt
- 1 cup milk
- 1 large egg
- 1/2 teaspoon vanilla extract
- 4 tablespoons unsalted butter
- 2 cups fresh berries (any combination of raspberries, blueberries, blackberries, or sliced strawberries)
- 3/4 cup sugar

1. Adjust an oven rack to the lower-middle position and heat the oven to 375 degrees. Whisk the flour and salt in a medium bowl. Whisk the milk, egg, and vanilla in a small bowl. Make a well in the center of the flour mixture and add the milk mixture to the well. Whisk until combined (a few small lumps may remain).

2. Following the photos, melt the butter in a 12-inch ovenproof skillet over medium heat. Pour the batter into the center of the skillet and let it level. Scatter the berries over the batter, leaving a 1-inch border around the edges. Sprinkle the sugar over the berries, again avoiding the outer 1-inch border. Bake until the edges are puffed and deep golden brown,

50 to 60 minutes. Transfer to a serving plate and serve hot.

Notes from the Test Kitchen

With its crispy, puffed edges, caramelized bottom crust, and saturated, sweet fruit filling, this recipe was a hit in the test kitchen. The original recipe called for a 13 by 9-inch pan, but our results were inconsistent and often soggy. We tried making it in an ovenproof skillet and this made the recipe sturdier; the bottom was consistently crisp and caramelized, and the top always puffed.

MAKING THE WAUKAU

1. Swirl the butter in the skillet until the butter melts. Pour the batter into the middle of the skillet, allowing the batter to self-level. Do not stir.

2. Scatter the berries evenly over the batter, leaving a border around the edges. Sprinkle with sugar, again leaving a border at the edges.

Chocolate Marlow

SHARRON EBERT | BROOKLYN PARK, MINNESOTA

A frozen chocolate and marshmallow mousse topped with graham crackers, Chocolate Marlow came upon the scene in the 1930s (along with the advent of affordable home refrigerators), with recipes appearing in regional newspapers. (We also found the recipe in the *Hershey's 1934 Cookbook*.) We could find no specific clues to the name Marlow, though we suspect it is a contraction of marshmallow.

SERVES 8

MOUSSE

- 2 cups mini marshmallows
- 2/3 cup milk
- 6 ounces semisweet chocolate, chopped
- 2 teaspoons vanilla extract
- 1 1/3 cups heavy cream

SUGARED CRACKERS

- 4 whole graham crackers
- 1 large egg white, lightly beaten
- 2 teaspoons sugar

1. **FOR THE MOUSSE:** Combine the marshmallows, milk, and chocolate in a medium saucepan. Cook, stirring constantly, over medium heat until smooth. Off the heat, stir in the vanilla. Pour the mixture into a medium bowl, cover with plastic wrap, and refrigerate until slightly thickened but not completely set, about 1 hour.

2. With an electric mixer at medium-high speed, beat the cream to soft peaks. Fold the cream into the chocolate mixture until incorporated. Scrape the mixture into a 2-quart soufflé dish. Cover with plastic wrap and freeze until firm, at least 1 hour.

3. **FOR THE SUGARED CRACKERS:** Adjust an oven rack to the middle position and heat the oven to 350 degrees. Place the graham crackers on a baking sheet, brush the tops with the egg white, and sprinkle with the sugar. Bake until the topping is golden brown, about 6 minutes. Let the crackers cool completely, at least 20 minutes, then break into large pieces.

4. To serve, dip the dish with the frozen mousse into hot water for 30 seconds. Scoop the mousse into individual serving bowls and top with a few pieces of sugared crackers. Serve. (The mousse can be frozen for up to 1 month; let the frozen mousse sit at room temperature for 30 minutes before serving. The crackers will keep in an airtight container for up to 4 days.)

Notes from the Test Kitchen

We thought this recipe was intriguing and very promising, but there were a few things that needed fixing. First, the texture was grainy because the recipe originally used water, not milk. Also, it called for whipping evaporated milk, which just didn't work well, turning slushy, not smooth. Whipped heavy cream improved the texture drastically. The recipe also called for topping the mousse with a layer of graham cracker crumbs. We liked the flavor, but not the gritty texture. We thought the sugared crackers gave the dessert an elegant touch.

Coffee Carnival

MARY COLE | TYNGSBORO, MASSACHUSETTS

A tapioca pudding flavored with strong coffee and finished by the addition of a hefty amount of whipped cream folded in just before serving, Coffee Carnival belies the simplicity of its ingredients. We found an early recipe in a 1923 promotional cookbook put out by Minute Tapioca. In the 1930s, similar recipes started appearing in newspapers all around the country—no doubt because Minute Tapioca was cheap, nourishing, and quick to prepare. It was invented in Boston in 1883, so it's not surprising that Mary's grandmother would have made this recipe. As Mary says, "My grandmother, Nana O'Connell, would make Coffee Carnival only twice a year, Thanksgiving and Christmas. It was definitely the dessert everyone looked forward to eating the most every holiday. I can still remember the anticipation I felt when sneaking a spoonful while no one was looking."

SERVES 6

- 2 cups strong brewed coffee, room temperature
- ¼ cup Minute Tapioca
- ½ cup sugar
- ¼ teaspoon salt
- 1 teaspoon vanilla extract
- 2 cups heavy cream

1. Combine the coffee, tapioca, sugar, and salt in a medium saucepan and let sit for 5 minutes. Bring the mixture to a boil over medium-high heat. As soon as the mixture comes to a full boil, remove it from the heat and stir in the vanilla. Transfer to a medium bowl, cover with plastic wrap, and refrigerate until well chilled, at least 2 hours.

2. With an electric mixer at medium-high speed, beat the cream to soft peaks. Fold into the tapioca mixture until incorporated. Serve. (The pudding can be refrigerated for up to 4 days.)

Notes from the Test Kitchen

The test kitchen was divided into two camps—those who liked tapioca pudding, and those who didn't. But when it came to this dessert, we were all sold. Coffee Carnival has all the flavor of a creamy cappuccino and the silkiness of cool coffee ice cream. Our only problem with the recipe was that it used a double boiler to cook the tapioca. The cooking process took a good 20 minutes, and the tapioca always felt a little blown out. We found it worked better to let the tapioca sit in the coffee for a few minutes to soften slightly, then bring the whole mixture to a boil. After the mixture came to a boil, we removed it from the heat. The pudding looked a little runny at first, but thickened as it cooled.

Caramel Dumplings

BETH ANNE CACKA | CANBY, OREGON

The simplicity and thriftiness of this recipe mark it in our minds as an heirloom recipe: A basic dumpling batter is made, and then placed on top of a basic caramel sauce and baked. It turns out that Caramel Dumplings were very popular in the 1930s, when they appeared in a number of newspaper cooking columns. The first cookbook where we could find a recipe, though, was Elizabeth Hedgecock Sparks's *North Carolina and Old Salem Cookery*, from 1955. Her recipe is nearly identical to Beth Anne's, though she embellishes her dumplings with pecans and heats the syrup to boiling before dropping in the dumplings. Beth Anne was given this classic recipe as a wedding gift from her grandmother. Serve with a dollop of whipped cream.

SERVES 6 TO 8

1¼	cups all-purpose flour
1½	cups sugar
1	tablespoon unsalted butter, softened
1	tablespoon baking powder
⅛	teaspoon salt
½	cup milk
1	tablespoon vanilla extract
2½	cups boiling water

1. Adjust an oven rack to the middle position and heat the oven to 350 degrees. Process the flour, ½ cup sugar, butter, baking powder, and salt in a food processor until combined. Add the milk and vanilla and process until the mixture forms a soft batter, about 30 seconds.

2. Place the remaining 1 cup sugar in a large ovenproof skillet. Cook over medium heat, without stirring, until the sugar begins to melt, 1 to 2 minutes. Cook, stirring constantly with a wooden spoon, until the sugar turns a deep amber brown, about 5 minutes. Very carefully, pour ½ cup boiling water into the sugar syrup and let the bubbling subside. Add the remaining 2 cups water and let the bubbling subside. Stir the mixture gently until completely smooth.

3. Using a ¼-cup measure, carefully drop the dumpling batter over the caramel syrup. Transfer the skillet to the oven and bake until the tops of the dumplings are well browned, 30 to 35 minutes. Let cool 10 minutes before serving. To serve, scoop the dumplings into individual serving bowls and spoon the caramel over the top. (The dumplings are best eaten on the same day that they are made.)

Notes from the Test Kitchen

Plump dumplings soaked with the hearty flavor of deep (almost burnt) caramel may sound like a strange combination, but the test kitchen loved this dish. When making the caramel, it is important to be especially careful, as the hot sugar can be dangerous to work with. To minimize the risk, we found that it was imperative to add only a little of the boiling water to the hot sugar at a time. The mixture will bubble violently, but that soon subsides. After the second batch of water is added and the bubbling again subsides, it is then safe to begin stirring the caramel until it is smooth. It is also important to know when to stir the sugar as it is melting. Stir before it begins to melt and the sugar will clump and the caramel will be granular. To avoid this, wait until the sugar begins to melt, then stir constantly until the sugar is completely melted and turns a deep amber color.

Falsha Strudel

JUSTINE STROMBERG | WOODINVILLE, WASHINGTON

Another name for Falsha Strudel might well be Mock Strudel since the word "falsha" comes from the German word *falsche*, which means false. A legacy from Justine's great-grandmother, this recipe captures the spirit of a strudel but is far easier. Here the dough is simply pressed into a standard 13 by 9-inch baking dish (with a portion of the dough reserved to form a crumb topping), and the "filling" is a simple mixture of jam and fresh fruit.

MAKES 24 SQUARES

DOUGH
2½ cups all-purpose flour plus ⅓ cup for topping
1 cup sugar
1 teaspoon grated lemon zest
½ teaspoon baking soda
½ teaspoon salt
3 large eggs
12 tablespoons (1½ sticks) unsalted butter, melted

FILLING
1 cup blackberry jam
2 tablespoons all-purpose flour
1 cup frozen or fresh blackberries

1. FOR THE DOUGH: Adjust an oven rack to the middle position and heat the oven to 350 degrees. Whisk 2½ cups flour, the sugar, lemon zest, baking soda, and salt together in a medium bowl. Beat the eggs and butter together in a medium bowl. Make a well in the center of the flour mixture and add the egg mixture. Stir together to form a moist and sticky dough.

2. Place one-third of the dough in a medium bowl. Add the remaining ⅓ cup flour, cutting it in with a fork until large crumbs form. Reserve for the topping. Following the photos, use the bottom of a measuring cup to press the remaining dough into the bottom of a 13 by 9-inch baking dish, forming a ½-inch rim of dough up the sides.

3. FOR THE FILLING: Mix the jam with the flour until smooth. Toss in the berries and arrange the mixture evenly over the dough.

4. Sprinkle the reserved topping mixture evenly over the fruit and bake until golden brown, about 30 minutes. Cool 10 minutes, then cut into squares. Serve warm.

Notes from the Test Kitchen
Justine's original recipe used hard-to-find black raspberry jam and did not call for berries, but we loved the flavor the blackberries added. Plus they cut the cloying flavor of the jam and provided an attractive texture to the strudel. Using a little bit of zest in the dough brightens the flavor of the berries. You can substitute raspberries and raspberry jam in this recipe without changing any other ingredients. If the measuring cup sticks while patting the dough into the pan, dip the bottom of it in flour as you work.

MAKING FALSHA STRUDEL

1. Press two-thirds of the dough into the pan using the bottom of a measuring cup and making a ½-inch-high rim up the sides of the pan.

2. Arrange the filling over the top of the dough, then sprinkle with the topping mixture.

Indian Pudding

THE EDITORS OF COOK'S COUNTRY

A dressed-up version of hasty pudding, Indian pudding is a very old New England dessert in which the warm flavors of molasses, ginger, and cinnamon transform cornmeal, milk, and eggs into an ethereal baked dish. Some version of Indian pudding probably existed from the earliest colonial times in America, when settlers realized that they simply had to accept Indian corn as a fact of life. We found three versions of Indian pudding in Amelia Simmons's *American Cookery* (1798). And of course the recipe is one of the hallmarks of Boston's famous Durgin-Park restaurant in Faneuil Hall. Certainly the recipe has evolved over time, and today you see lots of fussy variations, but we drew upon more traditional recipes to develop a foolproof version in our test kitchen—and one that wouldn't require all afternoon to bake.

SERVES 6

- 4 cups plus 2 tablespoons whole milk
- 1/2 cup mild molasses
- 1/4 cup maple syrup
- 1 teaspoon vanilla extract
- 1/2 teaspoon ground cinnamon
- 1/2 teaspoon ground ginger
- 1/2 teaspoon salt
- 3/4 cup yellow cornmeal, preferably stone-ground
- 2 large eggs, lightly beaten
- 1 teaspoon cornstarch

1. Adjust an oven rack to the lower-middle position and heat the oven to 275 degrees. Grease a 2-quart casserole dish or 9-inch soufflé dish. Cover the bottom of a roasting pan with a dish towel. Bring a kettle of water to a boil.

2. Bring 4 cups milk, the molasses, maple syrup, vanilla, cinnamon, ginger, and salt to a simmer in a medium saucepan over medium heat. Slowly whisk in the cornmeal. Reduce the heat to low and cook, stirring frequently, until the mixture has thickened and the whisk leaves trails when stirred, about 15 minutes.

3. Whisk the eggs, cornstarch, and remaining 2 tablespoons milk together until smooth, then slowly whisk into the cornmeal mixture. Increase the heat to medium-high and cook, stirring constantly, until large bubbles rise to the surface, 1 to 2 minutes.

4. Pour the cornmeal mixture into the prepared dish, wrap tightly in foil, and set inside the roasting pan. Place the roasting pan in the oven and carefully pour the boiling water into the pan until it reaches halfway up the sides of the dish. Bake until the pudding is no longer runny and has gently set, about 2 hours.

5. Remove the baking dish from the water bath and let cool on a wire rack for 20 minutes before serving. (The baked pudding can be cooled at room temperature for up to 3 hours before serving.)

Notes from the Test Kitchen
Most of the recipes we sampled were flavorless or too dense. To improve the pudding's flavor, we blended maple syrup and molasses to sweeten the pudding and added a shot of vanilla. For the creamiest texture, we realized that a water bath was necessary. The hot water surrounding the pudding moderates the temperature, thus preventing the custard from cooking too fast and drying out.

Single-Crust Pie Dough

MAKES ENOUGH FOR ONE 9-INCH PIE

1¼ cups all-purpose flour
1 tablespoon sugar
½ teaspoon salt
3 tablespoons vegetable shortening, cut into
   ½-inch pieces and chilled
4 tablespoons unsalted butter, cut into ¼-inch
   pieces and chilled
4–6 tablespoons ice water

1. Process the flour, sugar, and salt in a food processor until combined. Scatter the shortening over the top and continue to process until the mixture has the texture of coarse sand. Scatter the butter pieces over the top and process the mixture until it resembles coarse crumbs. (To make pie dough by hand, see page 175.) Transfer to a bowl.

2. Sprinkle 4 tablespoons of the ice water over the mixture. Stir and press the dough together, using a stiff rubber spatula, until the dough sticks together. If the dough does not come together, stir in the remaining water, 1 tablespoon at a time, until it does. Form the dough into a 4-inch disk, wrap tightly in plastic wrap, and refrigerate at least 1 hour. (The dough can be refrigerated, wrapped tightly in plastic wrap, for up to 2 days or frozen for up to 2 months. Let the frozen dough thaw on the countertop until malleable before rolling.)

3. Let the chilled dough soften slightly at room temperature before rolling it into a 12-inch circle on a floured work surface and fitting it into a pie plate. Following the photos, trim, tuck, and crimp the edges and freeze the unbaked pie crust until firm, about 30 minutes, before filling or baking.

4. For a prebaked piecrust: Adjust an oven rack to the lower-middle position and heat the oven to 375 degrees. Line the chilled pie crust with a double layer of aluminum foil, covering the edges to prevent burning.

5. Fill the crust with pie weights or pennies and bake for 20 to 25 minutes. After baking, remove the pie weights and foil and either let the crust cool (for a partially baked crust) or continue to bake for 10 to 15 minutes (for a fully baked crust).

Notes from the Test Kitchen
Traditional pie dough recipes call for either butter or shortening. Butter makes for the richest, most flavorful crust, but butter crusts can be difficult to prepare. Shortening lacks the flavor of butter, but makes the dough easy to work with and the crust exceptionally flaky. We found that combining the two fats gives you the best of both worlds: flavor and easy handling.

ROLLING AND FITTING PIE DOUGH

 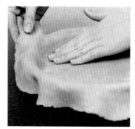  

1. Loosely roll the dough around the rolling pin. Then gently unroll the dough over the pie plate.

2. Lift the dough around the edges and gently press it down into the corners of the pie plate.

3. Trim the dough to within ½ inch of the pie plate. Tuck the dough underneath itself to form a rim that sits above the pie plate.

4. Use the index finger of one hand and the thumb and index finger of the other to create a crimped edge.

Double-Crust Pie Dough

MAKES ENOUGH FOR ONE 9-INCH PIE

2½ cups all-purpose flour

2 tablespoons sugar

1 teaspoon salt

8 tablespoons vegetable shortening, cut into
   ½-inch pieces and chilled

12 tablespoons (1½ sticks) unsalted butter, cut into
   ¼-inch pieces and chilled

6–8 tablespoons ice water

1. Process the flour, sugar, and salt in a food processor until combined. Scatter the shortening over the top and process until the mixture has the texture of coarse sand. Scatter the butter pieces over the top and process the mixture until it resembles coarse crumbs. Transfer to a bowl.

2. Sprinkle 6 tablespoons of the ice water over the mixture. Stir and press the dough together, using a stiff rubber spatula, until the dough sticks together. If the dough does not come together, stir in the remaining water, 1 tablespoon at a time, until it does.

3. Divide the dough into two even pieces and flatten each into a 4-inch disk. Wrap the disks tightly in plastic wrap and refrigerate for 1 hour. (The dough can be refrigerated, wrapped tightly in plastic wrap, for up to 2 days or frozen for up to 2 months. Let the frozen dough thaw on the countertop until malleable before rolling.) Let the chilled dough soften slightly at room temperature before rolling it out into two 12-inch circles on a floured work surface and fitting them into a pie plate.

Making Pie Dough by Hand

Freeze the butter in its stick form until very firm. Whisk together the flour, sugar, and salt in a large bowl. Add the chilled shortening and press into the flour, using a fork. Grate the frozen butter on the large holes of a box grater into the flour mixture, then cut the mixture together, using two butter or dinner knives, until the mixture resembles coarse crumbs. Continue as instructed in step 2 of the recipe.

MAKING A DOUBLE-CRUST PIE

1. After rolling out the top crust, loosely roll it around the rolling pin, then gently unroll it over the filled pie-crust bottom.

2. Trim all but ½ inch of the dough overhanging the edge of the pie plate with scissors. Press the top and bottom crusts together, then tuck the edges underneath.

3. Crimp the dough evenly around the edge of the pie, using your fingers.

4. Cut four 2-inch slits in the center of the top crust with a paring knife. Follow the recipe for any other instructions.

PIES, PUDDINGS, AND FRUIT DESSERTS **175**

CHERRY CHEDDAR BAR COOKIES

Cookies and Candies

Aunt Fannie's Toffee Chew Bars

SHELLEY HUBER | BOERNE, TEXAS

These chewy bar cookies are packed with brown sugar, nuts, and coconut—no wonder Shelley's family passed along this recipe. According to Shelley, these cookies were often the reward for helping her grandmother: "A workday at Grandma's house was always the same . . . delicious. A morning spent outside on yard work meant the best was yet to come: lunch. It always began with a steaming bowl of Campbell's chicken noodle soup perked up with chunks of melting cheddar cheese. And before we could leave the table, we were required to round out our lunch with sliced fresh fruit. But our sweetest reward for our workday at Grandma's was Aunt Fannie's Toffee Chew Bars. Aunt Fannie was my grandmother's sister-in-law and best friend. She insisted that Grandma serve her 'chews' warm from the oven with a tall glass of ice-cold milk."

MAKES 24 BARS

CRUST

- 8 tablespoons (1 stick) unsalted butter, softened
- 1/2 cup packed light brown sugar
- 1/2 teaspoon salt
- 1 cup all-purpose flour

FILLING

- 2 large eggs
- 1 cup packed light brown sugar
- 2 teaspoons vanilla extract
- 2 tablespoons all-purpose flour
- 1/2 teaspoon baking powder
- 1/4 teaspoon salt
- 1 1/2 cups sweetened, shredded coconut, toasted
- 1 cup sliced almonds, toasted

1. FOR THE CRUST: Adjust an oven rack to the middle position and heat the oven to 325 degrees. Line a 13 by 9-inch baking pan with foil, leaving overhang on all sides. Grease the foil. With an electric mixer at medium-high speed, beat the butter, sugar, and salt until fluffy, about 2 minutes. Add the flour and mix until combined. Press the mixture firmly into the prepared baking pan. Bake until golden brown, about 15 minutes.

2. FOR THE FILLING: Whisk the eggs, sugar, and vanilla together in a medium bowl. Add the flour, baking powder, and salt and whisk until combined. Stir in the coconut and almonds and spread the mixture evenly over the crust. Bake until lightly browned around the edges, 20 to 25 minutes. Transfer the pan to a wire rack and cool completely, about 2 hours. Using the foil overhang, lift the bars from the pan and cut into 24 bars. (The bars can be stored in an airtight container for up to 3 days.)

Notes from the Test Kitchen

We thought Aunt Fannie made a mean cookie, and we changed little about this recipe. One thing that we did notice was that the coconut and almond flavors were a little masked, so we chose to toast the coconut and almonds before stirring them into the batter. Also, these bars were very sticky, and were nearly impossible to remove from the pan. A well-greased foil sling is essential if you want to get the bars out in one piece.

Cherry Cheddar Bar Cookies

SUSAN BUSCH | WILLISTON, VERMONT

The surprising addition of cheddar cheese to these bar cookies caught our attention, plus they were very easy to make: One dough forms the base and the topping, and fruit jam is spread straight from the jar in between the two layers. This recipe dates back to Susan's grandmother; we're glad she located the recipe card. "I remember picking ripe cherries from my grandparents' tree that we would then use for baking. For those cookies, we would use fresh cherries and sharp yellow cheddar cheese, which always seemed strange to me. But the cheese gives the cookie a chewy texture and deep flavor."

MAKES 16 BARS

- 1¾ cups all-purpose flour
- ½ cup packed light brown sugar
- 1 teaspoon baking powder
- 1 teaspoon ground cinnamon
- 8 tablespoons (1 stick) unsalted butter, cut into ½-inch pieces and chilled
- 1 cup shredded sharp cheddar cheese (see note)
- ¾ cup cherry jam

1. Adjust an oven rack to the middle position and heat the oven to 325 degrees. Line a 9-inch square baking pan with foil, leaving overhang on all sides. Grease the foil.

2. Combine the flour, sugar, baking powder, and cinnamon in a food processor. Add the butter and cheese and pulse until the flour is pale yellow and resembles coarse cornmeal. (To do this by hand, grate frozen butter into the flour using the large holes of a box grater, add the cheese, then rub the flour-coated pieces between your fingers until the flour turns pale yellow and coarse.)

3. Press half the flour mixture firmly into the prepared pan. Bake until golden brown, about 15 minutes. Transfer to a wire rack and let cool slightly, about 10 minutes.

4. Spread the jam evenly over the crust, then crumble the remaining flour mixture evenly over the jam. Bake until the top is well browned, about 25 minutes. Transfer the pan to a wire rack and cool completely, about 1 hour. Using the foil overhang, lift the bars from the pan and cut into 16 bars. (The bars can be stored in an airtight container for up to 3 days.)

Notes from the Test Kitchen
The cheese added to this recipe reminded us of the slice of cheddar that often is served with a wedge of apple pie. It truly is an appealing sweet and salty pairing. We wondered what would happen if we used the preshredded cheese sold in resealable packages at the supermarket. We're happy to report that it worked great and, thanks to the cellulose powder that coats the cheese to prevent it from clumping, the crust and topping were crisper than when we shredded our own cheese. Either can be used, however.

Peanut Blossom Cookies

THE EDITORS OF COOK'S COUNTRY

When Freda Smith entered her Peanut Blossoms in the 1957 Pillsbury Bake-Off, little did she know that she had created a cookie sensation that would endure for nearly five decades. While she may not have won the $25,000 first prize, her chocolate-kissed peanut butter cookies quickly eclipsed that year's winner, a recipe for walnut-flavored butter cookies called Accordion Treats.

MAKES ABOUT 8 DOZEN COOKIES

- 2³/₄ cups all-purpose flour
- ¹/₂ teaspoon salt
- ¹/₂ teaspoon baking soda
- ¹/₂ teaspoon baking powder
- 1 cup roasted, salted peanuts
- 16 tablespoons (2 sticks) unsalted butter, softened
- ³/₄ cup packed dark brown sugar
- ³/₄ cup granulated sugar
- 1 cup creamy peanut butter
- 2 large eggs, room temperature
- 2 teaspoons vanilla extract
- 96 Hershey's Chocolate Kisses (from two 1-pound bags), wrappers removed

1. Adjust an oven rack to the middle position and heat the oven to 350 degrees. Line a baking sheet with parchment paper.

2. Whisk 1¾ cups flour, the salt, baking soda, and baking powder together in a medium bowl. Process the remaining 1 cup flour and the peanuts in a food processor until ground, then stir into the flour mixture.

3. With an electric mixer at medium-high speed, beat the butter and sugars together until fluffy, about 2 minutes. Add the peanut butter and continue to beat until combined. Add the eggs, one at a time, beating after each addition until incorporated, then beat in the vanilla. Reduce the speed to low, add the flour mixture in two batches, and mix until incorporated. Cover the bowl and refrigerate the dough until stiff, about 30 minutes.

4. Roll 1-inch balls of dough and space them 2 inches apart on a baking sheet. Bake until just set and beginning to crack, 9 to 11 minutes, rotating the baking sheet halfway through baking. Working quickly, remove the baking sheet from the oven and firmly press one Kiss in the center of each cookie. Return the baking sheet to the oven and bake until lightly golden, about 2 minutes. Transfer the baking sheet to a wire rack to cool for 5 minutes, then transfer the cookies directly to a wire rack to finish cooling. Repeat with the remaining cookies. Cool completely. (The cookies will be cool enough to eat after about 30 minutes, but the Kisses will take 2 hours to set completely.)

Notes from the Test Kitchen

Freda's recipe calls for creamy peanut butter, but we found that a mix of ground peanuts (which replaced some of the flour) and creamy peanut butter added deeper peanut flavor without compromising the texture (chunky peanut butter made the cookies craggy). The cookies were almost perfect, but we were frustrated by one thing: The residual heat in the cookies softened the kisses so much that they took at least four hours to firm up again. Strangely enough, placing the chocolates on the cookies during the last two minutes of baking helped them to firm up more quickly. (A little direct heat stabilizes and sets the exterior of the chocolate.) This recipe can be cut in half. Bake these cookies one batch at a time and be sure to use a fresh or cooled baking sheet for each batch.

Joe Froggers

THE EDITORS OF COOK'S COUNTRY

These wonderful flat, oversized molasses-spice cookies are moist, salty, rum flavored, and most unusual (and addictive). Joe Froggers date back more than 200 years to Black Joe's Tavern, located in Marblehead, Massachusetts, a seaside town about 25 miles north of Boston. Looking for authentic recipes, we tested as many as we could find from websites, cookbooks, and magazines, but they baked up hard, with no warm and salty rum flavor. The Marblehead Museum and Historical Society recommended we consult *The Spirit of '76 Lives Here* by Priscilla Sawyer Lord and Virginia Clegg Gamage (1971). The authors tell the story of Joseph Brown, a freed slave and Revolutionary War veteran who lived in Marblehead more than 200 years ago. Brown (known as "Old Black Joe") and his wife, Lucretia (affectionately known as Auntie Cresse), opened up Black Joe's Tavern in a part of Marblehead called Gingerbread Hill. Besides serving drinks (mostly rum), Joe and Auntie Cresse baked cookies: large, moist molasses and rum cookies made salty by the addition of Marblehead seawater. These cookies were popular sustenance on long fishing voyages, as they had no dairy to spoil and the combination of rum, molasses, and seawater kept them chewy for weeks.

According to Samuel Roads Jr.'s *History and Traditions of Marblehead*, published in 1879, the funny name for these cookies referred to the lily pads (similar in size and shape to the cookies) and large croaking frogs that would fill the pond behind Joe's tavern. Thus the cookies became known as Joe Froggers. At Marblehead's Abbot Public Library, the librarians produced recipes from local news journals and town cookbooks, such as the *Marblehead, Massachusetts, Baptist Women's Fellowship* (1965). These recipes first stirred molasses together with baking soda. The reaction between the two made the mixture bubble and froth, leaving the soda with little leavening power. That, combined with the absence of egg, explains why the cookies are so flat. Our version of this old-fashioned American cookie won't stay fresh for weeks at sea like the original, but it is so salty, spicy, sweet, and chewy we're not sure that matters.

MAKES 24 COOKIES

- $1/3$ cup dark rum (such as Myers's)
- 1 tablespoon water
- $1 1/2$ teaspoons salt
- 3 cups all-purpose flour
- $3/4$ teaspoon ground ginger
- $1/8$ teaspoon ground allspice
- $1/4$ teaspoon ground nutmeg
- $1/8$ teaspoon ground cloves
- 1 cup mild molasses (see note)
- 1 teaspoon baking soda
- 8 tablespoons (1 stick) unsalted butter, softened
- 1 cup sugar

1. Stir the rum, water, and salt in a small bowl until the salt dissolves. Whisk the flour, ginger, allspice, nutmeg, and cloves in a medium bowl. Stir the molasses and baking soda in a large measuring cup (the mixture will begin to bubble) and let sit until doubled in volume, about 15 minutes.

2. With an electric mixer on medium-high speed, beat the butter and sugar until fluffy, about 2 minutes. Reduce the speed to medium-low and gradually beat in the rum mixture. Add the flour mixture and molasses mixture alternately in two batches, scraping down the sides of the bowl as needed. Cover the bowl with plastic wrap and refrigerate until stiff, at least 8 hours or up to 3 days.

3. Adjust two oven racks to the upper-middle and lower-middle positions and heat the oven to 375 degrees. Line two baking sheets with parchment paper. Working with half of the dough at a time on a heavily floured work surface, roll out to $1/4$-inch thickness. Cut out cookies with a $3 1/2$-inch cookie cutter, spacing them $1 1/2$ inches apart on the prepared baking sheets. Bake until the cookies are set and just beginning to crack, about 8 minutes, switching and rotating the baking sheets halfway through baking. Cool the cookies on the baking sheets for 10 minutes, then transfer to a wire rack to cool completely. Repeat with the remaining dough. (The cookies can be stored in an airtight container for up to 1 week.)

Notes from the Test Kitchen

We found that we needed to make some adjustments to the old recipes we found to arrive at just the right flavor and chewy texture. We doubled the amount of rum most recipes called for and halved the water. We weren't going to call for seawater (although we did test it), but dissolving $1 1/2$ teaspoons of salt into the rum and water worked fine. Some recipes called for shortening (Auntie Cresse most likely used lard), but butter tasted better. Place only six cookies on each baking sheet—they will spread. If you don't have a $3 1/2$-inch cookie cutter, use a drinking glass. Use mild (not robust) molasses, and chill the dough for a full eight hours, or it will be too soft to roll out. Finally, be sure to use a fresh or cooled baking sheet for each batch.

May Day Cookies

ANGIE WHITTLE | SPRINGDALE, ARKANSAS

Since the recipe for these crispy molasses cookies originated in Arkansas, we would bet it was made originally with molasses distilled from sweet sorghum rather than sugar cane—a lengthy process that stretched from May to October in the Ozarks. We think Angie describes these cookies best: "Dark, spicy, and old-fashioned, they come from my great-grandmother, 'Granny,' Della McCoy Evans, born in 1883, Madison County, Arkansas. My father, now in his 70s, told me that she made these cookies often when he was a young boy. Granny stored them on a plate in a metal pie safe, which was a piece of furniture about three feet wide and shoulder high to an adult, and had two punched tin doors with shelves inside. If she made a large batch, she would store them in a lard bucket or syrup bucket. The molasses Granny used was made by a neighbor, and Daddy says they would help him make it every year, and the neighbor would give them a gallon of molasses for their labor."

MAKES 36 COOKIES

- 2 cups all-purpose flour
- 1/2 teaspoon baking soda
- 1/2 teaspoon salt
- 1 1/2 teaspoons ground cinnamon
- 1 teaspoon ground allspice
- 1/2 teaspoon ground nutmeg
- 3/4 cup mild molasses (see note)
- 1 large egg yolk
- 1/2 cup vegetable shortening
- 1/2 cup confectioners' sugar

1. Whisk the flour, baking soda, salt, and spices in a medium bowl. Whisk the molasses and egg yolk together in a measuring cup.

2. With an electric mixer at medium-high speed, beat the shortening and sugar together until fluffy, about 2 minutes. Reduce the speed to medium, add the molasses and egg yolk, and beat until combined. Add the flour mixture and beat until incorporated. Press the dough into a 4-inch disk and wrap in plastic wrap. Refrigerate until well chilled, at least 2 hours or up to 24 hours.

3. Adjust an oven rack to the middle position and heat the oven to 350 degrees. Line a baking sheet with parchment paper. On a lightly floured work surface, roll the dough out to a 1/4-inch-thick circle. Cut out rounds with a 2-inch cookie cutter, spacing them 1 inch apart on the prepared baking sheet. Bake until the cookies are set in the middle, 12 to 14 minutes. Cool the cookies on the baking sheet for 2 minutes, then transfer to a wire rack to cool completely, at least 20 minutes. Gather the scraps, reroll the dough, and repeat with the remaining dough. (The cookies can be stored in an airtight container for up to 3 days.)

Notes from the Test Kitchen

We tried mild, robust, and blackstrap molasses in these simple cookies but we found that mild molasses worked best, as it allowed the spices to take center stage. The vegetable shortening in these cookies makes them crispy, more akin to great ginger snaps. Be sure to bake these cookies one batch at a time and use a fresh or cooled baking sheet for each batch. Also, this dough is very tender. Intricate cookie cutters will be difficult to use; stick to simple circle shapes and you'll be fine.

Molasses Cookies

JERRI HANSEN | FORT COVINGTON, NEW YORK

The New England colonists used molasses as their primary sweetener in cooking and baking, so there's no doubt that cookies such as these have a long history. That said, we could not find recipes for molasses cookies in American cookbooks or newspapers until 1877; recipes and household news didn't really flourish in newspapers until after the Civil War. The recipe for these cookies, which are thick and chewy and stuffed with raisins and nuts, came from Jerri's grandmother: "My grandmother was a farmer's wife and would rather work outside than cook. When she baked it was always something easy and quick, and made enough for the cookie jar."

MAKES 48 COOKIES

- 3 cups all-purpose flour
- 1 teaspoon baking powder
- 1 teaspoon baking soda
- 1/2 teaspoon salt
- 1 teaspoon ground cinnamon
- 1/4 teaspoon ground cloves
- 1/4 teaspoon ground allspice
- 1/4 teaspoon ground nutmeg
- 8 tablespoons (1 stick) unsalted butter, softened
- 1 cup sugar
- 1/2 cup robust molasses (see note)
- 1/2 cup brewed coffee, room temperature
- 1/2 cup raisins
- 1/2 cup walnuts or pecans, chopped

1. Adjust two oven racks to the upper-middle and lower-middle positions and heat the oven to 350 degrees. Line two baking sheets with parchment paper. Whisk the flour, baking powder, baking soda, salt, and spices together in a medium bowl.

2. With an electric mixer at medium-high speed, beat the butter and sugar together until fluffy, about 2 minutes. Reduce the speed to medium, add the molasses, and beat until combined, about 30 seconds. Add the flour mixture and the coffee alternately in two batches, beating until combined. Using a rubber spatula, stir in the raisins and nuts.

3. Working with 1 tablespoon of dough at a time, shape the dough into balls. Place the balls on the prepared baking sheets, spacing them about 2 inches apart. Bake until the cookies have risen and are just set, 8 to 12 minutes, switching and rotating the baking sheets halfway through baking. Cool the cookies on the sheets for 2 minutes, then transfer to a wire rack to cool completely, about 20 minutes. Repeat with the remaining dough. (The cookies can be stored in an airtight container for up to 3 days.)

Notes from the Test Kitchen

Given all the ingredients in this recipe, we wondered if the type of molasses used would make a difference. It sure did; robust (dark) molasses beat mild (light) molasses hands down. Without it, the cookies lacked full molasses flavor. But don't be tempted to use blackstrap molasses; it will give the cookies an almost burnt flavor.

Originally this recipe called for a range of 3 to 3 1/2 cups of flour, but we found that no more than 3 cups was necessary. More and the cookies turned tough. This cookie is best baked until the tops are just set. Any longer and the cooled cookies will be hard and lose their chewy texture. Be sure to use a fresh or cooled baking sheet for each batch.

Iola's White Sugar Cookies

ANN MURPHY | ST. JOSEPH, MICHIGAN

Although we consider ourselves experts on the best sugar cookies, this recipe was somewhat of a revelation to us. Big, domed, and a cross between a cookie and a tender white cake, these cookies proved irresistible. We loved the simplicity of them and the fact that they weren't too sweet. This recipe was inspired by cookies made by Ann's grandmother. "My many memories of my grandmother Derby include her endless supply of sugar cookies: big, round, white, generously sugared, and so soft you could almost bend them in half. Grandmother was one of those natural cooks who baked by feel. My mother tried repeatedly to duplicate those wonderful cookies, once even sitting in Grandmother's kitchen writing down measurements and methods as Grandmother worked. Alas, even that valiant effort was not rewarded with success. I searched for the recipe for years (I am now a grandmother myself) before coming across Iola's White Sugar Cookies. They're delicious (and bendable) and extremely versatile." We're not sure who Iola is but we're glad that Ann discovered her recipe.

MAKES 24 COOKIES

- 3 cups all-purpose flour
- 1 teaspoon baking powder
- 1/2 teaspoon baking soda
- 1/2 teaspoon salt
- 8 tablespoons (1 stick) unsalted butter, softened
- 3/4 cup sugar
- 1 large egg
- 1/2 teaspoon vanilla extract
- 1/2 cup buttermilk

1. Whisk the flour, baking powder, baking soda, and salt in a large bowl.

2. With an electric mixer at medium-high speed, beat the butter and 1/2 cup sugar together until fluffy, about 2 minutes. Reduce the speed to medium, add the egg and vanilla, and beat until combined. Add the flour mixture and buttermilk alternately in two batches and beat until incorporated. Press the dough into a 4-inch disk and wrap in plastic wrap. Refrigerate until well chilled, at least 2 hours or up to 24 hours.

3. Adjust an oven rack to the middle position and heat the oven to 350 degrees. Line a baking sheet with parchment paper. On a lightly floured work surface, roll the dough out to a 1/4-inch-thick circle. Cut into rounds with a 2 1/2-inch cookie cutter, spacing them 1 inch apart on the prepared baking sheet. Sprinkle the cookies with some of the remaining 1/4 cup sugar and bake until just golden around the edges, 12 to 15 minutes. Cool the cookies on the baking sheet for 2 minutes, then transfer to a wire rack to cool completely, about 20 minutes. Gather the scraps, reroll the dough, and repeat with the remaining dough and sugar. (The cookies can be stored in an airtight container for up to 3 days.)

Notes from the Test Kitchen

We didn't expect to like a cookie with a scant 1/2 cup sugar in the dough, but this recipe actually became one of our favorites. Because these cookies have a cake-like quality, you don't want them to be overly large—we liked them best made with a 2 1/2-inch cookie cutter. Bake these cookies one batch at a time and use a fresh or cooled baking sheet for each batch.

Grandma Sylvia's Salt Butter Cookies

SUE GRAPEL | CHAPPAQUA, NEW YORK

Made with salted butter and a touch of whiskey, these chocolate-filled cookie sandwiches are unusual and old-fashioned. They are similar to a traditional French butter cookie, or *sablé*, which is often used as a sandwich cookie. These were clearly special cookies in Sue's family: "When I was 16 years old, I was diagnosed with a rare tumor in my leg. I was very lucky and the doctor was able to save my leg. Grandma showed up at the hospital with a large tin filled with her special cookies for the doctor. Years later, when I brought my son to the same doctor, he remembered my grandmother and her special cookies."

MAKES 36 COOKIES

COOKIES

- 2 large egg yolks
- 1 teaspoon vanilla extract
- 1 teaspoon whiskey
- 16 tablespoons (2 sticks) salted butter, softened
- 2/3 cup granulated sugar
- 2 1/4 cups all-purpose flour

FILLING

- 1 ounce unsweetened chocolate, chopped
- 1/4 cup water
- 2 cups confectioners' sugar

1. FOR THE COOKIES: Adjust an oven rack to the middle position and heat the oven to 350 degrees. Line a baking sheet with parchment paper. Whisk the yolks, vanilla, and whiskey together in a measuring cup.

2. With an electric mixer at medium-high speed, beat the butter and granulated sugar together until fluffy, about 2 minutes. Reduce the speed to medium, add the yolk mixture, and beat until combined. Add the flour and beat until incorporated. Shape the dough into ¾-inch balls and space half the balls 1 inch apart on the prepared baking sheet. Bake until lightly browned around the edges, 10 to 12 minutes. Cool the cookies on the baking sheet for 2 minutes, then transfer to a wire rack to

cool completely, about 30 minutes. Repeat with the remaining dough balls.

3. FOR THE FILLING: Combine the chocolate and water in a small saucepan and stir over low heat until smooth, about 5 minutes. Off the heat, whisk in the confectioners' sugar until smooth.

4. Following the photos, turn half of the cookies over (flat-side up) and spread with about 1 teaspoon of the filling. Top with another cookie. Let the filling set until hardened, about 20 minutes. (The cookies can be stored in an airtight container for up to 3 days.)

> ### Notes from the Test Kitchen
> These cookies have a wonderful sandy texture and rich butter flavor. The chocolate filling is a sweet complement to the simple cookie. Be sure to use a fresh or cooled baking sheet for each batch.

MAKING THE SANDWICHES

1. Spread 1 teaspoon filling over the flat side of half the cookies.

2. Top each chocolate-covered cookie with another cookie, pressing to adhere.

Benne Wafers

LINDA COTTER | SPRING BRANCH, TEXAS

Benne, or sesame, seeds have been around a long time, probably since African slaves arrived to work the rice plantations in the 1600s. According to a story by Craig Claiborne in the *New York Times* in 1950, "Legend has it that the slaves brought the seeds from Africa and sowed a few at the head of each row in plantation gardens to bring good luck." The cookies that are made from benne seeds can be either sweet and caramel-y, as they are here, or savory—perfect for cocktails. Either way, they have an intriguing history that is woven deeply into the fabric of Charleston, South Carolina. In fact, the word *benne* is African but exists in the Gullah language still spoken today in the Low Country, particularly the South Carolina Sea Islands, where Linda grew up.

MAKES 36 COOKIES

- $1/2$ cup all-purpose flour
- $1/8$ teaspoon baking powder
- $1/8$ teaspoon salt
- 6 tablespoons ($3/4$ stick) unsalted butter, softened
- $3/4$ cup packed light brown sugar
- 1 large egg
- $1/4$ teaspoon vanilla extract
- $1/4$ cup sesame seeds, toasted

1. Adjust an oven rack to the middle position and heat the oven to 325 degrees. Line a baking sheet with parchment paper. Whisk the flour, baking powder, and salt in a medium bowl.

2. With an electric mixer at medium-high speed, beat the butter and sugar together until fluffy, about 2 minutes. Reduce the speed to medium and beat in the egg and vanilla until combined. Add the flour mixture and beat until incorporated. Fold in the sesame seeds.

3. Drop heaping teaspoon-sized portions of dough onto the prepared baking sheet, spacing them about 2 inches apart. Bake until the tops of the cookies bubble and the edges turn deep brown, about 9 minutes. Cool the cookies on the baking sheet for 2 minutes, then transfer to a wire rack to cool completely, about 15 minutes. Repeat with the remaining dough. (The cookies can be stored in an airtight container for up to 2 days.)

Notes from the Test Kitchen

Crisp, translucent, and nutty in flavor, these benne wafers were a hit in the test kitchen. We loved the idea of sweet sesame flavor, but thought that the pretoasting of the seeds before baking might be an unnecessary step. It wasn't—untoasted, the seeds retained their blond color and were easily overwhelmed by the caramel flavor of the butter and brown sugar.

Like most cookies, it is important to allow the wafers to cool on the baking sheet for a minute or two before moving them to the cooling rack. For most cookie recipes, this allows the cookies to finish baking from the residual heat of the baking sheet, as well as letting them set up enough so that they don't fall apart when transferred. For benne wafers, this was especially important as these paper-thin cookies will otherwise bend and tear. Bake these cookies one batch at a time and be sure to use a fresh or cooled baking sheet for each batch.

Edna's Date-Nut Pinwheel Cookies

PATRICIA R. EPPLER | GLOBE, ARIZONA

Pinwheel cookies, in our opinion, are the ultimate holiday cookie. With their swirls of filling, they are festive and appealing—and endlessly variable. In addition to the old-fashioned date-nut filling here, which is quite common, they can be filled with jam, other fruit and nut fillings, or by combining two different doughs, typically vanilla and chocolate. They do take a little time to make, but once you've rolled the dough into a log and chilled it, you can have cookies at a moment's notice.

Patricia recalls her mother making these cookies in the 1960s: "My mother shared baking recipes with many of her friends. The recipe for these pinwheel cookies was given to her by Edna, the wife of our minister. For years, my mother would make batches of these cookies, baking some for Thanksgiving and saving some dough in the freezer until Christmas. Yes, EVEN in 1965 she had slice-n-bake cookies; you might even say that she was ahead of her time. The Christmas I met my in-laws-to-be, my mother packed my suitcase with frozen cookies, along with my clothes—and off I went to Arizona. My husband and his family became very fond of these cookies."

MAKES 32 COOKIES

FILLING

1³/₄   **cups dates, chopped fine**
²/₃   **cup granulated sugar**
²/₃   **cup water**
³/₄   **cup pecans, chopped fine**

DOUGH

3   **cups all-purpose flour**
¹/₄   **teaspoon baking soda**
¹/₄   **teaspoon salt**
2   **large eggs**
¹/₂   **teaspoon vanilla extract**
16   **tablespoons (2 sticks) unsalted butter, softened**
1¹/₄   **cups packed light brown sugar**

1. FOR THE FILLING: Bring the dates, granulated sugar, and water to a simmer in a medium saucepan over medium-high heat. Reduce the heat to medium-low and cook until the mixture becomes thick and syrupy, about 15 minutes. Set aside.

2. FOR THE DOUGH: Whisk the flour, baking soda, and salt in a medium bowl. Whisk the eggs and vanilla together in a measuring cup. With an electric mixer at medium-high speed, beat the butter and brown sugar together until fluffy, about 2 minutes. Reduce the speed to medium, add the egg mixture and flour mixture alternately in two batches, and beat until combined. Divide the dough into two pieces and flatten each into a 4-inch disk. Wrap each disk in plastic wrap and refrigerate until well chilled, at least 4 hours or up to 24 hours.

(Continued on page 194)

3. Following the photos, roll one disk of the dough between two sheets of parchment paper or waxed paper into a 14 by 12-inch rectangle. Remove the top layer of paper. Spread half the date filling evenly over the dough. Sprinkle with half the nuts. Starting at the short end, roll the dough into a tight log. Place on a baking sheet and freeze until firm, at least 30 minutes. Repeat with the remaining dough, date filling, and nuts. (The chilled logs can be wrapped tightly in plastic wrap and frozen for up to 1 month.)

4. Adjust two oven racks to the upper-middle and lower-middle positions and heat the oven to 350 degrees. Line two baking sheets with parchment paper. Working with one log at a time, cut the chilled log into ¾-inch-thick slices, spacing them 2 inches apart on the prepared baking sheets. Bake until the edges are golden brown and the centers are set, 18 to 25 minutes, switching and rotating the baking sheets halfway through baking. Cool the cookies on the baking sheets for 2 minutes, then transfer to a wire rack to cool completely, about 20 minutes. Allow the baking sheets to cool, then repeat with the remaining log. (The cookies can be stored in an airtight container for up to 3 days.)

Notes from the Test Kitchen
To make a pinwheel cookie, you need a paper-thin layer of cookie dough, which is hard to work with. We found that the dough was easier to deal with if rolled between sheets of parchment or waxed paper. If the dough becomes unmanageably soft, simply transfer it to a baking sheet and pop it in the freezer to firm up.

MAKING PINWHEEL COOKIES

1. Roll the chilled dough between two sheets of parchment paper into a 14 by 12-inch rectangle.

2. Spread half of the filling over the dough and sprinkle with half of the nuts.

3. Starting at the short end, carefully roll the dough into a log. Place on a baking sheet and freeze until firm.

4. Cut the chilled log into ¾-inch-thick slices and place on the prepared baking sheet.

Turtle Cookies

KRIS RASMUSSEN | MADISON, WISCONSIN

Inspired by the popular turtle candies of the 1950s, this cookie, with its pecan head and feet and chocolate shell, won the 1952 Pillsbury Bake-Off Contest. The original recipe was created by Beatrice Harlib, who credits one of her 10-year-old twin boys with the idea. These cookies became famous soon after the contest, appearing in newspapers around the country. Kris's recipe came from her mother and called for walnut flavoring, though we opted to use vanilla instead as it's easier to find.

MAKES 24 COOKIES

COOKIES

3	cups all-purpose flour
1/2	teaspoon baking soda
1/2	teaspoon salt
4	large eggs (2 whole, 2 separated)
2	teaspoons vanilla extract
16	tablespoons (2 sticks) unsalted butter, softened
1	cup packed light brown sugar
120	pecan halves (about 8 ounces)

GLAZE

4	ounces unsweetened chocolate, chopped
2	tablespoons unsalted butter
2	cups confectioners' sugar
4–6	tablespoons milk
2	teaspoons vanilla extract

1. FOR THE COOKIES: Adjust two oven racks to the upper-middle and lower-middle positions and heat the oven to 350 degrees. Line two baking sheets with parchment paper. Whisk the flour, baking soda, and salt in a medium bowl. Whisk the 2 whole eggs, 2 egg yolks, and vanilla together in a measuring cup.

2. With an electric mixer at medium-high speed, beat the butter and brown sugar together until fluffy, about 2 minutes. Reduce the speed to medium, add the egg mixture, and beat until combined. Add the flour mixture and beat until incorporated.

3. Lightly beat the remaining 2 egg whites in a shallow dish. Following the photos, arrange the pecans on the prepared baking sheets in clusters of 5 as follows: 1 for the turtle head, 2 for the arms, and 2 for the legs. Working with 2 tablespoons of dough at a time, form the dough into balls. Roll each ball in the egg whites, then place on top of each pecan cluster, pressing lightly. Bake until the cookies are golden brown, 16 to 18 minutes, switching and rotating the baking sheets halfway through baking. Cool the cookies completely on the baking sheets, at least 30 minutes.

4. FOR THE GLAZE: Heat the chocolate and butter in a small saucepan over low heat until smooth. Off the heat, stir in the confectioners' sugar, 4 tablespoons milk, and vanilla (add extra milk if the glaze is too thick). Dip the top of each turtle cookie into the glaze, creating a "shell." Let the cookies sit until the glaze hardens, at least 30 minutes. (The cookies can be stored in an airtight container for up to 3 days.)

MAKING THE TURTLES

1. Place a dough ball on top of each pecan cluster.

2. Dip the top of each baked and cooled turtle into the chocolate glaze.

Washboard Cookies

THE EDITORS OF COOK'S COUNTRY

These old-fashioned ridged cookies pack a big coconut and brown sugar crunch. Looking into the origin of these cookies, we found many early 1900s cookbooks that made mention of crisp coconut cookies, but we first saw the name "washboards" in midcentury cookbooks such as *Betty Crocker's Picture Cookbook* (1950). Thin, sweet, and crisp, these cookies are perfect with a cup of tea.

MAKES 36 COOKIES

- 2 cups all-purpose flour
- 1/2 teaspoon baking powder
- 1/4 teaspoon baking soda
- 1/4 teaspoon salt
- 1/4 teaspoon ground nutmeg
- 1 large egg
- 2 tablespoons milk
- 8 tablespoons (1 stick) unsalted butter, softened
- 1 cup packed light brown sugar
- 1 cup sweetened, shredded coconut

1. Whisk the flour, baking powder, baking soda, salt, and nutmeg in a medium bowl. Whisk together the egg and milk in a small bowl. With an electric mixer at medium-high speed, beat the butter and brown sugar until light and fluffy, about 2 minutes. Add the egg mixture and beat until well combined. Reduce the speed to low, add the flour mixture and coconut, and mix until just incorporated.

2. Following the photos, turn the dough out onto a lightly floured surface and, using floured hands, shape it into a 15-inch log. Flatten the top and sides of the log so that it measures 1 inch high and 3 inches wide. Wrap tightly with plastic wrap and refrigerate until firm, about 45 minutes. (The dough can refrigerated for up to 2 days or frozen for up to 1 month.)

3. Adjust two oven racks to the upper-middle and lower-middle positions and heat the oven to 350 degrees. Line two baking sheets with parchment paper. Remove the chilled dough from the refrigerator, unwrap, cut into

1/4-inch-thick slices, and arrange the slices 1 inch apart on the baking sheets. Dip a dinner fork in flour, then make crosswise indentations in the dough slices. Bake until the cookies are toasty brown, 15 to 18 minutes, switching and rotating the baking sheets halfway through baking. Cool the cookies on the baking sheets for 10 minutes, then transfer to a wire rack to cool completely. Serve.

Notes from the Test Kitchen

After trying many washboard cookie recipes, we learned a couple things: that we didn't like these cookies to be too sweet, and that we wanted a strong hit of coconut flavor. Multiple batches later, we had removed the white sugar and settled on using brown sugar only. We added a little nutmeg for flavor, and as much coconut as we could without turning the cookie into a macaroon.

HOW TO MAKE WASHBOARDS

1. Shape the dough into a 15-inch log. Flatten the top and sides of the log so that it measures 1 inch high and 3 inches wide.

2. Use the floured tines of a fork to gently press indentations into the dough slices.

Biscotti

JOEY RUDOLPH | WAUNA, WASHINGTON

In her book *Jewish Cooking in America*, Joan Nathan speculates that the large Jewish population in Piedmont, Italy, may have brought biscotti to Eastern Europe, where they were given the name *mandelbrot* (which means "almond bread"). These cookies were a popular Sabbath dessert because they kept so well and did not contain butter (though this one does). Joey recounted that this particular recipe likely came from his great-grandparents, who fled Poland, arriving in the United States via Ellis Island.

MAKES 40 COOKIES

- 3½ cups all-purpose flour
- 2 teaspoons baking powder
- ½ teaspoon salt
- ½ teaspoon ground cinnamon
- 4 large eggs
- 3 tablespoons lemon juice
- 2 teaspoons vanilla extract
- 8 tablespoons (1 stick) unsalted butter, softened
- 1 cup sugar
- 2 cups sliced almonds
- 1 cup dried apricots, chopped

1. Adjust two oven racks to the upper-middle and lower-middle positions and heat the oven to 350 degrees. Line two baking sheets with parchment paper. Whisk the flour, baking powder, salt, and cinnamon in a medium bowl. Whisk the eggs, lemon juice, and vanilla together in a measuring cup.

2. With an electric mixer at medium-high speed, beat the butter and sugar until fluffy, about 2 minutes. Reduce the speed to medium, add the egg mixture, and beat until combined. Add the flour mixture and beat until incorporated. Using a rubber spatula, stir in the almonds and apricots.

3. Divide the dough into two pieces and, working on a lightly floured surface, shape each piece into a 10 by 3-inch log, about 1 inch high. Transfer both logs to the prepared baking sheets. Bake until golden brown and a toothpick inserted in the center comes out clean, about 35 minutes, switching and rotating the baking sheets halfway through baking. Set the sheet on a cooling rack and cool for 15 minutes.

4. Raise the oven temperature to 400 degrees. Transfer the loaves to a cutting board with a wide metal spatula. Using a serrated knife, cut the logs on the diagonal into ½-inch slices and lay them flat side down on the parchment-lined baking sheets. Bake until lightly browned on both sides, about 8 minutes, flipping the slices over halfway through baking. Transfer the biscotti to a wire rack to cool completely. (The biscotti can be stored in an airtight container for up to 2 weeks.)

Notes from the Test Kitchen
These cookies are softer and moister than most biscotti due to the addition of butter and use of four whole eggs rather than the more customary whites. We tried other fruit and nut combinations and found that you can substitute an equal amount of pistachios and dried cherries, or pecans and dried cranberries.

Whoopie Pies

THE EDITORS OF COOK'S COUNTRY

Made of two chocolate cookie-like cakes stuffed to the gills with a fluffy marshmallow filling, the whoopie pie is our idea of a good sandwich. It turns out that Maine and Pennsylvania both claim whoopie pies as their own. Maine's earliest claim dates back to 1925, when Labadie's Bakery in Lewiston first sold whoopie pies to the public. As for Pennsylvania's claim on the pies, we found an article in the *Gettysburg Times* from 1982 that spoke of an old-fashioned chocolate cake sandwich with a fluffy cream center. While the name was different (gobs), the description (and a huge picture) showed that these were no doubt whoopie pies by another name.

SERVES 6

CAKES
- 2 cups all-purpose flour
- 1/2 cup Dutch-processed cocoa powder
- 1 teaspoon baking soda
- 1/2 teaspoon salt
- 8 tablespoons (1 stick) unsalted butter, softened
- 1 cup packed light brown sugar
- 1 large egg, room temperature
- 1 teaspoon vanilla extract
- 1 cup buttermilk

FILLING
- 12 tablespoons (1 1/2 sticks) unsalted butter, softened
- 1 1/4 cups confectioners' sugar
- 1 1/2 teaspoons vanilla extract
- 1/8 teaspoon salt
- 2 1/2 cups Marshmallow Fluff

1. **FOR THE CAKES:** Adjust two oven racks to the upper-middle and lower-middle positions and heat the oven to 350 degrees. Line two baking sheets with parchment paper. Whisk the flour, cocoa, baking soda, and salt in a medium bowl.

2. With an electric mixer at medium speed, beat the butter and brown sugar until fluffy, about 2 minutes. Beat in the egg until incorporated, then beat in the vanilla. Reduce the speed to low and add the flour mixture and the buttermilk alternately in two batches.

3. Using a 1/3-cup measure, scoop six mounds of batter onto each baking sheet, spacing the mounds about 3 inches apart. Bake until the cakes spring back when pressed, 15 to 18 minutes, switching and rotating the baking sheets halfway through baking. Cool the cakes completely on the baking sheets, at least 1 hour.

4. **FOR THE FILLING:** With an electric mixer at medium speed, beat the butter and confectioners' sugar together until fluffy, about 2 minutes. Beat in the vanilla and salt. Beat in the Fluff until incorporated. Refrigerate the filling until slightly firm, about 30 minutes. (The filling can be refrigerated for up to 2 days.)

5. Dollop 1/3 cup of the filling on the center of the flat side of six of the cakes. Top with the flat side of the remaining six cakes and gently press until the filling spreads to the edge of the cake. Serve. (Whoopie pies can be refrigerated in an airtight container for up to 3 days.)

Notes from the Test Kitchen
Although it's considered heresy in the whoopie world, we used butter instead of the shortening called for in most recipes. Moist and tender, these cakes were snatched up as fast as we could bake them. One word of caution when making whoopie pies: Don't be tempted to bake all the cakes on one baking sheet—the batter needs room to spread in the oven.

Brown Sugar Fudge

DANA RICHARDS | AKRON, OHIO

We have college girls of the 1880s from the Seven Sisters women's colleges to thank for Brown Sugar Fudge (and its spinoffs of various flavors). In fact, an apt name for this recipe would be Women's College Fudge, as we found many recipes and anecdotes about fudge in college archives as well as newspapers of the day that connected the confection to Vassar, Smith, and Wellesley. According to Lee Benning's book *Oh Fudge: A Celebration of America's Favorite Candy*, Brown Sugar Fudge has historically been known as Smith College Fudge or penuche. And the name "fudge"? We consulted the *Oxford Encyclopedia of Food and Drink in America*: "The name probably developed in 1888 at Vassar College . . . and refers to an expression young women might have used instead of swearing."

We don't know if Dana's grandmother's recipe had any connection to these lofty institutions, but her recipe is simple and old-fashioned. We liked Dana's seven-year-old son's comment that it "tastes like a miracle."

MAKES ABOUT 80 PIECES

- 3 cups packed light brown sugar
- 1 cup heavy cream
- 2 tablespoons unsalted butter
- 1 teaspoon vanilla extract
- 1/4 teaspoon salt

1. Line a 9-inch square baking pan with foil, leaving overhang on all sides. Grease the foil. Combine all the ingredients in a medium saucepan and bring to a boil over medium-high heat. Reduce the heat to medium-low and cook until the mixture reaches the soft-ball stage on a candy thermometer, about 234 degrees, 5 to 8 minutes (if you don't have a candy thermometer, see the note on page 203, checking the mixture after 5 minutes).

2. Remove the pan from the heat and allow to cool until just warm (about 120 degrees) and not yet firm, 35 to 45 minutes. Using a wooden spoon, stir vigorously until the mixture lightens and is no longer shiny, 6 to 10 minutes. Spread the mixture into the prepared pan and let sit until firm, about 1 hour. Using the foil overhang, remove the fudge from the pan and cut into 1-inch squares. (The fudge can be stored in an airtight container for up to 1 month.)

Notes from the Test Kitchen

We enjoyed this fudge for its simplicity and pleasant butterscotch flavor. We also liked its surprisingly light texture, the result of mixing the candy before spreading it in the pan. Since this fudge is called brown sugar fudge, we tested both light and dark brown sugars. The deep, molasses flavor of the dark brown sugar made the fudge too potent to eat, while light brown sugar worked great. We also tried this fudge with additions of chopped nuts and dried fruits. Raisins and other fruits seemed out of place, but 1/2 cup of chopped hazelnuts or pecans made the fudge taste like praline.

Mashed Potato Fudge

ARLENE CRUM | ORANGE, CALIFORNIA

If we called this candy Peanut Butter Fudge, no one would guess that it was mashed potatoes that provide its creaminess. Who would think that you could make candy from such humble ingredients? Most recipes for mashed potato fudge include chocolate, but this recipe tastes plenty rich without it. Arlene's recipe came from her mother, who was born in England in 1916 but grew up in Pennsylvania's Amish country. She recalls making this fudge years ago: "As a child, I was especially delighted to eat fudge made from potatoes! This recipe is important to me because, although we were a dirt-poor family, my mother and I had such fun together mashing the potatoes, carefully stirring in the peanuts, and impatiently waiting for the fudge to chill so we could enjoy it. Candy was a real treat."

MAKE 64 PIECES

- 1   russet potato, peeled and cut into 1-inch chunks
- 2   cups sugar
- 1   cup whole milk
- 1   teaspoon vanilla extract
- ½   cup peanut butter
- 1   cup dry-roasted peanuts, chopped

1. Bring the potato and water to cover to a boil in a small saucepan. Reduce the heat and simmer until the potato is tender, about 15 minutes. Drain the potato, then mash until smooth.

2. Line an 8-inch square baking pan with foil, leaving overhang on all sides. Grease the foil. Transfer ½ cup mashed potatoes to a large saucepan (discard the remaining potatoes) and add the sugar and milk; bring to a boil over medium-high heat, stirring occasionally. Reduce the heat to medium and cook until the mixture reaches the soft-ball stage on a candy thermometer, about 234 degrees, 15 to 25 minutes (if you don't have a candy thermometer, see the note on page 203).

3. Off the heat, add the vanilla, peanut butter, and peanuts, mixing with a wooden spoon until the mixture begins to thicken, about 5 minutes. Spread the mixture into the prepared pan and refrigerate, uncovered, until firm, at least 4 hours. Using the foil overhang, remove the fudge from the pan and cut into 1-inch squares. (The fudge can be refrigerated in an airtight container for up to 2 weeks.)

Notes from the Test Kitchen

We loved the creaminess that the potatoes added. Leftover potatoes also worked well. For the sake of convenience, we also tried using reconstituted instant potatoes and found the resulting candy to be stale tasting and runny. The original recipe called for Spanish peanuts, but testing showed that dry-roasted peanuts worked just as well. We also realized that this softer fudge keeps better in the refrigerator.

Buttermilk Candy

JOYCE VALENTINE | WOODWARD, OKLAHOMA

Essentially a white nut fudge, this creamy candy (as well as simpler boiled milk and sugar versions) dates back to the turn of the century (or even earlier). In a book from 1849 called *Complete Confectioner*, we found reference to the technique of adding a bit of acid to boiling sugar when making candy, which keeps it from becoming grainy. Here the buttermilk provides the acid and keeps the candy silky and creamy. We were not surprised that Joyce found the recipe in a newspaper years ago, as we discovered this exact recipe in a 1967 newspaper from Walla Walla, Washington, where it was called "an expected favorite during Christmas season in many mid-west homes." Says Joyce about the recipe: "This buttermilk candy recipe is very old and I have been making the candy for 40 years. I found the recipe in an old newspaper many years ago. I have never had a failure with it."

MAKES 64 PIECES

4 cups sugar
2 cups low-fat buttermilk (see note)
4 tablespoons unsalted butter, cut into 4 pieces
1 1/2 cups walnuts or pecans, chopped

1. Line an 8-inch square baking pan with foil, leaving overhang on all sides. Grease the foil. Combine the sugar and buttermilk in a heavy-bottomed saucepan and bring to a boil over medium-high heat. Reduce the heat to low and simmer until the mixture reaches the soft-ball stage on a candy thermometer, about 234 degrees, 35 to 40 minutes, stirring constantly. (If you don't have a candy thermometer, see the note at right.)

2. Off the heat, add the butter, mixing with a wooden spoon until the candy begins to thicken, about 5 minutes. Stir in the nuts until the mixture becomes difficult to stir, about 3 minutes. Spread the mixture into the prepared pan and let cool completely, at least 2 hours. Using the foil overhang, remove the candy from the pan and cut into 1-inch squares. (The candy can be stored in an airtight container for up to 2 weeks.)

Notes from the Test Kitchen

When shopping for buttermilk, we found that we had two options—low-fat buttermilk or fat-free buttermilk—and wondered if it would make a difference in the candy. It did. The fat-free buttermilk gave the candy a slightly gritty feel, while the low-fat buttermilk made the candy creamy. The buttermilk flavor also acts as a great background for just about any nut. We tried pecans, walnuts, hazelnuts, cashews, and peanuts, and all worked just fine.

If you don't have a candy thermometer, here's what to do. After the candy mixture has simmered for 15 minutes, you can test for the soft-ball stage by using a metal spoon to drop a small dollop of the hot mixture into a bowl of cold water. The mixture will cool instantly, and if you can form the mixture into a soft, pliable ball, the mixture has reached the correct temperature. If the mixture stays loose in the water and will not form a ball, it will need more cooking—check it every few minutes. On the other hand, if the mixture instantly seizes in the cold water into a hard, rock-like piece, it is overcooked and you must start over again. That's why it make sense to start checking the fudge early—and often—or invest in a candy thermometer.

Conversions

SOME SAY COOKING IS A SCIENCE AND AN ART. We would say that geography has a hand in it, too. Flour milled in the United Kingdom and elsewhere will feel and taste different from flour milled in the United States. So we cannot promise that the loaf of bread you bake in Canada or England will taste the same as a loaf baked in the States, but we can offer guidelines for converting weights and measures. We also recommend that you rely on your instincts when making our recipes. Refer to the visual cues provided. If the bread dough hasn't "come together in a ball," as described, you may need to add more flour—even if the recipe doesn't tell you so. You be the judge. For more information on conversions and ingredient equivalents, visit our website at www.cooksillustrated.com and type "conversion chart" in the search box.

The recipes in this book were developed using standard U.S. measures following U.S. government guidelines. The charts below offer equivalents for U.S., metric, and Imperial (U.K.) measures. All conversions are approximate and most have been rounded up or down to the nearest whole number.

For example:

1 teaspoon = 4.929 milliliters, rounded up to 5 milliliters
1 ounce = 28.349 grams, rounded down to 28 grams

VOLUME CONVERSIONS

U.S.	METRIC
1 teaspoon	5 milliliters
2 teaspoons	10 milliliters
1 tablespoon	15 milliliters
2 tablespoons	30 milliliters
1/4 cup	59 milliliters
1/3 cup	79 milliliters
1/2 cup	118 milliliters
3/4 cup	177 milliliters
1 cup	237 milliliters
1 1/4 cups	296 milliliters
1 1/2 cups	355 milliliters
2 cups	473 milliliters
2 1/2 cups	592 milliliters
3 cups	710 milliliters
4 cups (1 quart)	0.946 liter
1.06 quarts	1 liter
4 quarts (1 gallon)	3.8 liters

WEIGHT CONVERSIONS

OUNCES	GRAMS
1/2	14
3/4	21
1	28
1 1/2	43
2	57
2 1/2	71
3	85
3 1/2	99
4	113
4 1/2	128
5	142
6	170
7	198
8	227
9	255
10	283
12	340
16 (1 pound)	454

CONVERSIONS FOR INGREDIENTS COMMONLY USED IN BAKING

INGREDIENT	OUNCES	GRAMS
1 cup all-purpose flour*	5	142
1 cup whole wheat flour	5½	156
1 cup granulated (white) sugar	7	198
1 cup packed brown sugar (light or dark)	7	198
1 cup confectioners' sugar	4	113
1 cup cocoa powder	3	85
Butter†		
4 tablespoons (½ stick, or ¼ cup)	2	57
8 tablespoons (1 stick, or ½ cup)	4	113
16 tablespoons (2 sticks, or 1 cup)	8	227

*U.S. all-purpose flour, the most frequently used flour in this book, does not contain leaveners, as some European flours do. These leavened flours are called self-rising or self-raising. If you are using self-rising flour, take this into consideration before adding leavening to a recipe.

† In the United States, butter is sold both salted and unsalted. We generally recommend unsalted butter. If you are using salted butter, take this into consideration before adding salt to a recipe.

OVEN TEMPERATURES

FAHRENHEIT	CELSIUS	GAS MARK (IMPERIAL)
225	105	¼
250	120	½
275	130	1
300	150	2
325	165	3
350	180	4
375	190	5
400	200	6
425	220	7
450	230	8
475	245	9

CONVERTING TEMPERATURES FROM AN INSTANT-READ THERMOMETER

We include doneness temperatures in many of our recipes, such as those for poultry, meat, and bread. We recommend an instant-read thermometer for the job. Refer to the table above to convert Fahrenheit degrees to Celsius. Or, for temperatures not represented in the chart, use this simple formula:

Subtract 32 degrees from the Fahrenheit reading, then divide the result by 1.8 to find the Celsius reading.

EXAMPLE:

"Roast until the juice runs clear when the chicken is cut with a paring knife or the thickest part of the breast registers 160 degrees on an instant-read thermometer."

To convert:
160° F − 32 = 128°
128° ÷ 1.8 = 71° C (rounded down from 71.11)

Index

NOTE: *Italicized* page references indicate recipe photographs.